Context-Sensitive
Development

Context-Sensitive Development

How International NGOs Operate in Myanmar

Anthony Ware

Kumarian Press
An Imprint of Stylus Publishing

Context-Sensitive Development: How International NGOs Operate in Myanmar

COPYRIGHT © 2012 by Kumarian Press, an imprint of STYLUS PUBLISHING, LLC.

Published by Stylus Publishing, LLC
22883 Quicksilver Drive
Sterling, Virginia 20166-2102

Library of Congress Cataloging-in-Publication Data
Ware, Anthony, 1966–
Context-sensitive development : how international NGOs operate in Myanmar / Anthony
    Ware. — 1st ed.
    p.   cm.
Includes bibliographical references and index.
ISBN 978-1-56549-523-4 (cloth : alk. paper) — ISBN 978-1-56549-524-1 (pbk. : alk.
    paper) — ISBN 978-1-56549-525-8 (library networkable e-edition) — ISBN
    978-1-56549-526-5 (consumer e-edition)
    1. Non-governmental organizations—Burma. 2. International agencies—Burma.
    3. Economic development—Burma—Societies, etc. 4. Community development—
    Burma—Societies, etc. 5. Humanitarian assistance—Burma—Societies, etc. 6. Human
    rights—Burma. I. Title.
HC422.W27   2012
338.9591—dc23

                                                                        2012018526

13-digit ISBN: 978-1-56549-523-4 (cloth)
13-digit ISBN: 978-1-56549-524-1 (paper)
13-digit ISBN: 978-1-56549-525-8 (library networkable e-edition)
13-digit ISBN: 978-1-56549-526-5 (consumer e-edition)

Printed in the United States of America

All first editions printed on acid-free paper that meets the American National Standards Institute Z39-48 Standard.

Bulk Purchases: Quantity discounts are available for use in workshops and for staff development. Call 1-800-232-0223

First Edition, 2012
10 9 8 7 6 5 4 3 2 1

Contents

Tables and Figures

Tables

Figures

Abbreviations

ADB	Asian Development Bank
ASEAN	Association of South East Asian Nations
BIA	Burma Independence Army formed during WWII under Aung San, renamed Burma National Army after WWII
CPB	Community Party of Burma, known as the Red Flag communists
EIU	Economist Intelligence Unit of the London *Economist* magazine
ESCAP	UN Economic and Social Commission for Asia and the Pacific
EU	European Union
FAO	Food and Agricultural Organisation
FBO	faith-based organization
GDP	gross domestic product
GONGO	government organized/operated nongovernmental organization
ILO	International Labour Organisation
IMF	International Monetary Fund
INGO	international nongovernment organization
KMT	Kuomingtang Chinese Nationalist
LDC	least developed country, according to the UN list
LNGO	local nongovernment organization
MDGs	Millennium Development Goals
MoH/MOH	Ministry of Health, Government of the Union of Myanmar
MOU	memorandum of understanding

NDF	National Democratic Front, a loose coalition of pro-West/anticommunist ethnic groups along the Thai border, long supported by the United States as a buffer against the perceived communist threat
NGO	nongovernment organization
NLD	National League for Democracy
ODA	official development assistance
PPP	purchasing-power parity
QUANGO	quasi-autonomous nongovernmental organizations
RBA	rights-based approach (to development)
SLORC	State Law and Order Restoration Council, the ruling junta 1988–1997
SPDC	State Peace and Development Council, the ruling junta 1997–2011
UK	United Kingdom
UN	United Nations
UNDP	United Nations Development Programme
UNICEF	United Nations Children's Fund
US/USA	United States of America
USDA	Union Solidarity Development Association, a Myanmar state-controlled mass civilian, charitable, and development organization
USDP	Union Solidarity Development Party, the ruling political party since the 2010 elections, formed from the USDA and backed by the former SPDC
WHO	World Health Organization
YMBA	Young Men's Buddhist Association (1906–1921), modeled on YMCA, became GCBA

Acknowledgments

I am very grateful to Professor Matthew Clarke and Dr. Heather Wallace of Deakin University, as well as Dr. Morten Pedersen of the University of New South Wales, for their invaluable advice and assistance in preparing the manuscript of this book. These wonderful supporters have provided critical reviews of each chapter and given generous assistance with ideas and suggestions. I would also like to thank Val Hoare and my parents, Brian and Merla Ware, for proofreading the text.

A huge thank-you to my wonderful wife, Vicki-Ann Ware. Thank you for believing in me and giving me the time, encouragement, and space to complete this undertaking. Thanks for many hours of conversation about the ideas in the book and for critically reviewing each chapter. You are my best friend, and it is a privilege to be able to journey through this life with you.

Thank you also to my four wonderful children, Danielle, Alicia, Nathaniel, and Benjamin, who have had to endure Dad being absent or preoccupied so often. Thank you for enduring and bearing with me through this. You are awesome kids, and I am so proud of you and grateful for you.

Preface

I have spent the past two and a half decades physically, spiritually, and emotionally in Southeast Asia.

I first became intensely interested in Burma, as it was then, in the mid-1980s. For a teenager who had never traveled in Asia, and who was partway through a science degree, it was an odd attraction. I knew no one who had emigrated from Burma or anyone who had ever lived there. I had no family or friends who had even ever visited the country, and it was never in the media. I knew nothing about Burma, although I quickly began absorbing everything I could find out about its people, culture, politics, and history. For me, this was a spiritual experience, full of exotic, romantic imagery and idealism. It changed the course of my life irrevocably, becoming what could only be described as a strong sense of destiny, a life calling, to somehow bring something of benefit to this nation. This interest has only grown over the years.

I vividly remember the shivers of emotion when news broke of the mass demonstrations and Ne Win's resignation in 1988. I recall my horror at the brutal crackdown against demonstrators that August and the frustration that no more than two minutes of news made our TV screens for such a momentous event in the history of one of our Asian neighbors. The following year I had the opportunity to spend an evening with the first person off the first plane out of Burma after that event, a businessman whose account and recordings had been played endlessly on CNN and other news channels. I followed Aung San Suu Kyi's 1989 house arrest and the excitement then heartbreak of the 1990 elections. I began learning the Burmese language and reading Burmese history. Then finally I got to visit!

It was 1992, and my wife and I traveled in for a week with our baby daughter. Many expressed shock that we would take a young baby into such an isolated, underdeveloped, and unstable part of the world. That was during the height of the tension over the military's refusal to hand over power to the

National League for Democracy, after its decisive election victory. We made a few connections, but it quickly became apparent that Myanmar at that time was not welcoming to young, inexperienced, and idealistic volunteers connected to a small agency with no experience working in Myanmar. We went home disappointed and applied for a position in Thailand, instead devoting ourselves to the study of Thai language, history, and culture.

For the next decade I watched Burmese affairs from the relative comfort of Bangkok, busy with projects in that country, but occasionally visiting to monitor the changing situation in Myanmar. All the while I pondered two questions: (1) Given the restricted domestic and international situation, how could we gain access to work in needy communities in that country? And (2) if we did gain access, what could we do to work effectively with those communities without provoking a backlash by the authorities on either the people we worked with or ourselves? Visits to Laos, Cambodia, or the Burma border region only fueled these questions, which eventually led to this doctoral research.

By the early 2000s, as Prime Minister Khin Nyunt's limited expansion of the humanitarian space began to be felt, it became apparent that visa access to the country would be possible. But by then we were responsible for four young children, and the weight of this burden signaled it was time to return to Australia to attend to their needs. Still, the possibility of access only accentuated the questions in my mind of what an agency could do to be effective in that difficult sociopolitical context.

This research has thus been a very personal journey of discovery, the culmination of a lengthy and long-distance courtship, if you will, with an intriguing and complex country. I look forward to my own next steps, whatever they may be, but even more to what I hope will be a far brighter future for this land of dreams and possibilities.

Anthony Ware
Melbourne, December 2011

Prologue: Burma or Myanmar?

A Note on Names and Political Orientation

On June 18, 1989, the then-new regime, the State Law and Order Restoration Council (SLORC), changed the official English-language name of the country from "The Union of Burma" to "The Union of Myanmar." The government argued this change was to discard a name chosen by British colonial authorities, not the Burmese people, and that "Myanmar" is a more inclusive name. They argued that "Myanmar" is a transliteration of the official Burmese-language written form of the name of the country and that it reflects the name the Burmese people traditionally use for the nation—while "Burma" is derived from the name the Burmese people traditionally use for the majority Burman ethnic group only (Steinberg 2010b). The rejection of the regime's legitimacy to change the country's name by Aung San Suu Kyi and the National League for Democracy (NLD) has led to the choice over which name to use becoming a highly political and emotional one.

The origins and usage of these two names are disputed. Some contend a totally opposite position to the regime, that the name "Myanmar" is historically used of the dominant Burman ethnic group and "Burma" is the more racially neutral and inclusive. Hall (1956), for instance, writing during the democratic era in Burma (well before any of the current political issues), cites examples of inscriptions dating to AD 1102 and 1190 that refer to the ethnic group as *Mranma* and *Mirma*, respectively, as well as evidence that the Chinese knew the ethnic Burmans as the *Mien*. Some suggest "Myanmar" is simply an old written form of the name (Steinberg 2009). Others argue that both terms have long been in common usage and are as ancient as one another and that the general population does not distinguish between them (Houtman 1999). Still others argue that the name "Burma" was a distortion by the British of the Mon pronunciation of "Myanmar" and that since colonial times political leaders have wavered between the two terms as indicators of national (rather than ethnic) identity (Rozenberg 2009).

Holliday (2011a) observes that the name change was deemed necessary precisely because something had been lost in the British transliteration. He argues, however, that "Burma" remains the more suitable name to use at this time because the name "Burma" has better links to democracy, being the name used during the nationalist struggle for independence, as well as negotiations with ethnic minorities leading to the 1947 Panglong Agreement. "Myanmar," by contrast, he suggests has come to symbolize brutal military rule.

The name "Myanmar" was widely used prior to the three wars with the British to refer to the territory under the rule of the kings, but it fell from use during the colonial period (Badgley 2004b). It was used as late as the 1920s as the title of the leading nationalist organization of that period, the *Myanmar Athin Chokkyi* (the General Council of Burmese Associations), and in the 1940s by Prime Minister Ba Maw's *Myanmar Wunthanu Aphwe* (Myanmar Nationalist Organisation). U Nu, prime minister during the democratic era 1948–1962 and outspoken opponent of both Ne Win's regime and SLORC, expressed regret that he did not lead Parliament to change the name of the country back to "Myanmar" shortly after independence, to undo more of the colonial legacy (Rozenberg 2009).

Choice of name is quite confusing at an international political level. The United Nations (UN) and the Association of South East Asian Nations (ASEAN) have accepted the official English name "Myanmar." The European Union (EU), including the United Kingdom (UK), has officially adopted the clumsy formulation "Burma/Myanmar," although it often reverts to one or the other even in official communication. For example, the British Foreign and Commonwealth Office continues to commonly use "Burma" in its public communication (FCO 2011), and UK bills imposing financial sanctions from 2000–2005 used "Burma" (Treasury 2011), while the EU High Representative of the Union for Foreign Affairs and Security Policy commonly uses the formulation "Myanmar (Burma)" or simply "Myanmar" rather than "Burma/Myanmar" (EEAS 2011). Australia, Canada, and the United States of America (USA), among others, continue to recognize "Burma" as the official English-language name of the country in solidarity with Suu Kyi and the NLD.

The continued use of the name "Burma" by these nations in international settings is an ongoing point of irritation to the government. On the other hand, many exiles and migrants outside the country who adhere to "Burma" feel they are expressing the illegitimacy of the military regime by refusing to accept the name change. They see those who adopt "Myanmar" as having compromised with an illegitimate regime.

In recent years almost any analysis of the country became politicized, with the polarization within Myanmar studies reminiscent of tensions within Soviet and China studies at the height of the cold war (Selth 2010b). Recent academic studies of Myanmar largely come from one of two perspectives. As Robert Taylor (2008) expresses it, one wants to assess Myanmar against an external model, has a political "axe to grind," and sees Myanmar as "a case of deviancy from the norm of the contemporary republican nation-state in ideal modern form"; the other tries to play down comparative analysis and sees the situation in Myanmar "as emanating from its own logic . . . history, 'political culture,' or religious, structural, and institutional characteristics" and is in "danger of concluding that what is must be" (Taylor 2008, 222). In other words, is the Myanmar context "a problem to be solved or a political system to be understood and explained comparatively and historically" (Taylor 2008, 233)?

In such a highly politicized context, any choice of name risks criticism and causing offense. This research seeks a middle ground. The general population inside the country, particularly the ethnic Burmans, today does widely resort to the distinction between "Bama" and "Myanma" as markers of ethnicity and nationality, respectively, as the regime argues (Rozenberg 2009). Both names are used widely inside and outside the country referring to the political entity. However, the choice of using "Burma" or "Myanmar" still does carry deep political connotations for many people, particularly for those in the exile or diaspora communities. Steinberg laments,

> The name of the state has become a surrogate indicator of political persuasion and even projected legitimacy, causing considerable antipathy and confusion in both official and popular circles. . . . The use of one or the other name thus politically identifies the orientation of the writer or speaker. (Steinberg 2006, xx)

The final decision of the name adopted in this book is made out of respect for the fact that this research focuses on the work of nongovernment organizations (NGOs) and other development agencies who work inside the country, many officially with memoranda of understanding (MOUs) with the government. These development agencies, both local and international, almost exclusively use the name "Myanmar" in all written documentation. It is also noted that an increasing number of respected scholars appear to be adopting the name change. For example, Robert Taylor has recently switched from using "Burma" (1987, 2001) to "Myanmar" (2008, 2009). In response to the ongoing political reform, Australia has just adopted the use of the name "Myanmar," as of June 2012. Australia's foreign minister, Bob Carr, concluded that "it is time to start calling the country by the name it wants to be known" (Carr 2012c).

Throughout this book I have chosen to adopt the convention of Professor David Steinberg (Georgetown University), who, for simplicity and attempted neutrality, uses "Myanmar" to refer to the state post-1988 (although the name was actually changed in 1989), "Burma" to refer to periods prior to that, and "Burma/Myanmar" to indicate continuity (Steinberg 2006). The language will, however, be referred to as "Burmese," as it is more commonly known. "Burmese" (or "Myanmar") will refer equally to all ethnic groups in the country, and "Burman" will be used to refer to the dominant ethnic group.

When the regime changed the name for the state, it also changed the English spelling of many cities, districts, and geographical features. This book will also adopt the new spellings of place names rather than the traditional British spelling—for example, Yangon not Rangoon, Bago not Pegu, Ayeyarwady not Irrawaddy, and so on—for all post-1988 references for the same reasons, given these new names are now becoming more widely recognized, but use the old spelling in pre-1988 references.

Part 1

The Problem and Theory

Myanmar and Context-Sensitivity in Development

> It is quite unrealistic to pretend that in a country which is fundamentally authoritarian, an agency is going to come in and be able to run a project in a totally participatory manner. This would guarantee a draconian response from the government. (Philip Alston, former chair, UN Committee on Economic, Social, and Cultural Rights, 1995, 11)

After decades in relative obscurity and isolation, Myanmar is very much in the limelight. On November 7, 2010, the people of Myanmar went to the polls for the first time in more than twenty years, in elections widely condemned as a sham. Six days later, on November 13, 2010, opposition leader and Nobel Peace Prize laureate Aung San Suu Kyi was released after spending fifteen of the preceding twenty-one years under house arrest. At the time of Suu Kyi's release, there was an air of expectation in the international media, buoyed by the hope her release might bring greater freedom and political change. On the back of the publicity surrounding Cyclone Nargis in 2008, the global community anxiously searched for signs of a political breakthrough that could lay the foundations for economic and social improvement in the lives of the Burmese people.

As time passed, Myanmar began to recede from the international spotlight again, back into relative anonymity. But then a slew of announcements in the second half of 2011 and into 2012 raised hopes that political reform is very much underway, culminating in the election of Suu Kyi and forty-two other NLD representatives to Parliament in by-elections held in April 2012, and the subsequent visit of UK prime minister David

Cameron. Cameron's visit led to the suspension (not lifting) of most EU sanctions against Myanmar, hotly followed by an easing of sanctions by the United States. The eyes of the global community are once again fixed on Myanmar.

Rudyard Kipling, 123 years ago, described arriving in colonial Rangoon and seeing the golden spire of the Shwedagon Pagoda for the first time:

> A golden mystery upheaved itself on the horizon—a beautiful, winking wonder that blazed in the sun. . . . "There's the old Shway Dagon," said my companion. . . . The golden dome said, "This is Burma, and it will be quite unlike any land that one knows about." (Kipling 1889)

Burma then was an exotic tropical playground full of gems and teak, a peaceful Buddhist land of mystique filled with pagodas and monks, with a proud history and rich variety of fascinating cultures. It was a thriving, romantic colony, to become a setting for Oscar Wilde's amusing *For Love of the King* (1922), Noel Coward's satirical *Mad Dogs and Englishmen* (1931), and George Orwell's illuminating *Burmese Days* (1934). Burma was a hive of business investment, the latest colonial acquisition, the largest rice exporter in the world, and the busiest seaport in mainland Southeast Asia.

Much has changed, and Myanmar today occupies a very different place in the world, but Kipling's remark still seems highly appropriate: for most people, Myanmar today is "quite unlike any land that one knows about."

The Development Challenge

This book examines the manner in which international nongovernmental organizations (INGOs) work in Myanmar, as a case study exploring development that is sensitive to difficult sociopolitical contexts.

After North Korea, Myanmar has long been "the most obscure and obscured state in the contemporary world" (Steinberg 2010b, 1). It has long been a difficult context for the international community to understand; indeed, "few states in the contemporary world present the complexities that characterize Burma/Myanmar" (Steinberg 2006, xi).

Myanmar is a developing nation in which at least a quarter of the population still lives in extreme poverty (IHLCA 2011). Economic and demographic data on Myanmar have been of questionable validity since independence, which is an area of acute need. However, the depth of the humanitarian need can be quickly illustrated by observing that government investment in key areas such as health and education rank have long been among the lowest in the world (based on MoH 2008 figures; UNICEF 2003). Such low state investment in crucial areas of the economy has inevitably resulted in a wide range of significant developmental and humanitarian issues.

The poverty and vulnerability of the people are highlighted by the level of destruction caused by Cyclone Nargis, which struck Myanmar on May 2–3, 2008. Despite being only a category 3 cyclone, Nargis resulted in 140,000 deaths and caused "unprecedented destruction," affecting 2.4 million people across the Delta region of the country (TCG 2008). By way of comparison, as destructive as Hurricane Katrina was in New Orleans, more than 75 people were killed by Nargis for every fatality caused by Katrina, yet Katrina hit a more densely populated urban center with higher wind strength and a storm surge of similar magnitude.

Most countries with a level of underdevelopment and humanitarian need similar to that of Myanmar receive significant development assistance. However, bilateral aid and humanitarian assistance have been greatly restricted because of grave concerns by the international community about abuse of power, human rights violations, and suppression of democracy by the ruling elite. These concerns are reflected, for example, in the fact that the UN General Assembly has passed resolutions against human rights violations in Myanmar at every sitting since 1991. A special rapporteur for human rights has likewise been monitoring the situation in Myanmar on behalf of the Human Rights Council since 1992. These apprehensions have resulted in Myanmar being widely ostracized by the international community, and many countries have instituted sanctions in an effort to pressure the regime into reform. Prior to Cyclone Nargis, *official development assistance* (ODA) to Myanmar was the least of any of the UN *least developed countries* (LDCs), at just 5 percent of the average per capita assistance to these other needy nations (ICG 2008).

Thus, while the global community is concerned about the level of poverty and humanitarian need in the country, to the extent that it remains unconvinced about the sincerity of reform and poverty alleviation, it is divided over how best to respond to the humanitarian situation. When coupled with the restrictions applied by a government suspicious of the motives of outside organizations, it becomes clear that Myanmar has been a particularly difficult context for international development agencies to operate within over the past two decades. International agencies still face a very "complex political and bureaucratic environment" in Myanmar (ICG 2008, 15) and a "politically delicate situation" (CEC 2007, 28), and even INGO leaders who have spent some years in the country find some things "nearly impossible to understand" (Allan 2009).

The adaptations INGOs make to normalized global development approaches in response to this difficult sociopolitical context is the key theme of this book, a context restricted by a combination of challenging domestic politics and reactionary international responses. The research presented in this book demonstrates that a more nuanced understanding of each specific context and its historical antecedents aids an understanding of how to sensitively approach local complexity and that field staff with such nuanced contextual understanding than head office management should be more deliberately empowered to make such adaptations to the development approach.

In the field research reported in part 3 of this book, INGO managers working in Myanmar describe having faced a wall of negative sentiment from politicians, civil society, and the general donor community in the West, even from their own boards. They describe an environment of very restricted aid funding and mandates and contending daily with the restrictions and scrutiny of officials extremely suspicious about their motives, and officials concerned (rightly or wrongly) about potential negative side effects of their work on the security, unity, and sovereignty of the nation.

One result of these restrictions and political concerns over engagement in the country is that many major agencies have not worked in the country at all, and many others that do work in the country operate under only limited mandates. For example, significant multilateral agencies such as the International Monetary Fund (IMF), the World Bank, and the Asian Development Bank (ADB) all had no official presence or work in the country until this year, while the International Labour Organisation (ILO) and the United Nations Development Programme (UNDP) operate in the country on greatly restricted mandates. The Food and Agricultural Organisation (FAO) is possibly the only multilateral agency operating in Myanmar without any mandate restrictions, working directly with government departments. A similar situation exists within the INGO community. For example, World Vision was initially very divided over reentering the country during the 1990s, while Médecins Sans Frontières–France commenced work only to withdraw in a blaze of publicity in March 2006, expressing concern at the level of restriction and scrutiny imposed by the regime—while Médecins Sans Frontières–Holland remained active in the country. The International Committee of the Red Cross continues to work in the country but greatly restricted its activities after expressing similar concerns about government restrictions in 2007. Plan International, Opportunity International, and Habitat for Humanity, among many others, have all decided not to conduct any official work in the country at this juncture, after feasibility studies and funding limited projects via local NGO partners.

Prior to 1988, the regime's self-imposed isolation resulted in little opportunity for INGO programs. With greater opportunity after 1988–90, some voiced concerns that the very presence of INGOs added legitimacy to an illegitimate regime, thereby entrenching oppressive leaders, or that INGO activities were so restricted or manipulated as to be only of limited benefit (e.g., Vicary 2010). The debate was well summarized by Purcell (1997), although as time passed since the imposition of sanctions, the voices calling for noninvolvement diminished, while those calling for increased humanitarian engagement increased.

Even prior to Cyclone Nargis in 2008, none less than the special rapporteur for human rights in Myanmar began arguing,

> Humanitarian needs of the population in Myanmar must not be hostage to politics. . . . The international community has the duty to address the humanitarian needs in the country. [Thus UN decisions about human rights must be] guided by the best interests of children, women, people living with disabilities, those affected by diseases and minority groups. (Pinheiro 2006)

The devastation of Cyclone Nargis appears to have crystallized the view that we cannot wait for a change in government before humanitarian assistance is provided, with an approximate doubling of the number of INGOs negotiating MOUs (memoranda of understanding) and working directly in the country. This research therefore focuses on how INGOs have addressed and continue to address context-sensitivity issues rather than on whether to engage.

The confluence in Myanmar of very significant need with domestic and international restrictions created a difficult sociopolitical context for INGOs and other agencies that seek to bring poverty alleviation and development. Restricted resources, absence of some major multilateral agencies, limited mandates, authoritarian government, and deep reservations by international donors and governments have all added to the complexity. Nonetheless, approximately eighty INGOs had negotiated MOUs with the government and were operating development programs and projects aimed at alleviating the impact of extreme poverty in the country even before the political reforms began in earnest in 2011. These include some of the largest INGOs in the world; for example, World Vision, Oxfam (UK), CARE International, Médecins Sans Frontières–Holland, and Save the Children were all present, and the number of agencies continue to grow. In addition, a large number of other INGOs of various sizes work into Myanmar from outside the country, through partnerships with local (often unregistered) NGOs, businesses, civil groups, or other INGOs.

Research and Significance

This book explores how INGOs adapt their operations and projects to Myanmar, as a case study of context-sensitivity in order to maximize development effectiveness within a complex domestic and international sociopolitical context. It considers the state of the theory on context-sensitivity in development, analyzes the sociopolitical context faced by INGOs in Myanmar, and explores how the INGOs that are working in Myanmar contextualize their approach to this particular context.

The Research Question

The question explored throughout this book can be succinctly stated as follows: How do INGOs contextualize their operations and projects in order to be sensitive to the sociopolitical context they face in Myanmar, in an effort to maximize their effectiveness toward alleviating extreme poverty in this complex context? Specific aspects to this question consider ways INGOs contextualize their development approach when working directly with the extremely poor in local communities, in their relationships with other key stakeholders, and how they contextualize negotiating funding and access with both the domestic government and the international community. Answering these questions requires a theoretical base by which we might understand sensitivity to context in INGO development, as well as a detailed understanding of the sociopolitical context in Myanmar.

There are three aspects to the contextualization that will be explored in part 3 of this book. The first explores the ways in which INGOs contextualize their approach when working with the extremely poor in local communities, because of the wider sociopolitical factors. It examines how development principles or approaches, as expressed by these organizations globally, are applied in Myanmar. In other words, it explores what is done differently in working with communities within this sociopolitical context. It also considers what the people and communities themselves respond to, which is a significant question given the authoritarian nature of the regimes of the past decades, as well as how INGOs prepare for sustainability after the end of a project cycle in the face of a suspicious regime and donor restrictions limiting capacity building of the officials and agencies that might otherwise support development.

A second major aspect of this contextualization explores how the socio-political context of Myanmar changes the way INGOs relate to other stake-holders in development and poverty alleviation. These stakeholders include Myanmar government officials and agencies; local Myanmar civil organizations; other agencies in Myanmar; transnational civil society; international state actors; and the agencies' own boards, governments, and donors. This aspect explores, therefore, how INGOs express context-sensitivity in the manner in which they relate to each of these stakeholders, given the tensions within the domestic and international political relationships.

A third aspect to this contextualization research explores the complex set of restrictions INGOs have faced, from both the domestic government and the international community. It examines how INGOs negotiate with domestic and international actors for the humanitarian space and funding required to conduct projects effectively, what these negotiations mean for the development approaches of INGOs, and the role INGOs have played in expanding the humanitarian space within the ongoing reform.

Significance of the Research
Theory of Context-Sensitive Development
In development theory, "context" certainly includes local cultural factors. However, the greatest complexity in what might be considered difficult international contexts involve strained domestic and international political situations, both of which generally have long historical backgrounds. Chapter 2 therefore reviews the existing research regarding context and context-sensitivity in international community development. While in theory the global development dialogue has largely moved past universal prescriptions to recognize diversity, multiple paths, and unique contexts, this does not always operate in practice. No one has seriously advocated universal policy prescriptions for international development for decades, other than broad calls for things such as a gender mainstreaming and a rights-based approach to development. However, insofar as development studies and development practice have sought to identify commonalities across diverse contexts in order to ascertain and transfer at least broadly applicable lessons, if not universal principles and approaches to development, the dominant presentation of international development approaches and principles remains expressed in terms of norms.

Strong political and organizational normative forces undermine the theory and practice of context-sensitivity in international development, including the fact that large international agencies derive much of their legitimacy from normalized mission and strategy statements that they are then held publicly accountable against. This dominant presentation of development in terms of norms has resulted in insufficient articulation of how external development agencies ought to tailor what they do to specific contexts, and therefore that context requires renewed attention and theorization. This book suggests the need for the extension of the ideas of participatory development to also deliberately include the empowerment of agency in-country personnel within the meso-macro sociopolitical contexts, within which they are the primary actors. It suggests that ideas from social change theory and an extension of conflict-sensitive ideas are most relevant, extending the conflict-sensitive development ideas from overt, violent intrastate conflict to also include highly strained international relations of an isolated, so-called "pariah state." This research thus offers a contribution toward the development of such theory, particularly for complex international sociopolitical contexts like Myanmar.

Documenting Context-Sensitive INGO Development in Myanmar

The other significant contribution of this book is in documenting how INGOs create space and operate context-sensitively in Myanmar. There is a great scarcity of literature in this field. Part 3 of this book goes significantly beyond existing studies of INGO development work in Myanmar, presenting analysis of over ninety hours of primary interview data by the author and focusing specifically on the ways in which development agencies contextualize their approaches to maximize aid effectiveness.

There have been many studies of Myanmar politics and reports examining the pros and cons of sanctions, but while this body of research often mentions the humanitarian impact of the political stalemate, there has been very little research into aid effectiveness in Myanmar, much less any examination of how INGOs adapt their development approaches to operate most effectively within this context.

Selth (2010b) offers a timely survey of the Myanmar studies literature. He suggests that tension in Myanmar's international relations is reflected in a politicization and polarization within the field of Myanmar studies that is reminiscent of tensions within Soviet and China studies at the height of the cold war. Selth cautions that, as a result, a considerable amount of material published since 1988 must be treated with caution and that a number of myths and misconceptions have found their way even into the academic literature.

Selth concludes that the largest proportion of published research on Burma/Myanmar prior to 1988 broadly considers history, particularly the history of political development (or lack thereof) since independence. Since 1988 the major emphases have been on comparative politics, the state of Burmese political institutions, and the implications of these for a possible transition from military rule to democracy. Other areas of solid research publication have been strategic analysis of military capability, ethnic insurgency, and human security, with a number of major publications considering the decline of the economy since independence, as well as sociological or anthropological studies into the social, religious, cultural, and linguistic diversity in the country. This includes the role of Buddhism in Burmese society and the plight of ethnic and religious minorities.

Notably absent from Selth's survey are studies of the work of international development agencies, an area with very little published academic research. In one rare study, Inwood's (2008) master's thesis examines whether international development agencies provide effective humanitarian assistance in Myanmar. He particularly focuses on theories of humanitarian intervention and whether intervention based truly on humanitarian principles is possible in Myanmar. His research is based on thirteen semistructured interviews and two discussions with groups of representatives from INGOs, UN agencies, donor agencies, journalists, members of exile groups, and academics between May 2006 and May 2007 (i.e., prior to the "Saffron Revolution" and Cyclone Nargis).

Inwood's (2008) research provides a solid starting platform on which this current research can build, including findings showing that agencies in Myanmar believe

- poor governance is the central cause of poverty in the country, yet the humanitarian situation does still demand international intervention;
- assistance can and should be significantly increased to be closer to levels given to neighboring needy counties and should continue to be given via development agencies and not through partnership projects with the government;
- this humanitarian funding should not be conditional;
- the policies of both Western countries and ASEAN to bring about political change in Myanmar have failed, particularly the sanctions policy;
- gaining access to the humanitarian space in Myanmar remains a challenge, especially initial access for new agencies and access to more sensitive and poverty-stricken areas such as Kachin, Chin, and Karen states;

- visas and travel authority to remote sites remain a problem, with visas for consultants taking up to two to three months to obtain and with a one- to two-month delay on permission for in-country travel;
- small grassroots projects are the most effective means to deliver humanitarian assistance, and thus INGOs have a greater role to play within the current context than larger multilateral agencies; and
- agencies do actively self-censor their public information and promotion of their work so as to not attract adverse attention of officials. This affects working relationships between agencies.

In a smaller study relating to the same time period, Igboemeka (2005) considered the perceptions of development agencies on aid effectiveness in Myanmar. The research, on behalf of the UK Department for International Development (DFID), involved telephone interviews from Bangkok with twenty-six representatives from UN agencies, INGOs, and donor agencies over a five-day period. However, and notably for our study, only four of those interviewed were with INGOs.

Igboemeka found a lack of consensus among agencies on measurement of effectiveness and on how effectiveness might be improved in Myanmar. She did, however, find consensus that the most significant constraints to effectiveness are the highly politicized context, the highly restricted humanitarian space, an atmosphere of secrecy and self-censorship, limited financial and human resources, weak capacity, a lack of reliable data, and difficulty gaining access to needy areas of the country. Divergent aid policies by other countries in the region, particularly China and Thailand, were a further complication. Some practitioners saw alignment with government priorities as a crucial need to support poverty reduction and catalyze broader policy change, but there were conflicting views on this among her respondents. Donors from countries within the region were clear that state building should be an objective, while Western donors contested this view. Mistrust of international actors by Myanmar authorities was apparent, manifested in suspicion and controls on projects stringent enough to significantly constrain effectiveness. A major concern was that external actors do not recognize or reflect in-country understandings, leading Igboemeka to conclude that a more thorough understanding of the challenging context and its links to change processes is required by all actors.

In 2006 the International Crisis Group released a report on humanitarian aid in Myanmar (ICG 2006), concluding that access to vulnerable populations had improved during the preceding couple of years. By their assessment, the work of most agencies in Myanmar is better defined as providing humanitarian aid, rather than sustainable human development, and that the overall trend was for increasing humanitarian space.

In its report after Cyclone Nargis, the ICG (2008) further argued that development agencies, particularly INGOs, were being highly effective with very limited resources and that unprecedented cooperation between the government and international agencies in delivering emergency aid to the survivors signaled that it was time to normalize aid relations with Myanmar. By that, the ICG was recommending that all political conditionality and restrictions on aid, except the prohibition on direct budgetary support for the Myanmar government, be lifted, that substantial increases in aid be given to allow sustainable human development (not just humanitarian aid), and that economic sanctions that affect livelihoods of vulnerable groups be lifted, notably bans on imports of Myanmar garments and agricultural and fishery products and restrictions on tourism. Its subsequent report in the lead up to the 2010 elections (ICG 2009) observed that some government ministers had been particularly active, cooperating with humanitarian assistance organizations in continuing to expand this humanitarian space. The ICG suggested development cooperation was becoming a preferred means for many officials to project a more positive domestic public image, as they attempt to help secure their political futures beyond the 2010 elections.

DFID (2010) takes a contrary view, arguing that development and political progress cannot be separated in Myanmar. DFID emphasizes targeted sanctions as a means to push for political reconciliation and human rights. It does, however, argue that the work of INGOs in addressing severe humanitarian needs is making a real impact in the lives of the poor, particularly in health, education, rural growth, and capacity development of civil society.

A working paper by Duffield (2008), sponsored by the UN Humanitarian Coordinator and the Office for the Coordination of Humanitarian Affairs in Yangon after Cyclone Nargis, examines how development agencies operate in the "difficult environment" of Myanmar. This paper is not an evaluation of the aid program to Myanmar but an attempt to "place the humanitarian situation in a wider context." He finds that while levels of suspicion and restriction by the government are high, they are not exceptional. What is anomalous, he suggests, is the disproportionate effect external lobby groups have had on restricting aid funding and mandates, the polarizing lens of Western sanctions, and the climate of political isolation.

Duffield argues that fragile state approaches are not appropriate in Myanmar. Drawing instead on theories of humanitarian assistance, he concludes that a primary role for agencies working in Myanmar is "pushing back, containing or domesticating a colonially derived design of power." He concludes that development agencies create space for independent action in Myanmar through engagement and visibility with the Myanmar authorities, by disarming the arbitrary personal power of officials through co-option, and by constant reassurances to both sides of the polarized political discourse that they are adhering strictly to the principles of humanitarian assistance, namely,

> *humanity*: the centrality of saving human lives and alleviating suffering;

> *impartiality*: implementation of action solely on the basis of need, without discrimination between or within affected populations;

> *neutrality*: that humanitarian action must not favor any side in an armed conflict or other dispute; and

> *independence*: autonomy of humanitarian objectives from the political, economic, military, or other objectives that any actor may hold.

While each of these research papers provides useful starting material, the research in this present work goes significantly beyond each of these previous studies of INGO work in Myanmar to examine their context-sensitive development approaches in depth.

Definitions

Before proceeding, a few definitions are required.

NGO/INGO

The earliest definition of INGO is found in resolution 288(X) of the UN Economic and Social Council (ECOSOC 1950), which defines an INGO as simply "any international organization that is not founded by an international treaty."

In recent years the designation *nongovernment organization* (NGO) has come to take on a particular meaning. Operational Directive 14.70 of the World Bank defines NGOs, for example, as private organizations that pursue activities to relieve suffering, promote the interests of the poor, protect the environment, provide basic social services, or undertake community development. NGOs often differ from other organizations in the sense that they tend to operate independent from government, are value-based and are guided by the principles of altruism and voluntarism. (World Bank 1989)

INGOs are NGOs with international structures that involve the flow of leadership, staff, funding, policy, expertise, or projects from outside the country.

The World Bank divides NGOs into *operational NGOs*, whose primary purpose is the design and implementation of development-related projects, and *advocacy NGOs*, whose primary purpose is to defend or promote a specific cause and who seek to influence policies and practices. Using this terminology, this research considers operational NGOs more than advocacy NGOs, recognizing that most NGOs also advocate but that the primary activity of most NGOs in Myanmar is the design and implementation of development-related interventions. NGOs whose primary purpose is advocacy regularly critique Myanmar but do so from outside the country and largely do not engage communities, civil society, or government officials directly inside the country.

The website *NGOs in the Golden Land* (2010) defines an INGO as any organization that operates not only in Myanmar but also in other countries and that provides social goods to the people of Myanmar and operate somewhat independently from government structures. While this definition is more inclusive than exclusive and is broader than many definitions, it appears to reflect the view of a majority of INGOs in the country and is thus the definition used throughout this book.

Context

"Context" is a widely used term, but it is extremely difficult to define. Its breadth creates the possibility of being too broad a term to be usefully employed, and it risks being co-opted to refer to anything anyone wants it to mean, thus losing all meaning. Nonetheless, the term is in widespread use to embrace factors from the milieu or environment surrounding the development that affects operations or interventions.

In this book, "context" is used in line with the definition of the global consortium of INGOs, now known as the Conflict Sensitivity Consortium:

The operating environment, which ranges from the micro to the macro level (e.g., community, district/province, region[s], country, neighboring countries) . . . comprised of actors, causes, profile and dynamics. (Africa Peace Forum et al. 2004)

The Conflict Sensitivity Consortium (formerly Africa Peace Forum et al.) suggests that the context within which INGOs operate typically includes political, economic, sociocultural, and historical factors from the micro-level of the village community to the macro-level of the national and international scene. As discussed in chapter 2, the most significant aspects of context in the development studies literature apart from culture relate to politics, particularly *conflict* (a "conflict-sensitive approach") and state *fragility*. The most significant aspects of the Myanmar context spoken about in the Myanmar studies literature, discussed in detail in part 2 (chapters 3 and 4), are likewise largely sociopolitical and include traditional values about power and legitimacy, the history of the relationship with the West, the history of internal ethnic conflict, the impact of authoritarian rule on the people, international responses toward Myanmar, the state of the economy, and the humanitarian situation.

Context-Sensitive

"Context-sensitive development," therefore, is not a competing development approach but an extension of participatory development and conflict-sensitive development ideas to embrace the sociopolitical environment surrounding development. "Sensitive" means understanding these contextual factors and the interaction between them and development interventions and acting on the understanding of this interaction in ways that either align with these factors or always keep them clearly in mind, respecting the views and processes embodied by them and seeking to minimize negative impacts and maximize positive impacts while working for change (Africa Peace Forum et al. 2004).

Development

"Development" is a highly contested concept, in terms of both its meaning and its means of achieving outcomes. However, the intrinsic goal of development is to advance human dignity, freedom, social equity, and self-determination. A lack of development is characterized by poverty, social exclusion, powerlessness, poor health, and shortened life expectancy. Good development outcomes are best achieved when communities have ownership of the goals and processes and where there are participatory representation, social equity, transparency, and accountability mechanisms. Good development outcomes must also explicitly consider the importance of gender and diversity, as well as expand people's freedoms and experience of their inalienable human rights. Ensuring development outcomes are sustainable therefore requires any underlying factors contributing to underdevelopment be addressed, making sustainable development inherently political and requiring partnership and capacity building of both civil society and government agencies (UNDP 1996).

The UNDP defines "human development" as

> a process of enlarging people's choices. The most critical ones are to lead a long and healthy life, to be educated and to enjoy a decent standard of living. If these essential choices are not available, many other opportunities remain inaccessible. (UNDP 1990, 10)

INGO development is based on principles that

> emphasize that all persons share similar needs and desires, that individuals and associations of individuals can work together for the common good of humanity, that rational progress can be made towards individual and community well-being, and that all individuals are endowed with certain rights and responsibilities. (Tegenfeldt 2001, 109)

Development occurs in all societies. It involves processes that require an appreciation of existing endogenous strengths and (often) exogenous interventions. Successful development requires critical analysis, mutual learning, and acceptance of its paradoxes and dilemmas. To ensure that benefits of development are sustained, environmental concerns must be a central priority. There is no single measure of development, and assessment of development requires a range of indicators.

By contrast, humanitarian action focuses on saving lives and relieving suffering. Traditionally, humanitarian assistance has been based on the defining humanitarian principles outlined previously, of impartially alleviating suffering based solely on need, independent of the political, economic, or strategic objectives of any actors (IMGHD 2003). Seeking to remain apolitical, humanitarian assistance therefore commonly bypasses domestic governments and seeks to provide assistance directly to those in need. While often a short-term response to natural disasters, humanitarian assistance may also be a response to chronic need.

As has already been noted, NGO and multilateral development agencies have created space for development in Myanmar by adhering strictly to these humanitarian principles of assistance (Duffield 2008). As a result, throughout much of this book the terms "development" and "humanitarian" are sometimes used in conjunction with one another to refer to programs seeking development outcomes but whose implementation is based largely or exclusively on these traditional humanitarian principles.

This research focuses on how Western-based or Western-origin INGOs work context-sensitively in Myanmar, because of the specific issues connected with Western–Burmese relationships, both historically and currently. INGO work in Myanmar consists primarily of project-based community development interventions and work in areas of advocacy with government officials on behalf of communities and civil society.

INGOs are distinct from multilateral organizations, who are overseen by nation-states via the UN. Likewise, bilateral organizations are inherently linked with nation-states. Given the strained relationships between Myanmar and much of the international community, including the UN, tensions exist with the governments behind most bilateral and multilateral agencies. INGOs, on the other hand, have greater potential to offer humanitarian neutrality. Where their comparative neutrality is accepted by both sides, the possibility exists for INGOs to engage in action precisely because of their non-government status.

Development work may address a micro-, meso-, or macro-level, engaging individuals, communities, districts, nations, and international regions (Feeny and Clarke 2009). Broad-based, pro-poor macroeconomic growth may possibly be the most effective at lifting the largest number of people out of economic poverty, although even when countries experience rapid economic growth (as in many East and Southeast Asian countries over the past half century), many are left behind, and issues of marginalization and social exclusion are often not dealt with. Multilateral and bilateral agencies are often the best equipped to assist with macroeconomic growth, through institutional capacity building. INGO approaches are often more tailored to target disadvantaged and excluded communities and individuals.

Achieving significant macroeconomic growth in Myanmar will require substantial policy change, making this an inherently political path. Changes required will include integration into global trade and finance; reform of banking, taxation, infrastructure, and education; and stimulation of private entrepreneurship, savings, and investment. These preconditions for long-term macroeconomic development are not currently in place in Myanmar (Moore

2009, 2011). The absence of true rule of law and the unwillingness of the regime and the international community to partner in reforming these vital areas of the state and the economy to date have prohibited such growth, suggesting such broad macroeconomic development is still some way off. The significant thawing of relations between the international community and the Myanmar government is encouraging, but there remains a long way to go.

Micro- and meso-levels of development are more grass roots and bottom up, instigated by working directly with local communities and civil society. INGO development thus is not merely a stopgap while waiting for macroeconomic development. INGO development has a specific focus and a number of key strengths, most notably in that it targets assistance to the poorest, most vulnerable, and most marginalized, those who are the last to benefit from broader macroeconomic development, and that it primarily seeks to engage with and empower civil society and local communities (Malik 2011). This is in stark contrast to the work of multilateral and bilateral development agencies that often engage primarily with the government agencies and through them create the environment within which civil society and communities can be supported in development.

Most international donors require development assistance to Myanmar to bypass the government and be geared toward the alleviation of extreme poverty and capacity development of communities and civil society. These are activities in which INGOs excel and are commonly referred to as human or community development.

It could therefore be argued that INGO development is far better suited to current donor demands on assistance to Myanmar than multilateral development is. It is interesting to note that the UNDP operates in Myanmar under a restricted mandate preventing it from partnering with government agencies, and thus it also directly partners with civil society and local communities in a manner closely resembling INGO development.

Fieldwork

The most authoritative primary sources to use for information about INGO actions and projects are the key decision-makers in INGO country offices, generally foreigners with the role of country coordinator or a similar position description. It is these individuals who pursue or authorize development approaches in Myanmar or at very least pursue or authorize the local implementation of their organizational development approaches. After the survey of the literature regarding context in development and the Myanmar context, this research therefore then needs a window into their thoughts and actions on context-sensitive implementation of development within this environment.

Phenomenological Approach

The research methodology adopted to gain such an insight into context-sensitivity seeks to understand project implementation and effectiveness through the eyes of key INGO decision-makers and practitioners working in Myanmar. The fieldwork in this volume therefore primarily adopts a phenomenological approach.

Phenomenology "holds that any attempt to understand social reality has to be grounded in people's experiences of that social reality" (Gray 2009, 22). A phenomenological approach aims to gain understanding of subjective experience through an exploration of the personal perceptions of others (Denzin and Lincoln 2000), thereby exploring prevailing cultural or social understandings (Gray 2009). It aims to "get inside the social context of the phenomenon, to live it oneself, as it were, and look at the phenomenon more indirectly" (Titchen and Hobson 2005, 121). This is an inductive approach that seeks to find the internal logic of the subject and understand meanings from their perspective. It works with individuals and seeks to understand conceptual perspectives and understandings of their personal experience. A phenomenological approach therefore makes almost exclusive use of in-depth interviews.

Semistructured Interviews

Foreign and local managers of development organizations constitute a professional elite, and semistructured interviews are the preferred method of qualitative data collection from such elites because it gives participants more control and helps them to find inherent value in the research (Odendahl and Shaw 2001). Chain referral sampling was used to access informants, because of their connection through personal networks in the professional and expatriate communities. Such purposeful selection is particularly appropriate in circumstances such as this, where only a small number of people are qualified to be interviewed (Maykut and Morehouse 1994), and is ideal for reaching a sufficient number of information-rich key informants (Patton 1990).

Informants

The field research reported in part 3 draws on semistructured interviews with fifty-one key practitioners between 2009 and 2011. Most interviews were conducted face-to-face in Myanmar, were around one and a half hours in length, and were recorded and transcribed. A Delphi panel discussion was also used in Yangon during December 2009 to confirm preliminary findings.

Interview participants represent a broad spectrum of those working in the country, as follows:

- twenty-four current and one former country directors or senior advisers from twenty-one INGOs,
- four directors of INGOs who do not have MOUs and are therefore based outside Myanmar and work into the country from outside through partnerships,
- eight directors or advisers for local nongovernmental organizations (LNGOs),
- six country representatives or senior managers for UN agencies,
- three in-country coordinators for some of the largest international donors,
- four foreign journalists with extensive experience inside Myanmar, and
- one president of a GONGO.

The INGOs represented that can be named signify a broad spectrum of the organizations working in the country. These include World Vision, the largest INGO in Myanmar with approximately 1,200 local staff at the time of the interviews (400 were at that time on short-term contracts for Cyclone Nargis relief projects). Other major INGOs included CARE, Oxfam, and Médecins du Monde. They also include much smaller organizations, such as the Burnet Institute from Australia, working to build the capacity of local civil organizations in the area of health, and Terre des Hommes, Italy. They also include a number of faith-based organizations (FBOs), such as The Leprosy Mission International and Adventist Development and Relief Agency. The LNGOs represented in these interviews, likewise, cover a spectrum from the Shalom Foundation, one of the larger, better organized, and better funded LNGOs in the country, through to unregistered local organizations cautiously running community development programs, orphanages, and educational programs while attempting to not attract unwanted attention.

Many interview participants requested complete anonymity, while others requested that some comments be treated anonymously. Where participants agreed to allow responses to be on the record, interviews are referenced in text with author surname followed by organization and year. For example, (Tumbian, *WV* 2009) refers to the interview with James Tumbian, country director for World Vision Myanmar, during 2009. At the same time, however, all interviewees have been assigned a randomized number from 1 to 50, and any reference to anonymous parts of their interview is simply referenced by a number (e.g., Source 6).

A Note on the Reliability of Data

As was discussed in Ware (2011), economic and demographic data on Burma/Myanmar have been of questionable validity since independence, and the problem remains acute today despite improvements made through the concerted efforts of agencies after Cyclone Nargis. This paucity of reliable data is the result of several factors, including the regime having limited control over parts of the territory, limited resources for data gathering and analysis, and data being manipulated for internal and external consumption. Often this manipulation is by the officials and agencies that collect the data, "to please the top of the power hierarchy" (Steinberg 2006, xxvi). "The statistical record is particularly problem ridden, at best no more than a rough and unreliable picture, prone to understatement through incompetence . . . [or] exaggeration through politically driven manipulation," in which it is not always in the interest of middle-ranking officials to reveal what they know (Perry 2007, 16). There are also widespread suggestions that deliberate misinformation has been a regime survival strategy. As Rotberg (1998, 154) observes, "Economic data [on Burma] often have only a tenuous link to that which they purport to observe."

The government has not published a full annual statistical review since 1997–98, and the most recent formal census took place in 1983. As an illustration of the dearth in reliable data, Table 1.1 provides national population estimates from various agencies showing variation of up to sixteen million people over four years (a variation of up to one-third the estimated population) depending on the source and on the modeling used. With that rate of variation in data as fundamental as population, other data on poverty and the economy must be considered estimates at best.

This lack of reliable data and the difficulties gaining access means even respected academic researchers are often forced to rely on "informed hunches" (Taylor 2008, 219). Data are "negotiated more than they are observed in Myanmar," and political incentives favor overreporting by government officials (Dapice, Vallely, and Wilkinson 2009). There is "a manipulation of data culture" in which even INGOs are advised not to publish real data but to report figures as provided by government officials. Sometimes key figures released by

Table 1.1

Total Population of Myanmar Data, as Reported by Various Agencies

Source	Population (Million)	Year
ADB[a]	58.820	2008
ASEAN[b]	58.510	2008
DFAT (Aust)[c]	58.800	2008
EIU[d]	49.100	2008
IMF[e]	48.800	2008
MoFA[f]	52.400	2003
MoH[g]	56.620	2006
SDC[h]	48.400	2008
UN ESA[i]	50.519	2005
UNICEF[j]	48.798	2007
UN OHRLLS[k]	42.720	2004
WHO[l]	48.379	2006
World Bank[m]	49.200	2008

Source. Adapted from Save [the Children] in Myanmar & Matt Desmond (2009).
a. Asian Development Bank: Key indicators for Asia & Pacific (2009).
b. ASEAN Statistical Yearbook (2008).
c. Australian Department of Foreign Affairs and Trade: Burma Factsheet (2009).
d. Economist Intelligence Unit Country Report (May 2009).
e. International Monetary Fund (2008).
f. Myanmar Ministry of Foreign Affairs website (2008).
g. Myanmar Ministry of Health. *Health in Myanmar 2008*, Nay Pyi Taw. Refers Planning Department, Ministry of National Planning and Economic Development.
h. SDC: Mekong Programme website (info from BBC).
i. UN Department of Economic and Social Affairs, Population Division (2007).
j. UNICEF: At a Glance. Myanmar statistics (2008).
k. UN OHRLLS Country Profiles. Special Report (2006).
l. WHO World Health Statistics (2008).
m. World Bank: World Development Indicators (2009).

the government are rejected by the international community as clearly inconsistent with other information; for example, recent GDP figures for Myanmar were not accepted by the World Bank or IMF (ESCAP 2007). Other data are not produced at all, or the Myanmar government chooses not to make it public.

Igboemeka (2005) argues that this lack of reliable data is one of the most important limitations on aid effectiveness in the country but that deep political sensitivities make producing accurate data a challenge. Agencies are often unwilling to share the information they collect from their own operations with each other because of these political sensitivities. This may have improved somewhat with the coordination between agencies that emerged in the response to Cyclone Nargis, but it still remains an issue.

Inadequate and unreliable data are not unique to Myanmar. For example, similar issues are observed in Papua New Guinea and the Solomon Islands (Feeny and Clarke 2009). Still, Myanmar is the only member country of ASEAN that has not yet begun to formulate a national statistical development strategy and stands out as the country with the "least capacity" in ASEAN "to produce reliable and timely data even for the most basic statistics" (ESCAP 2007). The World Bank's *Statistical Capacity Indicator* (2009) for Myanmar has been revised downward significantly over the past three years (World Bank 2009; ESCAP 2007). The IMF regularly admonishes Myanmar to improve data and statistical reporting (Collignon 2001), but this also suggests a responsibility on the international community to work with the Myanmar government to help build data-gathering and data-integrity capacity.

Summary of Chapters

This book is structured in three parts. Part 1 sets up the theory and research design for examining context-sensitive development, part 2 explores the Myanmar context in detail, and part 3 presents and analyzes the fieldwork research findings documenting how INGOs implement context-sensitive development in Myanmar.

Part 1 consists of two chapters exploring the theory, literature, and research. This first chapter has introduced the topic, defined the research question, offered definitions of key terms, and outlined the research methodology used to gain the in-depth interview data with development practitioners reported in part 3 of the book.

Chapter 2 traces the evolution of thinking about context-sensitivity in international development from single pathway notions of economic development after World War II. It notes the development of country-specific plans, the recognition that every country faces a unique developmental environment, emphasis from developing nations on the need for greater sensitivity to their context, recent emphasis on cultural diversity, and the prioritization of community-led development and partnership with local organizations. It notes that apart from emphasis on culture, most context-sensitive development literature focuses on sociopolitical factors, with the complexity of conflict and state fragility requiring the greatest sensitivity. This chapter suggests that while the global development dialogue has moved past universal prescriptions to recognize diversity, multiple paths, and unique contexts, strong forces push development practice toward normative application. Despite emphasis on highly participatory development, local partnerships, and empowerment, what is widely overlooked is the ways in which international agencies themselves still need to contextualize their own actions to local, national, and international contextual factors.

Part 2 also consists of two chapters, exploring the sociopolitical context of Myanmar from a historical and then a contemporary perspective. Noting that Myanmar is marked by conflict and state fragility, and that the literature calls for development in such contexts to be grounded in an in-depth, historically informed understanding, chapter 3 offers a critical analysis of the historical antecedents to the current political crisis. It does this by examining three significant historical narratives: the traditional values established during centuries of monarchy, the impact of Western contact and colonialism, and the tumultuous period surrounding independence. It is argued that traditional perceptions about power and rulership, the conditioning history of interaction with the West, and the animosities of WWII and the post-independence civil war all continue to resonate within contemporary politics. "Without the study of [Burmese history], one's understanding of Burmese society subsequently, though not unimportant, is incomplete" (Aung-Thwin 1985, 1). This discussion lays a foundation to understanding the values of the political elite today and why they react in the ways they do and thus points to development approaches that are more likely to gain cooperation.

Chapter 4 then explores the contemporary sociopolitical, economic, and humanitarian context faced by INGOs working in Myanmar. The political context is analyzed by examining the values and strategic objectives of the four key actors in this drama: the *tatmadaw* (armed forces) and the ruling elite, Aung San Suu Kyi and the opposition movement, the ethnic minorities, and the international community. Then an analysis of the economy is presented, together with discussion of the causes of underdevelopment in the country. Finally, the humanitarian challenge facing INGOs in Myanmar is investigated by considering the extent of absolute poverty and multidimensional impacts it has within the country, the key challenge development INGOs seek to address.

Part 3 presents new field research exploring INGO context-sensitive development in Myanmar over three chapters. Chapter 5 explores interview results documenting the ways in which INGOs make their work in local communities context-sensitive, adapting to both the domestic context and the international context. Work in local communities is analyzed under the conceptual approaches to community development most commonly expressed during the interviews, namely, participation, equity, sustainability, active citizenship, and context-sensitivity. It is found that to be most effective, INGOs place more effort into making their programs more highly participatory in Myanmar than they would in other contexts within which they work, with a strong focus on equity and on sustainability by local communities themselves. Until very recently, however, they stopped short of capacity building local communities for active citizenship, preferring to adopt advocacy roles on behalf of communities.

INGOs likewise contextualize the way in which they negotiate their relationships with other stakeholders in Myanmar's development. Chapter 6 presents the interview results documenting the ways they negotiate these stakeholder relationships, finding INGOs approach working with local civil society, NGOs, regime officials, and even other INGOs quite differently in Myanmar than they would in most other countries. It is found that INGOs see a need to limit or proceed far more cautiously with many of these relationships within the Myanmar context than they would elsewhere. Again, this contextualization can be linked directly to restrictions stemming from both the domestic and the international political environment. Relationships with these stakeholders are analyzed under the ideas of partnerships, capacity building, advocacy, rights-based approach, and accountability.

Chapter 7 presents the perspective of the interview participants in regard to the restricted humanitarian space within which they operate, in terms of both domestic and international restrictions, and then analyses this restricted space from several theoretical perspectives. INGOs argue that the greatest constraints on their efforts toward immediate alleviation of extreme poverty do not come from the Myanmar government as much as from limited funding and restrictive mandates, requiring continual lobbying of their own governments, boards, and donors. This chapter therefore explores the theory behind the international pressure on Myanmar and the restrictions on the humanitarian assistance from perspectives of humanitarianism, international relations, contemporary political philosophy, and development theory. It concludes that while sanctions have a role in the socialization of norm-violating states and addressing structural causes of poverty, the international community has competing approaches and concerns toward Myanmar that need to be clarified. In the light of the effective approaches INGOs have found in Myanmar, and many significant tactical concessions made recently by the Myanmar government, this chapter argues that a repositioning by the international community that would significantly expand the humanitarian space is overdue.

Chapter 8 draws the book together, offering a range of conclusions from the research and synthesizing the findings. It reemphasizes the need for context-sensitive development and the theoretical perspective on conceptual ways to further facilitate this and discusses how INGOs conduct development context-sensitively in the context of contemporary Myanmar.

2

Context-Sensitive Development Theory

> Development is, perhaps, the world's most critical problem, incorporating most of the world's pressing issues. At the same time, the subject of development has retreated to increasingly simple formulae in the minds of many of the people and governments able to address it meaningfully. (Kingsbury 2008b, 6)

The International Labour Organisation (ILO) offers an interesting case study of an international agency adapting its approach in Myanmar to be sensitive to the context.

The global governing body of the ILO comprises representatives from UN states, employer groups, and employee groups. Its mandate is to promote rights at work, encourage employment opportunities, enhance social protection, and strengthen dialogue on work-related issues. It usually fulfills these aims by promoting social justice and rights, developing labor standards, and running technical partnership programs between governments, employers, and workers. However, restrictions required by the international community and the Myanmar government have limited the ILO's mandate in Myanmar to working solely for the elimination of forced labor and ensuring freedom of association in the country (see ILO 1998, 2002, and supplements 2007, 2008, 2009, 2010, and 2011).

Given this global mission statement and the narrow mandate for Myanmar, the ILO undertook some fascinating contextual work in Myanmar in the wake of Cyclone Nargis, highlighting the role of agency field offices in contextualization. The ILO liaison officer for Myanmar, Steve Marshall, described how he significantly innovated under the terms of his mandate from the ILO and the Myanmar government, documenting how the ILO has engaged in desperately needed community reconstruction and development within their mandate, in a highly context-sensitive manner:

> *During Nargis we did a specific project for the elimination of forced labor. We did it as a "good practice employment" project where we let some 150-odd contracts for infrastructure reconstruction work. These contracts were let with local village community committees, which were elected for that purpose. Those committees let local contracts to villagers. I only engaged civil engineers and liaison officers whose job it was to teach local communities the basics of governance and conflict of interest management, financial management, and to teach contractors things such as about competitive bidding, good employment, and things of that nature.*
>
> *So from October last year until the end of June 2009, we have been working in the Delta in quite a big way, in what I would see as being a community development activity which happens to produce some infrastructure as an outcome. It is clearly about good employment practices. It is clearly about getting citizens to understand the fundamentals of community activity, consultation processes, good governance activities, good employment practices, good payment of wages practices, and their fundamental rights under the existing law. (Not giving them any idea about what life could or should be like, but what they actually have the right to now.)*
>
> *There is not much point in giving someone a nice building and a nice farm and helping them plant a crop if they can't get their stuff to the market. So our project was about giving them mobility, between villages and from villages to markets. We built something like 85 km of raised concrete footpaths, we built 52–53 bridges, 25–26 jetties (not bamboo, but decent ones that will last). And this was ALL done by local contractors. Given the skills and resources, these communities employed locals from their area, and they own everything.*
>
> *I am currently negotiating with the government to continue that project in a non-Nargis environment, so we are looking at expansion outside of the Delta. . . . Obviously this goes to some very fundamental community development issues which will be critical if the government is moving to a form of democracy, because most people in these villages have got no understanding of the concepts of decision making for com-*

munity development. This is not a country where you make decisions . . .
so it is critical that people at a village level actually start to understand
concepts of community consultation, discussion of issues, and consensus
decision making.

Everything is being done in the name of forced labor and freedom
of association (laughs), because if I do it in any other name, the reality is
that I am breaching the resolution of our conference, and that gets me
in trouble. So, for example, this project is not a community development
activity—I sold it as being a project of education for the elimination of
forced labor. But the reality is that we have a very good community
development project, which has some very useful physical community
outcomes.

There can be no fixed and final definition of development; only suggestions of what it should imply in particular contexts. (Hettne 1995, 15)

Aid agencies have not advocated universal policy prescriptions for international development for decades, other than broad policies such as gender mainstreaming or rights. However, despite over thirty years of well-argued critique denouncing normative, one-size-fits-all formulations of development, top-down, externally driven, noncontextual development persists, and attitudes of modernity and neocolonialism continue to dominate much development thought and practice (Ife 2010). Rather than facilitating difference, this type of development acts more as a "homogenising conversion of extrinsic properties to a common conceptual core" (Bastin 2010). In this milieu,

diversity is seen as a deviation from the central axis of progress and so must be tamed and refined. . . . While paying lip-service to "difference"—the superficial characteristics and varying histories of groups—development programmes, including those of international NGOs, have never been patient with diversity. (Murphy 2000, 342)

On one hand, participation, empowerment, and the recognition of factors, such as culture and conflict, are very widely acknowledged to be essential for effective sustainable development. On the other hand, powerful forces still drive both development theory and practice toward normative approaches. This chapter explores that tension and the ideas of context-sensitive development through a review of the development studies literature, examining inadequacies in current theory and proposing steps toward a new model for context-sensitive development.

Agencies and donors recognize that every context is unique, that there is no template for development, and therefore that what works in one country may not work in another (Stokes 2010). Yet at the same time, development practice has sought at least broadly applicable lessons, if not universal principles, while large international agencies derive much of their legitimacy from key organizational mission statements resulting in their being held publicly accountable against normalizing criteria (Shutt 2009). Some specialists even argue that development studies is a normative discipline and should remain that way (e.g., Kilby 2010). Regardless, this chapter argues that the dominant presentation of development in terms of norms has resulted in insufficient articulation of the role of development agencies in tailoring what they do to specific contexts, particularly to difficult sociopolitical contexts such as Myanmar.

This chapter traces the evolution of context-sensitivity in the development literature, then examines the various aspects of context-sensitivity that are well reflected in it, namely, sensitivity to culture, conflict, and state fragility. The distinctive roles of various types of development agencies in different difficult political contexts are discussed. This chapter then examines participatory development as the model most widely adopted by the INGO development community to ensure context-sensitivity, noting the underlying assumption implicit in this model is that local knowledge, participation, empowerment, and partnership will make decision making inherently sensitive to context. Despite the strengths of this model in terms of local knowledge, cultural sensitivity, and devolved decision making, it is argued that this model is insufficient of itself to ensure sensitivity to more difficult sociopolitical issues, especially those involving significant national and international tension. The need for greater theorization of sensitivity to difficult sociopolitical context and the roles INGOs themselves need to play is thus argued. This chapter ends with a discussion of social change models and a proposed conceptual advancement arguing for an extension to the participation-empowerment model to also include the deliberate empowerment of INGO field staff by INGO head offices and hierarchies.

The History of Context-Sensitivity in Development Thought

The recognition that development needs to be sensitive to context is today widespread; indeed it is an almost implicit presupposition in most development thinking. However, arriving at this level of conceptual agreement has been a lengthy process, and this understanding is still subject to strong normative forces opposing effective contextualization in practice.

Modernity, Economic Development, and Modernization
Origins of the Idea of Development

The origins of the modern notion of development are said to date to innovations in ancient Greek and early Christian thought, as early Christians, in particular, reconceived history as a linear flow of time replacing older and more traditional ideas of history as a cyclical rotation of seasons (Rist 2002). Christianity postulated a definite beginning to time in the distant past, a present condition that included the offer of redemption in present and future circumstances, and a future consummation of all things at the end of time. While this reconception took some centuries to have its effect, the idea of a linear flow of time and the perception that history involves progress and development eventually led to the Enlightenment and became the foundational idea of modernity.

The dominant Western ideas about development are founded on the concept of modernity and the underlying notion of progress along a linear, cause-and-effect pathway. Bastin (2010) goes so far as to suggest that "development" is not a concept, in the sense that Deleuze and Guattari (1991) define the term, but a mode of practice based on the underlying concept of modernity. Deleuze and Guattari argue that such propositions are commonly confused with concepts but that concepts are distinctive by the inseparability of their components. Building on this philosophical reasoning, attempts to redefine the parameters of development fail because of the coherent and pervasive nature of the underlying concept being drawn on in development practice, namely, modernity.

The "development era" began in the late nineteenth century, the heyday of modernism. The popular adoption of the idea of development at this time paralleled acceptance of the theory of evolution and its application in social and cultural evolution (Nisbet 1969; Rist 2002). History came to be seen in evolutionary terms, with humanity continually evolving into more developed cultural forms. History was increasingly defined in linear ideas of progress, growth, and development, and the West, being wealthier at that point in history, was assumed to be more evolved than other societies, an idea with strong endurance.

Development was thus co-opted as a doctrine by the European colonial powers to justify colonial intervention on philanthropic grounds. It was widely argued that "higher races" had duties toward "lower races" to share the benefits of science and progress in a "civilizing mission" (Bernstein 2000; Rist 2002). Not doing so constituted "moral degeneracy." Colonialism was thus justified, in part, as the most efficient means to civilize less developed peoples. While local culture and other contextual differences were commonly noted during this period, development was framed in linear, evolutionary terms that sought to exchange this traditional culture for more developed forms (Rist 2002). Context was subjugated to evolutionary ideas.

Hildebrand (1848) was possibly the first to formalize this linear "stages" theory in economic development, a theme taken up by Schumpeter in his more well-known *Theory of Economic Development* ([1911] 1962). By the end of the colonial era, the linear development model with sequential developmental stages was firmly enshrined in economic theory.

Second Impetus for Development

A second, more contemporary, impetus for development came from post-WWII reconstruction, the formation of the United Nations, the cold war, and decolonization. During the cold war, offers of development assistance were wielded as tools to persuade poorer countries into one of the two ideological alliances, as was well illustrated by Harry Truman's famous 1947 *Truman Doctrine* speech. The United Nations' (1951) subsequent study of *Measures for the Economic Development of Under-Developed Countries* is clearly based on an implicit assumption that development in all societies would be triggered by investment in infrastructure and industrialization and result in a mass-production and consumption-based society. Lewis's *Theory of Economic Growth* (1955), highly influential in the West, required favoring an entrepreneurial capitalist class to facilitate economic growth. The paradigm was very much based on the linear stages theory.

Possibly the most influential Western articulation of development theory during this era was Rostow's *Stages of Economic Growth* (1960). Even the title highlights the dominance of the idea of linear progression. Rostow was a significant voice in US cold war modernist development and epitomizes the dominant ideology about the means of achieving rapid economic development in Third World countries. Rostow postulated a linear sequence of five universal stages of economic growth, from traditional society through to a mass-consumption economy, which all countries must pass through in economic development. His model characterized the preconditions for economic "take-off" as being linked to rapid culture change in which traditional values and behaviors are substituted with more developed, Western-like ones. These ideas became the conventional development wisdom during this period. Any contextual differences between developing nations were subjugated to the idea of linear development toward a more advanced Western norm.

Challenges to the Linear Model
The Rise of Country- and Context-Specific Development

One of the earliest development economists to challenge this model and argue for country-specific solutions was Hirschman (1958). While still referring to "advanced" and "backward" countries, and speaking of processes and sequences, he introduced the idea of context into development. This theme was taken up by Seers (1969), whose seminal paper redefined development from economic advancement measured by national product into "the realisation of the potential of human personality." This, he argued, requires not only the reduction of poverty, unemployment, and inequality but also adequate education, freedom of speech, and national political and economic sovereignty. Economic growth, he argued, could just as easily contribute to social and political problems as solve them.

Seers then examined nation-specific strategies for development, arguing that development for underdeveloped countries today is an entirely different task from that faced by, say, Britain or France in the nineteenth century (Seers and Joy 1970). Development is not a single linear progression of stages but depends on historical and contemporary context. Marris (1970, 103) likewise argued that "there are all kinds of issues which cannot be solved by any dogmatic prescription," while Streeten (1970) suggested that the real challenge is finding the appropriate means for each context. Because contexts change and our understanding of them is not good, development cannot be a set of predetermined steps but must adapt to changing circumstances. The following year Simon Kuznets won the Nobel Prize for "insight into the economic and social structure and process of development." He concluded that underdeveloped countries possess different characteristics and exist in contexts very different from those faced by industrialized countries when they developed, helping put an end to the simplistic view that all countries go through the same linear stages.

Almost a decade later, Seers (1977) lamented that the simplistic linear growth paradigm remained because of its simplicity and that it offered an easy, "objective" basis for project evaluation. Development, he insisted, has not occurred unless inequality and poverty are reduced, requiring development to be country specific and involve cultural politics. He predicted, however, a long lag before widespread implementation of these ideas.

Basic Needs, Developing Nations, and Human Development

Voices for more context-sensitive development grew throughout the 1970s and 1980s. The ILO launched a mission for equitable distribution in 1970, drawing on social rather than economic indicators of development (Seers 1977). The ILO then began arguing for development targeting *basic needs*, defined as basic goods (food, shelter, clothing, etc.), basic services (education, health, etc.), participation in decision making, basic human rights, and productive employment (McGillivray 2008). These needs are contextual; thus cultural fit became seen as essential for sustainable development. One precondition for satisfaction of basic needs is "shared cultural understanding of techniques previously learned by the people" through the transmission of cultural knowledge (Doyal and Gough 1991).

As developing nations have gained a voice in the development dialogue, they have likewise called for greater emphasis on context. For example, the UN *Declaration on the Right to Development* (1986) originated with the Non-Aligned Movement and was articulated in relation to its call for a *New International Economic Order* (Gouwenberg 2009). The preamble to the declaration describes development as

> a comprehensive economic, social, cultural and political process . . . [of] the entire population and of all individuals . . . a many-faceted concept which encompasses the whole human being in all the aspects of her or his basic rights . . . in the context within which the individual must live . . . [and] the community to which she or he belongs. (UN 1991, article 17)

The inaugural UN Development Programme's *Human Development Report* (1990) took up this theme and proposed a new composite human development index to replace economic indicators as the standard measure of development. This shift was based largely on the work of Nobel Prize laureate Amartya Sen (1993, 1999a), whose *Capability Approach* proposed development as an expansion of "capabilities," creating freedom for people to do and to be, to exercise various "functionings." Nussbaum (2000) defined these as things like life, health, bodily integrity, emotions, practical reason, affiliation, play, and control over one's environment.

Such has been the change in the understanding of development as being person focused and contextual that now leaders in the developing world who have no specific background in development studies, such as Myanmar opposition leader Aung San Suu Kyi, can confidently deny the previous development mantra:

> The history of the world shows that peoples and societies do not have to pass through a fixed series of stages in the course of development. . . . The true development of human beings involves much more than mere economic growth. At its heart there must be a sense of empowerment and inner fulfilment. This alone will ensure that human and cultural values remain paramount. (Suu Kyi 1995a, 17)

Acceptance of Need for Context-Sensitive Development

Most scholars, international agencies, and donors today would agree that "development programs must involve a capacity for modification to local circumstances, according to local criteria . . . to suit local needs. . . . [This] highlights and illustrates the broader principle of modification to context at every level" (Kingsbury 2008a, 223). Furthermore,

> the diversity of contexts in which NGOs operate [and] the importance of understanding those contexts [means] assumptions . . . are not necessarily transferable from one place to another, and misunderstandings are often rooted in cultural differences. . . . Development interventions [must] be based on a deep understanding of the local context. (Brehm 2000, 1)

A realization of the need for development to be sensitive to context is today almost universal, and recognition of context is widely considered an essential first step toward effectiveness. For example, recent reviews of AusAID's programs by the Office of Development Effectiveness concluded that the most important factor for program effectiveness was understanding and being "flexible to the country context" (Davidson 2010). The review found that forms and institutions should not be imported from other contexts. Several other reviews agree, emphasizing, "Aid programs must be adapted to individual country circumstances. One size does not fit all—not even among countries categorised as fragile states" (Baird 2009, 14).

It needs to be recognized that what constitutes good practice in one context may not work in another. Perhaps, then, an essential fundament of good practice is recognition that any practice needs to be designed with a close appreciation of the local context. . . . It cannot be overstated how important an understanding of context is to the effectiveness of aid. Gaining that understanding is not just about analysing the nature of the current government; it is also about knowing and understanding the key agents of change and continuity in any society. (Hall and Howell 2010, 7, 24)

Aspects of Context-Sensitive Development

In suggesting that context-sensitive development has become widely accepted in development theory, it is worthy of note that the term "context" is rarely defined and is rarely connected to discussion of the roles and dynamics such sensitivity might imply. A survey of the literature shows that sensitivity to two major types of context are documented, namely, sensitivity to unique cultures and sensitivity to difficult political contexts, particularly those suffering conflict and state fragility.

Sensitivity to Unique Cultural Contexts
Culture and Economic Development
Foremost within the idea of sensitivity to context in the development literature is the aspect of culture. Indeed, the term "context" is commonly used interchangeably with the term "culture." "Culture" is one of the most complicated and disputed words in the English language (Williams 1993), with many conceptual problems stemming from widespread use without agreed definition (Keesing and Strathern 1998). The modern anthropological meaning of the term, first established by Tylor in 1871 (Kroeber and Kluckhohn 1952), defined "culture" as a "complex whole which includes knowledge, belief, art, law, morals, custom, and any other capabilities and habits acquired by man as a member of society" (Tylor [1871] 1958). The oft-quoted conclusion of Kroeber and Kluckhohn (1952, 357), after surveying 164 definitions of culture, is that "culture consists of patterns, explicit and implicit, of and for behavior acquired and transmitted by symbols. . . . The essential core of culture consists of traditional . . . ideas and especially their attached values." While anthropologists have since raised many other definitions and challenges to the idea of culture, culture, broadly conceived of in this manner as a collective, coherent system of learned ideas, behaviors, values, and symbols, is widely

adopted in the development literature. In this, every culture is unique and thus requires sensitivity.

Prior to the 1970s, development was largely equated with modernization, and culture was associated with anthropology (Schech and Haggis 2000). Tradition and modernity were seen as a dichotomy, and development's interest in culture was to seek ways to transform traditional behavior and values into more Western forms (Braden and Mayo 1999; Williams 2004). Hoselitz (1952, 9) set the scene during the cold war era in the very first article of the journal *Economic Development and Cultural Change*. Discussing "Non-Economic Barriers to Economic Development," he argued that development required a complete reorientation of cultural norms and values, lamenting "the obstinacy with which people hold to traditional values even in the face of a rapidly changing technology."

Modernization theorists of the era discussed traditional cultural elements they believed must change for economic development to occur. For example, Hoselitz cited key Buddhist and social elements of Burmese culture as good examples of obstacles to economic advancement, while Hagen (1957) saw loyalty to family in China as an obstacle. Belief that traditional culture was a barrier to development, and that rapid cultural change into modern, Western-like forms was integral to economic development, was further reflected in Lerner's 1958 modernization text, *The Passing of Traditional Society*.

Culture at the Heart of Human Development
Perspectives have changed as our appreciation of other peoples has deepened. Sensitivity to culture emerged as a central consideration in the development dialogue during the 1990s and is now at the heart of mainstream development (Radcliffe 2006a). This new emphasis on culture has far-reaching implications and constitutes a major challenge to rethink development; only some of the issues presented by culture are being fully addressed in the discourse at this time. Schech and Haggis (2000) offer a comprehensive discussion of the tools offered by cultural studies, postcolonial studies, and postmodernism for this task. In "How Does Culture Matter?" Sen (2004) refers to culture as a resource in development study and practice.

The centrality of sensitivity to culture, at least in theory, has been widely expressed by development agencies over the past two decades. This is illustrated by a brief survey of recent discussion of culture by UN agencies but extends far wider than just the United Nations. For example, in January 1988, while launching the *World Decade for Cultural Development*, UN secretary-general Javier Pérez de Cuéllar observed that development had often failed, because the importance of the human factor—that complex web of relationships and beliefs, values and motivations, which lie at the very heart of a culture—had been underestimated in many development projects. (foreword to UNESCO 1995, 22)

In 1991 UNESCO established a World Commission on Culture and Development. De Cuéllar, now president of that commission, declared in its first report, *Our Creative Diversity,*

By 1988, it was already clear to us that development was a far more complex undertaking than had been originally thought. It could no longer be seen as a single, uniform, linear path, for this would inevitably eliminate cultural diversity and experimentation, and dangerously limit humankind's creative capacities. (UNESCO 1995, 22)

Our Creative Diversity argues that cultural diversity is a source of innovation and that development must offer the freedom to choose a satisfying and valued way of life in any culture. "Development divorced from its human or cultural context is growth without a soul." Then, in 2001 UNESCO explicitly linked cultural diversity with human rights, arguing that cultural diversity is a key factor in rights-based development, "one of the roots of development . . . a means to achieve a more satisfactory intellectual, emotional, moral and spiritual existence" (Article 3, UNESCO 2001). The UNDP concurs: "Cultural liberty is a human right and an important aspect of human development" (UNDP 2004, 6).

This recognition has ignited debate about development approaches that are more culturally sensitive. For example, a 2009 UNESCO symposium titled *Culture and Development* spent considerable time discussing the question, "How can culture, in its broadest sense, be more effectively integrated into local, national and regional development programmes?" One participant insightfully suggested, "Perhaps it is time to concentrate on the development dimension of culture, rather than the cultural dimension of development" (UNESCO 2010, 18).

A similar discovery of cultural diversity can be seen within the World Bank. In 1996 the World Bank put a task force together to consider the social dimensions of development, which led to the 1998 *Conference on Culture in Sustainable Development.* In opening the conference, the bank president remarked,

You simply cannot have development without a recognition of culture and of history. . . . Without cultural continuity, without a preservation of the things that matter in a society, there can be no stable development. (Wolfensohn 1998, 5)

He opened the follow-up 1999 *Culture Counts* conference saying,

Reducing poverty is not just about increasing productivity and income, but just as fundamentally about enabling people to have a broad sense of well-being and opportunities to express and make choices about their lives. And who can doubt that recognition and expression of cultural diversity is not fundamental to social well-being? (Wolfensohn 2000, 10)

The World Bank president, together with the archbishop of Canterbury, formed the now recently disbanded World Faiths Development Dialogue (WFDD) in 1998, seeking contribution from religious institutions into the bank's consultations for the *World Development Report* decadal report. The WFDD immediately urged an understanding of development that includes social, political, environmental, cultural, and spiritual, as well as economic, elements (Tyndale 1998). A follow-up report by the WFDD titled *Cultures, Spirituality and Development* (2001) offers a model of how this might work. Arguing that development will be successful, even in material terms, only if it takes into consideration the cultural and spiritual dimensions of people's lives, it proposes "a more truly participatory methodology than is usually the case" (WFDD 2001, 7). The WFDD insists that the people who are directly impacted by any change must play a conscious role in decision making that may result in aspects of traditional life being sacrificed. While not the first to suggest highly participatory development, the group clearly articulates a recognition that cultures continually evolve by the choices of people, thus linking culture-sensitive development with a process in which individuals and communities are truly empowered to accept, reject, adopt, or modify any development recommendations presented by outsiders, with full understanding of the implications of their decisions.

These examples clearly illustrate the extent to which at least the rhetoric of culture-sensitivity has become integral to the development dialogue. Nonetheless, concern continues to be expressed that despite decades of such critique and widespread acceptance of the importance of culturally sensitive development, "governments, development organisations and donors are [still] failing to engage with a crucial component of development by ignoring culture" (Commonwealth Foundation 2008a, 2). Somehow, the foundation challenges, current theory has not articulated how to move from assertions of the importance of cultural diversity to policy and strategy that provide for it in practice (Commonwealth Foundation 2008b).

Sensitivity to Difficult Political Contexts

In addition to the need for sensitivity to unique cultures, the development literature recognizes the need for sensitivity to certain difficult sociopolitical contexts. Development is particularly difficult in states embroiled in or just coming out of conflict, in states marred by poor governance and weak institutions, and in states with very strained relationships with the international community over concerns about human rights and regime legitimacy. The development literature addresses the first two of these contexts. This book extends this analysis to the third.

Conflict-Sensitive Development

Conflict is the sociopolitical context most widely addressed in the development literature. It is widely recognized that conflict inhibits development, and the link between poverty and conflict is well demonstrated (Kaldor 1999). Development is more arduous and dangerous in conflict situations and requires greater flexibility and adaptability (Kreimer et al. 1998). Social structures, ethnic divisions, poverty, and autocratic political systems can all fuel conflict, so the nature and delivery mechanisms of development can have serious ramifications (Clarke 2006; Clements 2006). Broad-based economic growth lifting masses out of poverty is impossible in countries that cannot guarantee public safety (AusAID 2005). Conflict is also the most common difficult political context for development. For example, over three-quarters of Australia's bilateral aid goes to countries that are experiencing, recovering from, or acutely vulnerable to conflict. AusAID claims that development assistance, when implemented sensitively, while far from a panacea, is one of the most effective foreign policy tools to reduce the incidence and severity of conflict in affected countries.

The idea of "conflict-sensitive development" is more recent than "culture-sensitive development" but has nonetheless quickly become well recognized. Momentum for conflict-sensitivity began with publication by the Development Assistance Committee of the Organisation for Economic Co-operation and Development of *Guidelines on Conflict, Peace and Development Cooperation* (OECD 1997). This report represented a significant shift in thinking, recognizing that development has the capacity to contribute proactively to conflict prevention and peace building if the root causes of conflict are understood and explicitly addressed and if societal capacity to manage differences without violence is strengthened. It likewise recognized that careless development can exacerbate conflict by fueling long-held fears and provoking unintended negative reactions.

Early in the discussion, Minear and Weiss (1993, 18) proposed eight principles for humanitarian work in conflict situations. These include non-partisanship, independence, appropriateness, contextualization, and that humanitarianism should overshadow sovereignty. The term "conflict-sensitive development" itself was introduced in a briefing paper submitted to this OECD committee by a group of INGOs (International Alert, Saferworld, and IDRC 2000). This consortium defines conflict as "two or more parties [who] believe that their interests are incompatible, express hostile attitudes or take action that damages other parties' ability to pursue their interests" (Conflict Sensitivity 2004). Thus, most conflict is not yet or not currently violent.

This grouping of INGOs, formalized in 2008 as the Conflict Sensitivity Consortium and funded by DFID, now consists of 37 major organizations. The consortium defines "conflict-sensitive development" as work that remains aware of local conflict and divisions,

> systematically taking into account both the positive and negative impact of interventions, in terms of conflict or peace dynamics, on the contexts in which they are undertaken, and, conversely, the impact of these contexts on the interventions. (Conflict Sensitivity 2009)

Conflict Sensitivity produced a manual, *Conflict-Sensitive Approaches to Development, Humanitarian Assistance and Peacebuilding (2004),* that provides a set of tools for conflict-sensitive practice. The group argues that conflict-sensitive development must commence with detailed analysis of the context, its causes, all actors, and their dynamic interaction. It specifically insists on interventions being based on an in-depth understanding of the political, economic, sociocultural, and historical context and the structural and proximate causes of conflict, including the triggers provoking fears and reactionary responses. Conflict-sensitive development requires a detailed understanding of the interaction between interventions and the context (Conflict Sensitivity 2011).

Humanitarian intervention in contested situations is always highly political, and thus conflict-sensitive development places an emphasis on dialogue, mediation, and full participation by all actors *(Conflict Sensitivity 2004)*. To omit actors increases the possibility of increased tensions. Conflict-sensitive development involves a delicate balance between demand for human rights standards, the achievement of peace and sustainable development, and ensuring injustice and inequality do not become further entrenched *(Conflict Sensitivity 2004)*.

Conflict-sensitive development seeks to ensure "human security," defined in the UNDP *Human Development Report* (1994) as "freedom from want" and "freedom from fear" and thus seeks to reduce reasons to fear others. Conflict most commonly stems from grievances over political, social, and/or economic inequalities; thus vital aspects of conflict-sensitive development include strengthening governance and civil society, facilitating dialogue and cooperation, developing mediation and participatory processes, and promoting human rights and democratization (OECD 1997). Conflict-sensitive development requires consolidation of relationships between actors and strengthening of institutions capable of containing and transforming conflict (Clements 2006). A series of recently published case studies concur that INGOs working in conflict contexts need to focus on (1) building and sustaining constructive relationships between actors and (2) addressing political, socioeconomic, and ethnic inequalities, not just poverty reduction, and that elite capture of development assistance is a major contributor to exacerbated conflict (Godnick and Klein 2009; Amarasuriya, Gündüz, and Mayer 2009; Alexander, Gündüz, and Subedi 2009; Banfield and Naujoks 2009).

A World Bank (2006) study found that the most common development mistakes made in conflict zones all result from conducting insufficiently detailed political analysis, underestimating the influence of local politics, and assuming that democracy would of itself promote peace. The bank finds that working in a conflict or postconflict situation requires an in-depth analysis of sociocultural, institutional, historical, and political dynamics of the conflict and consideration of the various stakeholders, social dynamics, vulnerabilities, social capital, and preexisting levels of participation and equity. It concludes by stating that programs need to be particularly context driven in conflict-affected settings.

The level of ethnic and political conflict within Myanmar means that these are all significant factors for context-sensitive development in that country, which we will explore as a case study in the following chapters. However, Myanmar itself has also been embroiled in a nonviolent but very real conflict with the international community, primarily the West, and this book seeks to extend these ideas about conflict-sensitivity into this realm of nonviolent conflict between pariah states and the international community. A deep under-standing of the historical and contemporary Myanmar sociopolitical context will therefore be a major feature of the next two chapters of this book.

Development in Fragile States

A second difficult sociopolitical context addressed in the development litera-ture is sensitivity to state fragility. Research into development in fragile states is only very recent, almost entirely in the past couple of years, and scholars note a considerable gap in the literature on development in such contexts (Baliamoune-Lutz and McGillivray 2008; McGillivray and Feeny 2008; UNU 2008). The *Failed States Index* (Foreign Policy 2010) and the *Index of State Weakness in the Developing World* (Rice and Patrick 2008) are generally taken to measure vulnerability to total collapse of the institutions of state and there-fore inability to provide security and basic services to the people. These indexes therefore comprise a rough measure of the difficulty of conducting develop-ment in countries suffering breakdown of law and order, armed conflict, weak-ness of state institutions, and so on. "Failed" or "weak" states are, therefore, in effect, either fragile states or states in the midst of conflict.

Focus on development in fragile states commenced only recently, when the OECD released two key documents on the subject (OECD 2007a, 2007b). State fragility is understood as arising primarily

> from weaknesses in the dynamic political process through which citizens' expectations of the state and state expectations of citizens are reconciled and brought into equilibrium with the state's capac-ity to deliver services. (OECD 2007a, 7)

The central objective of development in such fragile states is therefore to "build effective, legitimate, and resilient state institutions, capable of engaging productively with their people to promote sustained development" (OECD 2007a). The focus is on peace building, state building, and national reform to reconstruct institutions able to overcome weak governance and is most often required in states emerging from conflict or other disasters that impair state capacity. This makes the role of the major multilateral and bilateral agencies particularly important to development in fragile states.

The OECD list of recommendations for working in fragile states in-cludes (1) take context as the starting point; (2) do no harm; (3) focus on state building; (4) prioritize prevention; (5) recognize links between political, se-curity, and development objectives; (6) promote nondiscrimination; (7) align with local priorities; (8) coordinate between international actors; (9) act fast but stay engaged long enough; and (10) avoid pockets of exclusion (OECD 2007b). The conclusion is that

> the complexity and context specificity of the state-formation process, as well as limits of external influence, means that sustained, serious efforts as well as research and policy innovation are needed urgently. (OECD 2007a, 7)

Recent analysis by Wesley (2008) concluded that the two biggest factors that must shape contextual responses in failed states are sensitivity to contested notions of the form and legitimacy of the state, and postcolonial sensitivities.

Most observers believe the OECD's central objective of building "effective, legitimate, and resilient state institutions capable of engaging productively with their people to promote sustained development" is not currently possible in Myanmar, and governance in Myanmar would not normally be described as being either weakly held or the result of temporary fragility. Nonetheless, the new United Nations University World Institute for Development Economics Research (UNU-WIDER) project on *Fragility and Development* adopts a slightly different definition of "fragile state" as one wherein governments cannot or will not provide an environment for households to reduce or cope with poverty and other risks to well-being (UNU 2008). This definition is more relevant to Myanmar. AusAID (2010) expands this definition to include all countries that face particularly grave poverty and development challenges, that are at risk of further decline, and whose state structures lack the capacity or political will to provide public security, good governance, and economic growth.

Most fragile states are engaged in violent conflict or have just emerged from conflict (OECD 2007a; UNU 2008). Political contestation, together with either weak or recalcitrant governance, results in the international donor community having grave concerns about the prospects of poverty reduction in fragile states and thus restricting aid (Baliamoune-Lutz and McGillivray 2008). Addison (2005), for example, presents research showing a high recidivism rate of countries in falling back into conflict within five years. Certainly, fragile states cannot absorb as much aid as stable ones. Several studies confirm that absorptive capacity is reached somewhere between 15 and 45 percent of GDP, and thus fragile states can efficiently absorb only approximately one-third the amount of aid more stable countries can (Anderson 2005; McGillivray and Feeny 2008). Nonetheless, research also confirms that most fragile states are underaided, meaning they could efficiently absorb greater amounts of aid than they currently receive (McGillivray and Feeny 2008).

Donors overreact in limiting funding to fragile states. Anderson (2005) confirms that, up to this absorptive capacity, aid can still be very effective in reducing poverty even in very poor policy environments. He therefore argues strongly against attempting aid conditionality with fragile states, highlighting research showing that attempts to impose reform through aid conditionality is almost always ineffective. Browne (2007) believes that the major reason donors and agencies overly restrict funding to fragile states is a poor understanding of the context.

Development in Isolated (Pariah or Rogue) States

A third type of difficult political context for development is politically isolated states. Isolation is most commonly the result of concern over violation of international norms, usually norms to do with human rights, governance, or regime legitimacy, and the response of the regime to international actions against the state. While such states often list high on the *Failed States Index* and the *Index of State Weakness* in the Developing World, they are typically led by regimes in firm control of the country and that possess a range of strong state institutions used in the administration of the country, such as the armed forces. These states, however, are internationally politically isolated because they lack legitimacy in the eyes of the international community and thus have poor relationships with the United Nations and other states (often particularly with the West).

These isolated states are therefore sometimes labeled "pariah" or "rogue" states, characterizations that have both been applied to Myanmar. The term "pariah states" has been defined as states characterized by

> precarious diplomatic isolation, the absence of assured, credible security support or political moorings within big-power alliance structures, and . . . [being] the targets of obsessive and unrelenting opprobrium and censure within international forums such as the United Nations. (Harkavy 1981, 135)

The term "rogue state" is sometimes unilaterally applied by the United States, and occasionally by other Western states, to isolated states it sees as being totalitarian, having a strong disregard for human rights, and possessing or having aspirations to possess weapons of mass destruction in order to bolster their oppositional position to international norms (Bleiker 2003). In other words, it is applied to states that the West believes need to be watched, contained, and controlled. Both these terms, however, are controversial and confrontational and as such are more likely to provoke animosity than induce change.

Bleiker recasts so-called "rogue states" as norm-violating states that respond to coercive and aggressive demands from the West with similarly confrontational brinkmanship. The label demonizes states

> severely hinder[ing] both an adequate understanding and a possible resolution of the crisis. The rhetoric of rogue states is indicative of how US foreign policy continues to be driven by dualistic and militaristic Cold War thinking patterns. (Bleiker 2003, 731)

More productive discussion will focus on the isolation, the conflict in relationships with the global society of states, and the strain in the social compact between the rulers and the people. Pariah states commonly attract calls to restrict humanitarian aid, as part of socialization pressure on the regime to change. The lack of international trust also restricts development funding over questions of aid deliverability and fungibility, as well as sustainability, effectiveness, and risk of prolonging the rule of the sanctioned regime. Humanitarian budgets to pariah states are therefore generally heavily restricted. Unfortunately there is little academic literature considering aid effectiveness or context-sensitivity in countries facing this sort of international sanction. This book seeks to begin to address that lack of research.

It is noted that development in isolated pariah states is limited not by an inability of state institutions, as it is in "fragile" states, as much as by severe strain in the international relationships that could otherwise facilitate the global partnerships required for effective long-term macroeconomic development and by aid budgets restricted by a lack of trust. Bilateral and multilateral aid and development agencies, bound as they are to state actors with whom the isolated state has poor relationships and who generally prefer to work in partnership with government departments, commonly suffer mandate restrictions from both the international community and the domestic regime. Pressure is often also placed on INGOs to refrain from involvement in such states, and INGOs that do engage can be viewed with suspicion by both sides and affected by the strained international relations.

This book argues that INGOs, as nonstate actors, have the potential for better access and broader mandates to operate in such contexts under humanitarian principles and that this should be seen as an extension of conflict-sensitive development to the level of nonviolent international tension. The distinctive development approaches common to many INGOs, working predominantly with local communities and civil society more than government departments, and a focus on alleviating extreme poverty rather than on addressing macroeconomic development concerns also potentially facilitate their ability to work more effectively in these states. This book seeks to document sensitive approaches in such a context.

Participatory Development as INGO Context-Sensitivity

The Participatory Development Model

Recognition of the need for sensitivity to local context, as seen in this survey of the literature on economic development, really began in the 1970s. Coming from a sociological field perspective, Freire, in his *Pedagogy of the Oppressed* (1972), argues that traditional processes of teaching in which a teacher transfers knowledge to students is both ineffective and a form of oppression. This, he suggests, is especially true in development. Learning, according to Freire, should be a process of people rethinking their own assumptions and acting on their own ideas, not merely consuming the ideas of others, but he lamented that the poor were trapped in a "culture of silence" and lacked a voice in development. This paradigm has become the foundation underlying participatory approaches to development.

Building on this foundation, Chambers (1983) brought the idea of participatory development into the mainstream development thinking. Chambers conceptualizes poverty not as a lack of income, assets, services, or even knowledge by the poor but as powerlessness to do anything about their situation because of marginalization. Highlighting cultural differences, biases, and the different (often inappropriate) knowledge outsiders bring to development contexts, Chambers argues for a reversal in the management of development that transfers decision making primarily into the hands of those embedded within a local context. Chambers therefore popularized the idea of empowerment through highly participatory, beneficiary-led development as the basis for successful, sustained development.

Participation, Chambers argues, empowers "those who are most marginalized, powerless and poor to achieve a better life for themselves" (Chambers 2005, 97). This happens "when individuals and organised groups are able to imagine their world differently" and take action to change their circumstances (Eyben, Kabeer, and Cornwall 2008, 3). Chambers advocated methodologies in which local knowledge, participation, and decision making are made central to the planning and management of projects. His initial Participatory Rural Appraisal (PRA) approach relied on outside development workers to carry out the inquiry (Chambers 1994), but his later Participatory Learning and Action (PLA) further restricted the role of outside development workers to a facilitator of the process of local people sharing and reflecting on their knowledge.

Many quickly agreed with Chambers. For example, Edwards (1989) provocatively suggested in "The Irrelevance of Development Studies" that development research was having little impact on poverty because it thought in terms of transfer of goods, skills, and information and had failed to come to grips with local knowledge. "Problems are often specific in their complexity to particular times and places." Like Chambers, he advocated "popular participation" as the means to take into account contextual factors known to the locals, but often overlooked by outsiders, as the basis for effective development.

The participatory development model involves, of course, far more than merely participation. The model requires effective empowerment through various capacity building, capacity-development activities, training in human rights and advocacy, and so on (Cornwall 2002; Mohan 2007), which is why these aspects of development receive major emphasis in contemporary development theory and practice. It also calls for partnership with local civil society in implementation of programs in communities, and alignment between the priorities of agencies and those of government departments, all in order to allow recipients and partners to exercise control over program design and implementation, ensuring development is contextual and sustainable.

This participatory development model revolves around six power-and-relationship concepts now in common usage: participation, empowerment, ownership, partnership, accountability, and transparency (Chambers 2005). Such participatory development has now become central to development theory and is now widely accepted as a minimum requirement for successful and sustained development outcomes.

> It was only in the 1990s that [participation] entered almost every field development activity. . . . By the turn of the century, the words participatory and participation were embedded in development speak. . . . In the early years of the 21st century, participation, in name if not in reality, is now part of almost every development activity. (Chambers 2005, 101)

Fowler (2000a) suggests this participatory model of development has been widely adopted because it is perceived to address the key reasons aid was considered to have been failing at the time, namely, (1) a lack of sensitivity to the underlying environment (context), (2) a lack of ownership by recipients, and (3) inappropriate donor behavior, specifically aid conditionality and poor coordination. By contrast, it is believed that emphasizing participation, empowerment, and partnership will make decision making inherently more context-sensitive, build ownership, and overcome both aid conditionality and a lack of coordination. Many development INGOs therefore advocate participatory, beneficiary-led, or beneficiary-driven development, which seeks to empower and build the capacity of recipients to actively contribute to or lead the development decision making at every stage, as the solution to issues of sensitivity, ownership, and coordination.

NGO Generations and Participation

One way of highlighting how integral participatory development ideas have become to development thinking is by consideration of NGO typologies. Korten's (1990) well-known typology of "generations of NGOs" well illustrates the growing emphasis on participation and empowerment. Korten describes four generations of NGOs as being (1) relief and welfare, (2) community development, (3) sustainable development, and (4) people's movement. As NGOs increasingly involve communities in the design, delivery, and management of projects, they are said to become second-, third-, or fourth-generation NGOs. The implicit assumption within such stylized typologies is that community participation increases throughout the progression and that this is inherently proper (Clarke 2009). It is believed that increased community involvement at all stages of a development intervention is more likely to have a sustained impact because of (1) better identification of development needs and their causes; (2) better account taken of local resources and strengths, thus less reliance on external inputs; and (3) better management of the project through community decision making, which will then more likely continue after the external funding has ceased (Uphoff, Esman, and Krishna 1998; Dale 2004).

One additional observation to draw from such stylized typologies is that as organizations move through this progression, from first- and second-generation NGOs to third- and fourth-generation ones, the more consideration of context has moved from a deliberate and conscious facet INGOs must be mindful of to something it is assumed recipients inherently facilitate.

Critique of Participation as Context-Sensitivity

Shifting primary responsibility for context-sensitivity from the development agency to the recipients is both the strength of the participatory model and its greatest weakness. The model facilitates contextualization to the extent that participants and partners understand their own context, have a voice, and are empowered to make adaptations. This model may therefore work well in ensuring that local knowledge and cultural traits are identified, but without further definition of the role of outside agents, it does not of itself necessarily address issues of equity, power, conflict, marginalization, or lack of understanding of national or international sociopolitical contextual factors.

Oakley (1991) sees three fundamental obstacles to the success of participatory development at the community level: (1) structural obstacles, such as political power dictating direction or excluding some from decision making; (2) administrative obstacles, such as centralized government administration retaining control over resources and thereby over decision making; and (3) social obstacles, such as divisions keeping some marginalized within communities:

> Participation occurs within a particular context and will be influenced by the [political,] economic and social forces that mold that context. (Oakley 1991, 14)

After years of participatory development experience, Guijt and Shah (1998) elaborate similar concerns. Their primary issue is that participatory development approaches communities as if they are discrete and socially homogenous entities, looking for a single, coherent, consensual community view to emerge. Intracommunity divisions and inequalities are largely overlooked, undervaluing the positive contribution external agents could otherwise take in addressing marginalization and thereby allowing participatory approaches to reinforce the very power relations they seek to overcome. Cooke and Kothari (2001) express similar concerns, going so far as suggesting that participation bears within it a "tyrannical potential" for oppressing the poor and marginalized and demanding a rethink of the entire participatory model. It has been argued that the majority of participatory projects fail in their aim of reversing local power hierarchies, with "conservatism, convenience, and risk aversion" (Cleaver 2001) resulting in inequitable participation that reflects preexisting power relations based on factors such as gender, age, wealth, ethnicity, religion, and politics.

It has also been argued that, despite the rhetoric, most decision-making power in the majority of participatory projects has ultimately remained with the implementing agency (Mosse 2001). "Local decision-making is most likely to produce results sensitive to local needs and desires, [yet] such decision-making may still require [outside] assistance" to create the circumstances for that change and to provide information, assistance, and advice to enable informed and equitable decision making (Kingsbury 2008a, 224). Without additional definition of the role of facilitators and INGO staff in contextualization, not all decisions taken at a local level are appropriate (Kingsbury 2008a, 224). Some, based on desperation, are very short-term focused, others are based on limited understanding, while others are made out of deference to power holders, including the INGO. This is particularly true in difficult sociopolitical contexts. Several specific concerns are noted, as follows.

Whether Participants Are Empowered in Relation to Local Elite

Given these obstacles, concern must be expressed about how well this participatory model sufficiently empowers participants in difficult contexts, whether communities or partner organizations, to make development decisions that are counter to elite interests. O'Leary and Nee (2001) note that traditional, hierarchical societies hold an expectation that the people who have knowledge, resources, and power (high status) should give advice, manage, and control and that this militates strongly against real transfer of control and decision making. This is particularly true in conflict zones, failed states, and pariah states, where other significant forces can work directly against empowerment, actively marginalizing some and disempowering others through fear. In difficult political contexts such as these, participants are highly likely to defer to the established orthodoxy of prevailing power structures, not being sufficiently empowered to make contributions that challenge a fragile status quo.

Empowering highly marginalized participants is predicated on obtaining cooperation of the empowered elite, those whose power has created the people's marginalization, then communicating this permission to act to those previously marginalized in a way that demonstrates their freedom and safety. In difficult political contexts, these empowered elite may include figures connected to a military or militia, governing regime, or dominant ethnic group, for example, and gaining their cooperation is far from assured. INGO staff and facilitators have a significant and highly contextual role in creating such a safe space for participants and/or in making contextualized decisions on behalf of disempowered communities.

Whether Participants Are Empowered in Relation to the Development Agency

It is just as difficult for most individuals, communities, and partner organizations to challenge the perceived orthodoxy of the development agency. The agency, in effect, becomes another elite whose preference should be deferred to, particularly when it controls access to funding and its representative facilitates decision making within the community. Craig and Porter (1997) refer to this as "framing," the tendency for development workers and agencies to subtly, even unconsciously, circumscribe local participants' influence over the development agenda. Fowler (1998) argues that participation, empowerment, and partnership are the three most abused concepts in development, concluding that despite best intentions, empowerment is far more difficult to achieve than is commonly acknowledged, making it far more illusion than reality.

Critique has already been noted suggesting agencies commonly really allow only superficial variation, while at a deeper level treating contextualization as a deviation (Murphy 2000). Reviews of community-led participatory development regularly conclude that top-down assumptions continue to alienate participants (e.g., Kasongo 1998; Watson 2006), leading Ishizawa (2004) to argue that most development practice is "insidiously violent" by claiming to give voice to the marginalized while limiting assumptions and implicit values to the agency's way of seeing the world. Most participatory practice, he argues, neglects to incorporate any means to allow expression of different ways of being and ways of seeing, and recipients are thus not empowered to contextualize in ways that challenge agency orthodoxy.

One key driver of such orthodoxy is international efforts toward improving development effectiveness. By identifying commonalities across diverse contexts and seeking to identify best practices, development is commonly presented in terms of norms, principles, and approaches. The fact that these are only intended to be broadly applicable is often "obscured by global comparative analysis, presented as global conclusions" (Shutt 2009).

A second, related cause counteracting empowerment in participatory development is that decisions are often predetermined by assumptions about the need for coordination with wider programs and goals (Weitz 1986). Recent conversations between the key staff from the Institute of Development Studies (University of Sussex) and a number of large INGOs in the United Kingdom highlighted the strong normative pressure that organizational vision, mission, and strategy documents instill (Shutt 2009). It was acknowledged that while INGOs aspire for documents to be framed only in the most general of terms and for field staff to translate these into more situated strategies that such contextualization would create serious legitimacy issues for unelected publicly funded organizations. Translating INGO mission and strategy statements into context-specific applications would mean "different approaches may need to co-exist within one organisation, jeopardizing normative legitimacy as well as raising operational and 'brand' problems" (Shutt 2009, 22). Allowing adaptation of approaches to local contexts would cause "significant stress within the organisation" (Ossewaarde, Nijhof, and Heyse 2008).

Normative pressures are further compounded by management practices aimed at building organizational culture. For example, during interviews reported later in this book, a number of senior INGO staff expressed concern that the common policy of rotating key international staff between fields to strengthen organizational linkages and learning is most unhelpful to contextualization. Wallace, Bornstein, and Chapman (2006) likewise argue that the centralized managerial structures adopted by large INGOs do not easily admit expressions of cultural diversity. Craig and Porter (1997) argue that the need to be accountable to donors through effective management and evaluation is "deeply contradictory" to the goals of participatory development. The tools of participatory development can be used to equally promote either participation or control. A fundamental change is therefore required in the way development organizations and professionals operate before participatory development can achieve its lofty aims.

This is well illustrated by research in which INGO field staff with Médecins Sans Frontières–Holland were interviewed about organizational and operational principles (Hilhorst and Schmiemann 2002). This study found that most field-workers reconstructed their own set of operating principles on the field, in response to the contextual demands they face, often in contradiction with organizational policy and stated global organizational values. Murray and Clarke (2008) found something similar among staff deployed after the Boxing Day tsunami in 2005. A third example can be found in the World Bank's *Civic Engagement, Empowerment and Respect for Diversity* program, which aims to empower recipients to adapt programs through participation. A recent evaluation found that in practice the World Bank's monitoring and evaluation systems prevent most proposed contextualization (Brunner 2004).

There is strong evidence that these systemic normative pressures create a tension within INGOs between "field-oriented" staff, who advocate the need for flexibility in response to the local context, and "organization-oriented" staff, who seek consistent polity across the organization (Suzuki 1998). Fechter and Hindman (2011) document some of this in terms of the ways field staff negotiate the often conflicting and contradictory aspects of their role. Sumner and Tribe (2008) speak of strongly contrasting policy and practice-related dimensions of international development. National staff and local NGO partners of INGOs often find their more culturally aware views regularly conflict with INGO institutional values or approaches, leading to common accusations of development models being "imposed" on locals from the outside, despite the ideals of partnership, participation, and contextualization expressed by the agency (Shutt 2009). Thus, it is rare for participants to seriously challenge perceived development agency orthodoxy.

Whether Participants Are Sufficiently Aware of Macro-Contextual Factors

A third concern with how well participatory development facilitates context-sensitivity is whether participants, be they communities or partner organizations, sufficiently understand macro-sociopolitical contextual factors development needs to take into account, such as the nuances of strained international relations.

The participatory development model is based on the principle of prioritizing decision-making authority to be given to those with local knowledge. For communities and LNGOs, this correlates broadly to local cultural understanding and local political dynamics. In this sense participatory development is a major advance, taking sensitivity to local culture and local power into consideration. Culture (including local politics) was being rediscovered during the 1970s and 1980s, as this model was being developed and popularized. However, during this era many of the current tensions in international politics were subsumed by the global political machinations of the cold war. Today's difficult failed and pariah state contexts are more recent phenomena, involving relatively new and difficult political dynamics. It has already been noted that in conflict zones, failed states, and pariah states, information is often incomplete or manipulated as a means of control. The understanding of local communities and partners may not be sufficient for these dynamics, and participatory methodologies were not designed with this limitation in mind. The actor with local knowledge in this instance is more likely to be the senior in-country staff of the INGO, and an extension of the participatory model to this situation would imply the need for INGOs to empower and delegate significant decision making at this level to country offices.

To illustrate the point, the UNDP *Human Development Report* (2010) ranks Myanmar as the fifth least-free press in the world, exceeded only by Eritrea, North Korea, Turkmenistan, and Iran. Most marginalized groups therefore live in comparative ignorance of even national, let alone international, factors affecting their situation. This raises the question of how well, for example, rural or ethnic minority communities in Myanmar could appropriately tailor development programming decisions to fit with international donor attitudes, transnational advocacy campaigns, donor-country sanctions, donor conditionality, or even recent domestic policy concessions that the regime is reluctant to promote for fear of impact on its political legitimacy.

Minimizes or Ignores Sensitivity by Agencies in
Dealing With Other Stakeholders

The final concern with relying on participatory development to facilitate context-sensitivity is that it results in a lack of definition of the sensitivity to context that INGOs themselves need to enact, particularly in their relationships with other stakeholders. In other cultural and political contexts, the way people are valued, knowledge is transferred, change is handled, and decisions are made—even leadership style, ethics, values in relating to people, relationships, exclusion, gender, and power—can all be very different, yet there is a scarcity of literature on how INGOs might approach context-specific factors such as these (Jackson 2003). Beyond cultural dynamics, INGOs find themselves embroiled as unwilling participants in highly strained political relationships that have a direct impact on development effectiveness. INGOs, as outside agents, need to actively contextualize the way they relate to the other stakeholders, in ways that participation and partnership alone do not facilitate.

This book does not suggest that INGO in-country staff do not take an active role to ensure sensitivity to such sociopolitical factors, especially in their stakeholder relations. Most certainly do, and chapters 5 to 7 of this book documents how field staff had done this in one specific context. However, this research suggests that the development literature has not adequately theorized or described this vital role played by local offices of the INGO, and therefore taking this role often creates unnecessary internal organizational stress.

Thus, while on one hand the global development dialogue has moved past universalist prescriptions to recognize cultural diversity, multiple pathways, and unique contexts, and while most international development agencies work hard to ensure that their interventions are participatory and through local partnerships, strong forces still persist that in practice limit participants' empowerment to contextualize. Development theory lacks clear understanding of the role of the international agency itself in ensuring this contextualization, beyond ideas of ensuring participation, partnership, and capacity building. It is particularly difficult to genuinely empower people in difficult political contexts, such as conflict zones, failed states, and pariah states, where local power structures seek to marginalize and control people, and the poor lack awareness of macro-contextual factors. It is equally difficult to empower people to challenge the normative forces of development agency orthodoxy, especially in states where local participants are placed in a very awkward position between domestic political objectives and those of INGOs funded by states their own governments are in conflict with.

Conceptualizing INGO Context-Sensitivity

These limitations suggest current participatory theory does not adequately describe the role of the INGO, particularly in difficult sociopolitical contexts. Greater clarity of the role INGO staff need to play is required to ensure context-sensitive development occurs without diminishing the empowerment of partners and recipient communities. Radcliffe (2006b) recently called for such a detailed understanding of the roles of the various diverse actors in bringing context into development, including how, when, and where they do so and their differing relationships within the context. She argues that if actors and institutions remain invisible, responsibility for roles and change cannot be attributed to actors with agency.

This need is clearly illustrated in a recent evaluation of INGO programs training workers from local NGOs for village community development work in Cambodia (O'Leary and Nee 2001). They found that local NGO workers were not effective in fostering genuine change at the village level because they themselves were unconsciously struggling to reconcile the demands of their development work with cultural and social expectations. They concluded, "[INGO] capacity building practitioners and trainers need to understand more explicitly what the people whose capacity they are endeavoring to strengthen are facing regarding the dilemmas of development practice" and need to more fully contextualize their own role to that (O'Leary and Nee 2001, ix). They raise specific concern that the power imbalance inherent in the INGO having power over which projects to fund means INGO staff must far more deliberately address power and cultural sensitivity issues. What is needed is a "theory of practice that is organic and not a set of rules, steps or tools" (O'Leary and Nee 2001, 119).

Directed Social Change and Culture Change Theories

Recent development studies research has derived renewed inspiration from social change and culture change theories:

> Development practice is informed by theories of change, but individuals and organisations may not make them explicit. Practitioners may be unaware of the extent to which strategic choices and debates are informed by disparate thinking about how history happens and the role of purposeful intervention for progressive social change. (Eyben et al. 2008)

Social change theories constitute a diverse literature, from Marxist ideas of social revolution, to ideas of social action and social movements, to functionalist ideas that interpret society as a structure composed of interrelated norms, customs, traditions, and institutions (McLeish 1969). Eyben et al. (2008) suggest that the most theoretically comprehensive ideas about social change relevant to development practice are contained in Rogers's (2003) *Diffusion of Innovations*, a work first published in 1962. Rogers postulates that new ideas, behavior, or technology is innovated then diffused throughout a social system, individual to individual, based largely on psychological and motivational factors and mediated through changed knowledge, attitudes, and behavior of individuals. This approach is sometimes criticized for its behaviorist and rational-choice assumptions, and omission of analysis of power and structural inequality, but with this critique in mind, it does inform much contemporary theory (Eyben et al. 2008).

The theory of diffusion actually dates to the nineteenth century, when it was seen as a key mechanism of social/cultural evolution. It was argued that cultural traits are evolutionary adaptations to the human environment, and thus that as some parts of humanity were more developed than others (i.e., the West), it was natural for these ideas and products to be taken up by all other cultures (Patterson 1998; Naylor 1996). Such evolutionary thinking continued to dominate anthropological discussion of social change through to the mid-twentieth century. For example, Steward (1955) described a linear evolution of cultures moving toward some ultimate highly developed state, echoing the still-popular ideas of Tylor ([1871] 1958). Their interest was in what stage of the process various cultures were at, and the means to facilitate diffusion of more advanced ideas into these less culturally evolved contexts.

Most anthropologists, however, abandoned such evolutionary structural analysis by the early to mid-twentieth century, in favor of a more functionalist conception of social change with a community and individual perspective (Naylor 1996). Acculturation became the key focus, defined as the study of "when groups of individuals having different cultures come into continuous first-hand contact, with subsequent changes in the cultural patterns of either or both groups" (Redfield, Linton, and Herskovits 1936, 149). This shift was trigged by Malinowski (1929), who called for a "practical anthropology" that could assist people with the process of culture change. As the number of ethnographic studies examining these processes grew, Redfield, Linton, and Herskovits (1936) called for research into the process of acculturation stemming from cultures in contact (per Herskovits 1937). These anthropologists went on to draw a distinction between directed change, with change advocated by those outside the group, and nondirected change introduced by group members themselves borrowing from other groups (Redfield, Linton, and Herskovits 1936).

During the 1950s and 1960s, such "development anthropology" appropriated anthropological insights to improve the effectiveness of directed culture change, within the cold war modernization paradigm of international development. These anthropologists produced a number of handbooks for development field-workers (e.g., Goodenough 1963; Arensberg and Niehoff 1964, 1971), the most well-known being Rogers's *Diffusion of Innovations*, to which Eyben et al. (2008) refer. In this same period Christian missionaries began to articulate a "missionary anthropology" in similar applied anthropological terms. See, for example, Nida (1954, 1960) and Luzbetak's (1963) seminal missionary training handbook.

More recently anthropologists have become alarmed at the way "applied" anthropology was appropriated to strengthen colonialism, Christian missionary enterprise, and cold war development practice, leading most recent anthropologists to focus more on critique of development itself from a postcolonial or postdevelopment perspective than on the dynamics of social change in development. However, these social change theories still offer fresh inspiration and understanding when taken in addition to more recent understandings about empowerment, development of capacity and capabilities, and so on, rather than replacing them, and remaining mindful of issues of local power and inequality (Eyben et al. 2008).

The common theme of these models, as epitomized by Rogers (2003), is that change originates with an idea, whether invented or borrowed, that modifies, subtracts from, or adds to existing belief or practice. In successful social change, ideas diffuse through the group via human interaction mediated through change agents, either totally spontaneously or through planned action, until it is accepted by most individuals because it meets a felt need (Naylor 1996). Key concepts in this model are innovation, acculturation, diffusion, agents of change, barriers to change, fit, felt needs, and knowledge and information as empowering actors.

Process and Agents of Directed Social Change
Innovation and Diffusion

The role of innovation in social change was first expressed by Linton (1936), with its importance as possibly the central dynamic behind change best articulated by Barnett (1942, 1953). Innovation speaks of the way people recognize the need to change in response to changing conditions or see an opportunity and develop new ideas, behaviors, or products (Barnett 1942). Innovation occurs continually, although most innovation is transitory and does not diffuse significantly. Occasionally a new idea, behavior, or product diffuses and is accepted by a majority of the group, and only then can it be said that culture has changed. People are most motivated toward change that meets felt needs and when there is a high degree of "fit" between the proposed change and existing forms, meanings, and functions (Foster 1962).

Innovators may come up with ideas on their own (in which case changes are usually incremental syntheses of existing cultural material into new forms), or they may borrow ideas from other cultures (in which case larger changes are possible).

Acculturation

Acculturation is the process of adopting ideas from contact with other cultures (Foster 1962; Naylor 1996). Most culture change is the result of borrowing from other cultures, if not pressure from the outside imposing change on the group. However, it has long been recognized that borrowed ideas, behaviors, or products will almost always undergo further innovation to the new local context.

Positivism would deny any difference between cultural traits and any ascribed *meaning*; however, constructivists like Linton (1936) postulated that every cultural trait consists of a directly observable cultural *form*, carries within it a culturally ascribed underlying *meaning* (often not consciously articulated), and is used to fulfill a *function*. It is *forms* that are most often exported between cultures, but because of their subjective nature, *meaning* and thus *function* are commonly redefined in the new culture as a result. Thus, without innovation, exporting development approaches and norms (*forms*) is likely to result in the underlying *meanings* being reinterpreted, to the frustration of field-workers (Nida 1954, 1960; Rogers 2003). Conversely, since any truly universal development principles are likely to be *functions* with important associated underlying *meanings*, effectively exporting a principle to a new context will almost always require a changed *form* to maintain its distinctive *meaning* and *function*.

> Throughout history, it has been repeatedly observed that while societies may adopt similar material items or other innovations, they do so only after altering them to suit their own particular cultural contexts and needs. (Naylor 1996, 207)

The key role of the innovator in such acculturation is therefore the contextual-ization of the same *meaning*, by reinterpreting and adapting the *form*.

Recent development studies research reconfirms similar findings. Øyen (2002) studied how "best practices" in development are identified and how field-workers attempt to transfer them from one context to another. Øyen struggles to find literature documenting how a best practice might be success-fully transferred to another context without loss of the very elements that make it a best practice. She contends that what is usually transferred is the "physical idea" (the *form*), which commonly leads to resistance or failure. Miller (2002) agrees that seldom can a best practice be taken over in its original *form* and implemented successfully in a new context without adaptation.

Diffusion and Agents of Change

For social change to occur, a new or borrowed idea must become adopted by a majority of the group, ultimately becoming part of the learned patterns it passes on (Naylor 1996). This places interactions between people, and indi-vidual behavior and choice, at the center of the diffusion and social change process—and identifies social, cultural, and psychological aversion to destabi-lizing stress as strong barriers to social change (Foster 1962, 1969).

For diffusion to permeate a majority of a group, it thus usually needs to be driven by one or more change agents who assume responsibility for persuading other people to accept and adopt the proposed change (Redfield, Linton, and Herskovits 1936). Innovators may promote their own ideas or products, but commonly innovators are not the ones who are most effective as agents pro-moting the change, influencing opinion leaders through diffusion networks (Rogers 2003). Such change agents may be individuals or groups (e.g., pro-fessional agencies, companies, government, or civil organizations) who have an interest in persuading people to accept the new idea, behavior, or product (Barnett 1942). The role of change agents is well recognized, and acceptance or rejection of change is linked in large part to the prestige, personality, relation-ship networks, and affiliation of these advocates, as well as compatibility with the needs and motivations of recipients (Barnett 1942).

Facilitators of Change: Insider and Outsider Roles

Most culture change is the result of "cultures in contact" (adopting the termi-nology of Herskovits 1937). A good deal of that change is the result of outside advocacy and planning, and in that sense it is directed. The work of outside fa-cilitators is central to most development practice and is a good example of di-rected change given most development agencies bring with them certain ideas and principles they advocate for adoption (directly or indirectly) as part of the development process—ideas such as normative human rights, gender equity, democracy, liberal economic systems, or individualism.

Directed social change models propose a distinction between the roles of insider agents and those of outsider agents (Barnett 1953). The outsider role is often described as being a *facilitator*, to introduce and advocate new ideas through the provision of knowledge, information, and raising awareness, while insider roles include *receptors*, *innovators*, and *advocates* of change (Kraft 1979, 1996). Outside *facilitators* should attempt to de-Westernize or decontextualize the central ideas back to underlying values and meaning (Schineller 1990; Conn 1984). *Receptors*, community or opinion leaders, regulate access for messages into their communicational space, then *innovators* redesign borrowed ideas to best fit the local context, before *advocates* drive the diffusion of revised ideas. Kraft (1979, 2005) argues that it is usually *meaning* or *function* outsider *advocates* really propose, and thus that to preserve the same *meaning* into the new context insider, *innovators* must be empowered to contextualize the *form* in any way that preserves *meaning*. The result is something with equivalence in the new context, even if superficially it does not appear the same.

Sharp distinction between insiders and outsiders is, however, problematic, in that it pays insufficient attention to issues of power, exclusion, and inequality within social groups. Latour (2005) cautions that "society" continues to experience transformation and that networks and social group boundaries are always transient. Analyses that attempt to provide social explanations for phenomena by assuming a stable and defined social context are therefore an oversimplification. Both elite and marginalized people exist on the edges of any social group, and distinct divisions over gender, ethnicity, religion, military service, political affiliation, and the like often exist within a social group. Sharp distinctions are confronted by the question of who constitute insiders and to what sense culture is shared, by whom. A sympathetic foreign development worker may become accepted as more an insider by a marginalized group than privileged elite nominally of the same culture.

Accepting the problematic aspects of too broad a generalization and too clearly distinguished roles, this model remains useful in highlighting a different but complementary role for outside facilitators. Most change is the result of outside influence, and even many locally driven social change processes sooner or later invite an outsider intermediary to support the process (Guijt 2007). Recent focus within development studies has been on the role of outside agents in providing knowledge and information to participants in a manner that empowers them as actors with agency:

Facilitation is the process of enabling social actors [individuals, groups, collective movements, organizations, and institutions that undertake actions to bring about social change] to reflect on their assumptions and make informed choices about approaches to and forms of knowledge and learning to use in strategies for social change. (Taylor et al. 2006, 13)

Key roles for outside facilitators of change are the deliberate provision of knowledge, helping parties interact around the way they see their problems, improving problem-solving capabilities, and helping participants develop techniques for open discussion and handling confrontation (Chin and Benne 1976). Culbert (1976) speaks of a five-stage model of "consciousness-raising" by facilitators of social change, by assisting people to recognize how the current system works, identify what it is that concerns them, understand their relationship with the system, formulate alternatives, and identify ways to effect change for the group.

Extension of Current Model: Two INGO Roles
Putting together the participatory development model, the ideas of conflict-sensitive development, and social change theory and recognizing there is a range of levels of context from micro to macro, it is possible to construct a picture of the roles that different development actors play in participatory, sociopolitical, context-sensitive development.

Suzuki (1998) and Shutt (2009) have already noted a division within INGOs between "field-orientated" staff, both expatriates and nationals, who advocate the need for maximum flexibility in response to the local context, and "organization-oriented" staff who seek consistent polity across the organization. Half a century ago Goodenough (1963) highlighted this same tension between field agents being more community-centered in their approach and agency-centered staff who endorse contextualization in principle but struggle with allowing diversity of implementation in practice. A useful way of considering this long-standing field-oriented–organization-oriented dichotomy within INGOs is by noting that country field offices and head offices themselves operate within different contexts and therefore legitimately have different roles to play as agents in social change.

Figure 2.1 offers a visual representation of the major actors in context-sensitive development, highlighting the roles they play in context-sensitivity according to the participatory development model and social change theory.

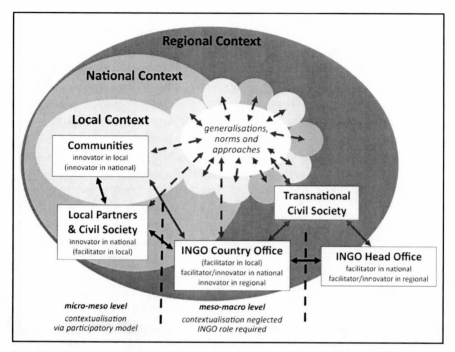

Figure 2.1 The roles of various development actors in context-sensitive development. *Source.* Author's own work.

The participatory development model of empowerment and partnership has the potential to facilitate contextualization at the micro-meso level, through local knowledge and decision making taking into consideration unique cultural contexts and (sometimes) local power dynamics. The model suggests that wherever it is possible to do so, local communities should be empowered, as insiders within their local context, to choose which ideas to receive and how to innovate on them and therefore to control the planning and implementation of development within their local context. This may not be fully possible in difficult political contexts, in which case local NGO partners and INGOs may sometimes need to take on some of these roles on their behalf, paying particular attention to power dynamics in the process.

Local NGO and civil society partner organizations are embedded within district or national contexts, not local contexts. Social change theory recognizes development action by these agencies is usually as outsiders to local contexts, and thus the participatory development model suggests that under normal circumstances their role in community contexts is as facilitators rather than innovators: creating the space for community empowerment and decision making, providing ideas, helping participants rethink the way they see their problems, and helping address equity, communication, and problem-solving deficiencies. Occasionally, in difficult sociocultural contexts, local NGO and civil society partner organizations may need to take a more active lead in these activities, as well as to ensure sensitivity to national and regional factors local participants may be unaware of.

Local NGO and civil society partners are, however, themselves insiders within district or national contexts, and at these levels it is important for them to be the active agents of contextualization to the greatest extent possible. They should be empowered, as insiders, to choose which ideas to receive from a general pool of international norms and approaches and to innovate with them to drive development at this level, which would include areas such as engaging in advocacy, setting up partnerships, setting goals, and so on. Again, in difficult political contexts, country office INGO staff may need to take on these roles on their behalf, being mindful to ensure context-sensitivity in the process. Some INGOs, particularly where there are insufficient local NGO and civil society organizations of sufficient capacity to partner with, directly implement some of their programs through national field staff, meaning INGO field staff sometimes also take on the role of facilitating development at the community level themselves, although much of the development literature suggests this is not ideal in the longer term.

The participatory model largely sees INGO country staff as facilitators building the capacity of local NGO and civil society partner organizations. Any further role of the INGO in ensuring context-sensitive development is, however, generally neglected in development theory. Social change theory, however, recognizes that the INGO country office is itself embedded largely within the national context and definitely within international regional politics, while the INGO head office is much more removed from both these contexts. As such, the INGO country office has a significant role in context-sensitive development at the national and international regional levels and should be empowered by its head office as such. This is also implied by the conflict-sensitivity and fragile states literature, which charges the development agency to take an active role in understanding the context and dynamics and make contextualization a high priority. How to do that, however, without disempowering communities or partners is not spelled out in the literature.

In practice, most INGO country offices do attempt to contextualize in the face of strong normative forces, but this practice often creates a tension within the INGO structure. Social change theory suggests legitimizing their role, focusing their role within the levels of context in which they take primary responsibility, such as stakeholder relationships. This model argues strongly for the deliberate and planned empowerment of INGO country offices and field-workers by INGO head offices for their role in adapting development approaches to ensure context-sensitive development.

Conclusion

This chapter has traced the growth of the now widespread recognition of the need for context-sensitive development, reflected in the literature primarily in terms of sensitivity to culture and political context. The most difficult political contexts for development contextualization are those involving conflict, state fragility, or international political isolation of regimes (so-called "pariah states"). Myanmar falls into the latter category. INGOs can potentially have more freedoms and wider mandates to operate in such internationally isolated states than multilateral agencies, because isolation stems from strained relationships between state actors, and multilateral agencies have stronger connections to international state actors embroiled in the tensions.

The means by which INGOs, in particular, attempt to ensure contextual development has therefore been discussed in detail. It has been found that the INGO approach to development assumes that highly participatory development based on empowerment, partnership, and capacity building inherently ensures decision making is context-sensitive. While there are a lot of strengths and validity in this approach, concerns with the underlying assumption have been raised in connection with development in difficult states such as Myanmar, including whether participants are sufficiently empowered to contextualize in relation to both local elite and the development agency, whether they are sufficiently aware of national and international political factors, and that this model minimizes or ignores the role agencies should play themselves in their dealings with stakeholders.

Directed social change theories have been reviewed in an attempt to explain the role and dynamics of outside agents interacting with local actors in the process of development, and from these a conceptualization of the roles of the various actors has been proposed. This model for context-sensitive development extends the participatory development model to propose multiple layers of context and that actors embedded in each layer of context are best placed to innovate within that context, while the role of those largely outside each context is to provide knowledge and information and potentially advocate options derived from generalized development norms and approaches as discovered across many other contexts. Innovation of ideas to enable them to fit the local context is best done by those within each level of context.

It has been noted that INGO head and country offices exist in different contexts and therefore legitimately have different roles to play. This model therefore adds to the participatory development model by suggesting that the role INGO country offices and field-workers already play in contextualizing organizational approaches to local cultural and political factors must be recognized in the theory, and deliberate, planned empowerment of INGO country offices and field-workers for this role must be facilitated by INGO head offices. It does, also, highlight the importance of INGO country offices and field-workers having a comprehensive understanding of the cultural, sociopolitical, and economic context they work within.

The following two chapters explore this sociopolitical and economic context for Myanmar and the historical antecedents that help explain the nature and pervasiveness of certain aspects of the contemporary context.

Part 2

Myanmar: A Historically Informed Analysis of Context

3

Burmese Days: Antecedents of the Sociopolitical Context

It would be [as much] an error to dismiss the Burmese past as irrelevant to the present or the future, as is often done in policy circles, as it would be to ignore contemporary realities and solely concentrate on history. (Steinberg 2006, 37)

Splashed across world newspaper headlines in January 2011 was the story of a letter written on pure gold sheet inlaid with rubies, contained in an elephant tusk, that had been sent to King George II by Burmese king Alaungpaya in 1756 (e.g., Ward 2011). The letter had now, finally, been fully translated at the Leibniz library in Hanover (see Figure 3.1). The letter is addressed to

> the most meritorious and supreme [king] master of all the parasol-bearing kings . . . lord of ruby, gold, silver, copper, iron, amber and precious stone mines, lord of white elephants, red elephants and elephants of various colours . . . the English king who rules over the English capital. (Leider 2009, 74–75)

Presenting his findings to the Académie des Inscriptions et Belles-Lettres in Paris on January 21, 2011, lead researcher Jacques Leider confirmed that amid the valuable gems and flowery language, Alaungpaya offers his permission for a British settlement and harbor to be built in the city of Pathein, ostensibly to encourage trading cooperation between the two countries.

As the story goes, in 1751 the Frenchman Sieur de Bruno arrived in Bago (the former coastal capital) just as King Alaungpaya was founding the third Burmese empire. In July 1751 de Bruno pressed Pondicherry for a few hundred well-disciplined French troops, boasting they could gain control of the Ayeyarwady Delta (Hall 1956). When the British governor of Madras heard the rumors, he preemptively sent a force that gained possession of the island of Negrais (a large island near Pathein, in the Delta region devastated by Cyclone Nargis in 2008). The English then tried to establish a friendship with Alaungpaya; however, Alaungpaya protested that he wanted to deal directly with a king as an equal, not with a mere trading company. Thus, in 1756 he wrote the now famous gold letter to King George II, offering recognition of the British presence at Negrais in exchange for the opening of trade and a supply of arms, as initiation of relations between the two countries. However, the story goes that by the time the letter was handed to King George II by Secretary of State William Pitt, a treaty had already been signed with the French, and orders had subsequently already been sent to abandon the unprofitable Negrais settlement (Harvey 1925). So King George II simply sent the letter to the royal library in Hanover, where it has long been thought of as a royal treasure from an unknown Indian prince (Leider 2009).

When Alaungpaya received no official reply from King George II to his overtures of friendship, despite the military incursion into his territory, he concluded that he had been either tricked or insulted. Thus when the Mon in the region near the British rebelled in 1759, and rumors suggested the English were supplying them with arms, Alaungpaya ordered the complete destruction of the remaining Negrais settlement—an act that became infamous and known to the British as the Negrais Massacre.

This whole episode is merely one more sorry tale of a litany of failed communication and bad experiences between Burma/Myanmar and the West, stretching over four centuries.

The Need for Historical Analysis

The international community's deep concerns over human rights abuses and governance failures in Myanmar have already been noted, as has the decades-long political impasse between the military, ethnic minorities, and the democracy movement. Despite the unexpected pace of recent reform, political values very foreign to Western observers still emerge daily in the power struggle between hard-liners, reformers, and opposition groups. Together with the fact that Myanmar has been equally plagued by long-standing poor international

Figure 3.1 The Golden Letter from Alaungpaya to King George II, 1756, now in the Gottfried Wilhelm Leibniz Library, Hanover, Germany. (Photograph © Gottfried Wilhelm Leibniz Bibliothek, Hanover)

relations, these factors point to the need for an in-depth historical understanding of underlying political priorities and sensitivities if development approaches are going to garner support and avoid exacerbating tensions.

The limited literature on development in difficult political contexts, as explored in chapter 2, emphasizes states experiencing conflict or fragility. Myanmar typifies both. Political and ethnic conflict is pervasive and has often been violent, with Myanmar being home to some of the longest running armed civil conflicts in the world (Smith 1997). It is also a fragile state. Foreign Policy (2010) ranks Myanmar as the sixteenth most vulnerable state to failure, and the Brookings Institute places it as the seventeenth weakest state, equal with North Korea as the world's most repressive autocracy (Rice and Patrick 2008). Only Somalia is weaker across Brookings' basket of political indicators.

The common thread running through this literature on development in difficult political contexts, as previously discussed at length, is the importance of grounding development in particularly historically informed understandings of the context. Most development mistakes in conflict-affected areas result from insufficient analysis of the sociocultural, institutional, historical, and political dynamics and an assumption that democracy alone will promote peace (World Bank 2006). In fragile states, historically contested notions of the state and postcolonial sensitivities are also issues (Wesley 2008). For these reasons a thorough examination of the historical origins of the contemporary conflicted politics and the strain in the state-society contract is required.

This is consistent with the research of Igboemeka (2005), discussed previously, who found that a more thorough understanding of the challenging Myanmar context and its link to change processes is required. It is also consistent with Myanmar studies literature, which regularly highlights the central importance of history and traditional culture to understanding contemporary society and politics (Steinberg 2010b). While it is tempting to ground a historical analysis largely on the two decades since the failed 1988 to 1990 push for democracy, or since the 1962 military coup, political analysis that fails to take adequate account of the longer history of how the Burmese state came to its current condition is simplistic, if not irrelevant (Taylor 2005; Guo Xiaolin 2009).

This chapter, therefore, offers brief analysis of the monarchical, colonial, and postcolonial antecedents to the current political context. It is widely recognized that the modern Burmese state, as reestablished by military regimes since the mid-1980s, has been built "in a new guise on the foundations of its monarchical and colonial predecessors" (Taylor 2009, 375). This historical analysis is therefore presented through these three major narratives related to the major time frames: (1) traditional perceptions about power, rulership, and political legitimacy, understandings that were relatively persistent over almost a millennium prior to the arrival of colonialism; (2) the impact of the colonial experience and history of interaction with the West, and the new security concerns this brought; and (3) the contribution of the crises at independence, and postcolonial sensitivities.

These three narratives form an important foundation for understanding the values, policies, and attitudes of many of the political elite in Myanmar today. Ultimately it is the leadership of individuals that has shaped Myanmar's modern history, and that history has been marred by some seriously poor policy decisions. However, these narratives illuminate the background structural context within which these leaders have acted, highlighting the fears and overreactions that many outside attempts to facilitate political change and economic development have provoked. They form an important foundation for identifying approaches more likely to receive cooperation than evoke reactions and suggesting altruistic motivations the political elite may hold, around which agreement on development and poverty alleviation policies might coalesce.

First Narrative: Historical Burmese-Buddhist Political Ideology

In the Tradition of Ancient Burmese Kings

The "guiding framework" of the modern Burmese state was laid at Bagan, the first Burmese empire, traditionally dated AD 1057–1287 (Aung-Thwin 1985, 199). Significant aspects of continuity persist, with echoes of traditional values resonating within contemporary Burmese politics (Taylor 2009). Steinberg (2006, 2010b) calls these "residues" from the past, legacies continuing to reverberate within notions of kingship and statecraft, in patterns of power and authority, and in their relationship with Buddhist concepts. Any understanding of contemporary Burmese society is thus incomplete without study of the structure and political values of these ancient Burmese empires.

All postindependence regimes have directly appealed to precolonial images of rulership to reinforce their own legitimacy (Matthews 1998).

> The cultural frame in which the military as well as the civilian political leadership of Burma have defined and claimed legitimacy has been the traditional culture with its age-old symbolic images. (Mya Maung 1991)

For example, during the WWII Japanese "independence," the Burmese civilian head of state, Dr. Ba Maw, adopted the title "Adipati Ashin Mingyi," which translates literally as "lord royal head of state" or according to Lintner (1991) "Lord of Power, the Great King's Royal Person," a title with clear "historical resonance going back to the Burmese kings" (Taylor 2009, 286). British rule and modernity did not change

> the more fundamental attitudes toward power, authority, hierar-
> chy, and governance that still profoundly influence how power is
> perceived and executed. . . . The colonial era . . . reinforced tradi-
> tional patterns of control, and emphasis on Buddhism as a reaction
> against rule that was widely interpreted, at least by Burmans, as
> illegitimate. (Steinberg 2006, 29)

There is good evidence that each of the senior generals heading the state since 1962 have, likewise, seen themselves within the tradition of the great Burman kings (Haacke 2006; Steinberg 2010b). Lacking democratic legitimacy, these generals have "behaved as if they were continuing in a royal tradition," adopting agendas that traditionally conferred legitimacy on rulers, namely, achieving unity, stability, and development and protecting independence, together with overt Buddhist patronage (Selth 2010a, 21).

Abundant illustrations support this view. For example, Ne Win (1962–88) married a descendant of the last Burmese royal family, then began appearing at state functions dressed in classical royal regalia and performed the kingly ceremony of raising the spire in a pagoda-building project (McCarthy 2008). Likewise, before Saw Maung (1988–92) was deposed, he too dressed in royal regalia and performed royal rituals, declaring himself a reincarnation of King Kyanzittha (1084–1112), son of Anawrahta, who founded the first Burmese empire (Steinberg 2010b). Than Shwe (1992–2010) refurbished the Shwedagon Pagoda with half a ton of diamonds, rubies, and sapphires and another 210 kilograms of gold and brought a tooth relic from China that was carried all over the country in a chariot drawn by an elephant in full regalia (Jordt 2003). He also constructed a facility in Rangoon to house all the white elephants being discovered throughout the country.

> During the time of the Buddhist kings, white elephants signified
> the purity and morality of a particular monarch's rule . . . (these
> new ones) supposedly proving beyond reasonable doubt the moral
> fitness of the SPDC. (Skidmore 2004, 88)

Than Shwe's move of the capital from Yangon to the newly constructed city of Naypyidaw in 2005 offers a further example. While there are several other likely strategic motivations, including undoing some of the colonial legacy and reconnecting with historical Burman ethnic roots (Seekins 2009), the move clearly appealed to traditional ideas of royal legitimacy (Maung Aung Myoe 2006). Burmese kings signaled the beginning of a new dynasty by moving their capital to a new site and built an elaborate new palace and royal pagoda. The name "Naypyidaw" translates as "seat of kings" (Seekins 2009) or "royal national site" (Steinberg 2010b, 16) and was a term used in precolonial times to refer to the royal city. Further reinforcing this view are the ten-meter-high bronze statues of the three most venerated warrior kings erected prominently in the city, the founders of the three Burmese empires, kings Anawrahta (1044–77), Bayinnaung (1551–81), and Alaungpaya (1752–60), pictured in Figure 3.2. Official invitations to the stake-driving ceremony for the replica of the historic Yangon Shwedagon Pagoda opened with the phrase "Rajahtani Naypyidaw," literally "the royal capital where the king resides" (Maung Aung Myoe 2006, 14).

Together, these actions suggest that the various regimes' ideas about political legitimacy have been heavily drawn from these precolonial models, under a veneer of modernity.

Figure 3.2 Senior General Than Shwe inspecting troops in front of the statues of the warrior kings Anawrahta, Bayinnaung, and Alaungpaya in Naypyidaw on Armed Forces Day 2007. (Photograph © Agence France-Presse)

Authoritarianism and Traditional Values

Appeal to these traditional sources of political legitimacy has been an ongoing practice in Burmese politics. Even during the democratic period prior to the 1962 coup, Maung Maung Gyi expressed concern that political power was being arrogated by authoritarian leaders through appeal to precolonial values and beliefs and that these values were broadly held by the entire population, not just the political elite (Maung Maung Gyi 1983). Reflecting on Ne Win's regime after the coup, he argued,

> Authoritarian rulership thrives only on authoritarian soil, that is, the type of nation that accepts an authoritarian regime. Had the social-political values of the nation been nonauthoritarian, the military, once they had straightened out the chaotic situation of the country, would be expected to return to the barracks, or else the public would use pressure to throw out the military from power. (Maung Maung Gyi 1983, 3)

Steinberg (2006) similarly argues that popular uprisings in Burma, from classical times until the 1988 demonstrations, were not designed to change the system as much as to substitute who was in command. This may have begun to change more recently, as people have become more aware of democracy, although arguably people still seek better living conditions and well-being more than principally a change in the form of government. Collignon (2001) substantiates this argument by correlating mass demonstrations with serious deterioration in economic circumstances, rather than inherently being a response to immediate political trigger events, concluding,

> The SLORC-SPDC generals [have] found more legitimacy in the traditional views of Burmese culture than the modern concept of human rights . . . the root of Burma's problems may not just be the SLORC-SPDC—it may be Burma itself. . . . The problem is the cognitive model on which Burmese society functions. . . . A military *regime* . . . can lay claim to legitimacy in the framework of the traditional cognitive model of Burmese society. (Collignon 2001, 79–80, 83)

Maung Maung Gyi suggests that colonialism had a minimal impact on these traditional values, arguing that the British "never seriously attempted to win the imagination of the people . . . to their ideals"; since they "were never in close touch with the people . . . the medieval Burmese mind underwent no essential change" (Maung Maung Gyi 1983, 8–13). He concludes that colonial rule actually reinforced more than challenged authoritarian ideas about power and rulership. By the time of the Japanese invasion during WWII, just fifty-six years after the British conquered Mandalay, most Burmans looked forward nostalgically to the establishment of a new version of that vision (Taylor 1987).

Buddhist Basis of Traditional Legitimacy

Buddhism is the cornerstone of Burmese culture and central to traditional ideas about political legitimacy (Rozenberg 2009). "Burmese polities have defined themselves in terms of Buddhist sources of legitimacy for more than a millennium" (Schober 2011), with all postindependence governments incorporating Burmese-Buddhist elements into their political ideology for legitimacy and nation-building purposes (Philp 2004). Many have claimed that the SLORC/SPDC regime possessed no legitimacy at all, because of their repression and ineffective rule. However, while their legitimacy has certainly been contested (Steinberg 2006), they did derive sufficient legitimacy from traditional values to control not only the population but also the military and the elite.

Since the time of King Anawrahta, whenever Burmese rulers have faced an erosion of political legitimacy, they have returned to Buddhism to define their political values (Houtman 1999).

The most comprehensive ethnographic study of Theravada Buddhism in Burma was conducted by Spiro (1982), who completed his fieldwork during the 1950s, during the democratic era. According to Spiro, while the radical soteriology of attaining *nibbana* may be the goal of many monks, it is not practical or desirable for a majority of laypeople. Paying lip service to doctrines of *dukka* (suffering) and *tanha* (desire), he suggests laypeople aspire to a future in which their desires are instead satisfied through the accumulation of *kamma* rather than by attaining *nibbana* and escaping *samsara* (cycle of rebirth). For most Burmese this means aspiring to a better rebirth, with the outcome being an emphasis on merit-making and amassing *kamma*. In the 1950s Spiro found laypeople in poor rural villages in Upper Burma investing between 30 and 40 percent of their net disposable income into merit-making.

Inscriptions as early as Anawrahta show many Burmese kings even viewed the accumulation of *kamma* as a direct means of attaining *nibbana*, bypassing the need for ascetic meditation (Aung-Thwin 1985; Koenig 1990). Those with large stores of *kamma*, those with *hpoun* (merit, glory), were highly respected. Since social position is the most clear, outward indicator of *hpoun*, and because social position brings additional ability for further merit-making, advancement in social position became a major ambition for most lay-Buddhists. In practice, most Burmese modify central Buddhist concepts to see *dukka* (suffering) as being caused not by *tanha* (desire) per se but by the frustration of desire, making accumulation of *hpoun* a central pursuit (Koenig 1990); "when applied to the laity at least, merit, wealth, and power thus became conceptually interchangeable" (Aung-Thwin 1985, 46).

These traditional ideas continue to some extent today, influencing the legitimacy-seeking behavior of the Myanmar elite. Burmese military rulers since 1962 have all exhibited a "deep and unfeigned reverence for Buddhism, and there is no room for such claims to moral legitimacy in regularly corrupt, nepotistic, late capitalistic dictatorships" (Skidmore 2004, 60). Rather, such merit-making is far better explained as recourse to traditional political legitimacy (Jordt 2001). (The Buddhist value placed on merit-making likewise goes a long way toward explaining the existence and nature of Burmese civil society today, with its strong emphasis on charity.)

Traditional political legitimacy is derived from these ideas of *kamma* and *hpoun* and their corollary for political leadership, *dhammaraja* and *cakkavatti*. The *dhammaraja* is an ideal of rulership known throughout Burmese history, one who uses his great *kamma* to restore political, moral, and religious order—an almost messianic role (Aung-Thwin 1983, 1985). It was the central organizing model of kingship during the third Burmese empire (1752–1886), linking political power with religious ideas and ritual practice (Schober 2011). The *dhammaraja* was expected to unify factions and install a higher moral order, creating an environment of peace and prosperity within which people could spend time gaining merit. Kings used this concept to legitimize conquests as wars to seek holy relics and proselytize, limiting the power of the *sangha* (monkhood) to apolitical roles as an act of purification (Aung-Thwin 1979, 1983).

A *cakkavatti* was similar, in Burmese thought being an enlightened being who delays entrance into *nibbana* to serve as a universal monarch, conquering the world and implementing *dhamma* out of concern for the welfare of people everywhere (Taylor 2009). The concept is thus likewise messianic, similar to the Mahayana *bodhisatta*, except that a *cakkavatti* adopts the wearisome task of political rulership and military conquest as the means to help others find the path (Aung-Thwin 1983; Tambiah 1976).

Dhammaraja and *cakkavatti* are ideals of rulership. Tambiah (1976) is convinced that Ne Win's Buddhist observance was carefully constructed to lay claim to the role of *cakkavatti*, while many saw U Nu's religious patronage as a sign he was a *dhammaraja* (Schober 2011). Aung San Suu Kyi, likewise, has appealed to the duties expected of a *dhammaraja* to challenge the regime and to elaborate her political ethos (Suu Kyi 1995b).

Kammaraja is a recent analytical term, coined to embrace the essential characteristic of both *dhammaraja* and *cakkavatti*, namely, rule by right of possessing the most abundant store of merit among the laypeople. It therefore describes the moral, *kammic* legitimization of kingship (Aung-Thwin 1985). It is, nonetheless, a circular argument: a king is proven to be the most worthy person to rule by virtue of being the ruler. Because they possess superior *hpoun*, such kings were considered to be future Buddhas. For example, the name Alaungpaya is an appellation meaning "Buddha to be" (Maung Htin Aung 1967, 168). The weakness of this belief, though, is that "it confers legitimacy on *any* political regime—not only on the regime in authority, but on the regime that usurps its authority" (Spiro 1982, 443).

> Karma plays a curiously paradoxical role. Conferring legitimacy on the regime in power, and at the same time providing an incentive for the overthrow of that regime, this doctrine has played an important part in the political instability that has persistently plagued Burmese history . . . (providing) powerful incentives for the . . . extraordinary incidence of usurpation of royal power. (Spiro 1982, 440–42)

Burmese chronicles record the mythical origins of kingship after eons of moral decay under democratic social structures. That decay led to a need for individuals with superior moral qualities (greater *hpoun*) to sacrificially accept a role to lead the people "to prevent society from lapsing into anarchy" (Koenig 1990, 65). The ruler's role is thus not to serve the people per se but to bring order from chaos by serving *dhamma* (Aung-Thwin 1985). It should be noted that this ancient concept was overtly and explicitly appealed to as recently as 1829 in *The Glass Palace Chronicle* (Pe Maung Tin and Luce 1923), a royal chronicle commissioned by King Bagyidaw to bolster his legitimacy after losing the First Anglo-Burmese War.

Seven Perceptions of Authority and Rulership Within This Ideology

Based on the preceding analysis, the "important residues" of ancient Burmese political ideology that reverberate within contemporary politics, with implications for contemporary INGO development work, could be summarized in terms of the following perceptions of authority and rulership.

Perceptions by Rulers (Those With Authority)

1. Legitimacy: Merit, Order, and Control

Kamma provides a powerful moral authority to the social order. As the pinnacle of the social order, rulers represent "the culmination of an incredible storehouse of merit" (Spiro 1982, 139). In theory, Burmese kings had absolute power, something the most charismatic figures claimed to wield. Demonstrating that their *hpoun* was flourishing allowed rulers to lead with "overwhelming reverence and awe" and keep the loyal following of the people (Spiro 1982, 140). However, most were caught in a web of competing interests, with power limited by the need to manage rivals, the monkhood, enemies, and the natural environment (Silverstein 1977; Steinberg 2006; Taylor 2009).

The legitimacy of rulers was thus determined by how much of this theoretically absolute control they could demonstrate militarily, politically, economically, and spiritually (Taylor 2009). For example, powerful kings had large militaries and an inclination toward preemptive military action (Maung Maung Gyi 1983; Matthews 1998; Taylor 2009). In 1862 (not a time of war), King Mindon's army was estimated at over 1 percent of the population, a proportion larger than today (Taylor 2009). Likewise, kings managed or removed rivals, unified factions and conquered states under loyalty to themselves, controlled business and trade, managed a "redistributive" economy with royal monopolies in key industries, and demonstrated their authority over the monkhood (Aung-Thwin 1979, 1985, 26–30; Lieberman 1980; Taylor 1987). One major difference between early modern Burma and European states was the Burmese prevention of the emergence of private wealth independent of royal favor, totally obscuring the development of a feudal system (Taylor 1987, 27). Strong kings likewise periodically demonstrated their control over the *sangha* (monkhood) through "purification" and reform, while remaining their chief patron (Aung-Thwin 1979, 1985; Lieberman 1980).

Reflections of similar perceptions of power can be seen even in the responses to the 2007 demonstrations led by the sangha, the Saffron Revolution, and Cyclone Nargis in 2008. The importance contemporary Burmese rulers continue to place on security, control, and prosperity to build their legitimacy is also significant.

2. Moral Responsibility: Order, Reformation, and Merit

Kammaraja legitimacy comes with moral responsibility. Merit and enlightenment must be used to establish political and moral order and work for the welfare and salvation of the people. Given the belief that kingship arose to correct the failure of democratic rule, the responsibility of rulers is not to serve the people by providing freedom, law, order, peace, opportunity, or prosperity as much as to build an ordered state around themselves in which *kammic* authority flows from the top down, unity is maintained, morality is upheld, and state merit-making is undertaken. Likewise, under this traditional ideology royal patronage of religion is a nationally important moral responsibility, matching the importance of providing order, security, and prosperity. The religious patronage of the current and former rulers has already been noted, and their attempts to lead the people in moral reformation are clearly apparent.

3. Nature of Authority: Personalized, Centralized, and Hierarchical

Power within this traditional ideology is finite and personalized (Steinberg 2006, 37–38), in contrast to modern Western theory in which power is considered infinitely expandable and most effective when delegated or shared. It is common in traditional societies for power to be seen in zero-sum terms as a "limited good." In Burma, this traditionally stemmed from the belief that rulership legitimacy derived from finite, personal *hpoun*. As a result, loyalty rightly belongs to the individual, not the institution, and only responsibility, not authority, can be delegated; delegation of authority is both illogical and destructive without conditions that retain ultimate control (Steinberg 2010b). This is the basis of Burmese patron–client entourage systems and a contributor to the rationale for a quarter of the new parliament being military appointees. Delegating power unconditionally could be perceived as a dereliction of duty. Within this worldview, information, an expression of power, likewise cannot be shared without control being maintained (Steinberg 2010b). While private ownership of property was recognized in ancient Burma, ultimate ownership by the king meant even free subjects could be required to provide either labor or property to any royal project (Aung-Thwin 1985). Contemporary labor and property rights violations are largely a continuation of such traditional practice.

Perceptions by the Ruled (Those Under Authority)

4. Responsibility When Strong: Comply

Unsurprisingly, many successful Burmese kings were not popular during their reign. Proverbs compared kings with natural calamities: something to avoid whenever possible and as an evil to be endured (Koenig 1990; Silverstein 1977). On the other hand, the central role the ruler plays in creating merit-based well-being makes compliance a moral good: "a quasi-religious duty" (Silverstein 1996, 213). In line with Buddhist teaching that the individual is responsible for his or her own fate, the average peasant "did not expect the state to do anything to improve his life, [showing] stoic acceptance of misfortune and the government's excessive demands and victimization" (Silverstein 1977, 10). As a result, the response when kings were strong was to try to avoid interaction with their representatives wherever possible (Than Tun 1983) and comply whenever they did have contact.

5. Responsibility When Weak: Challenge

Coercion, always inherent in the exercise of secular authority, diminishes merit, and thus Burmese kings engaged extensively in merit-making activities to counteract the negative impact of the use of force (Koenig 1990). However, overly authoritarian rule could rapidly diminish *hpoun*, legitimizing revolt. Whenever the kingdom appeared weak or in disunity, whenever the response to a significant natural disaster was inadequate, and in times of transition, rivals almost invariably rebelled (Aung-Thwin 1985). Revolt and regicide were particularly common in Burmese history, and revolts led by formerly loyal followers were easily justified. Overthrow of a monarch immediately transferred their legitimacy to the usurper. The revolts after British annexation of both Lower and Upper Burma and the civil war immediately following the assassination of Aung San both fit this model, which also partly explains the hesitant response to offers of assistance following Cyclone Nargis.

Perceptions About Competing Power

6. Response to Internal Rivals

In this political landscape, it was important for kings to end lesser rivalries by uniting them to each other and the throne. Strong kings thus placed a major emphasis on establishing unity between factions and on attempting to create a homogenous population from culturally varied conquered communities (Taylor 1987). This has continued to be the model for most government attempts at ending the ethnic problems plaguing the country. Permitting the continued existence of rival political power shows weakness, whether that is a rival leader or institution (Steinberg 2006; Silverstein 1977). As leaders earn legitimacy by winning pledges of loyalty from rivals or eliminating them, princes and possible heirs were closely watched while nobles were prevented from emerging as a class with independent rights. Writing prior to the 1962 coup, Pye noted,

> Although not untypical of traditional systems, the violence and cruelty of the Burmese kings is legendary. . . . There are few cultures that attach greater importance to power as a value than the Burmese. (Pye 1962, 67, 146)

7. Response to Competing External Powers: Nondependence

Burmese rulers have been labeled isolationist, intransigent, and xenophobic since eighteenth-century British trade and diplomatic contact (e.g., Donnison 1970, 55; Hall 1956). These are not recent perceptions. The response of many Burmese kings to contact with external powers was to belittle envoys, delay them for considerable periods, engage in grandiose ceremony, and take uncompromising, belligerent positions (e.g., Donnison 1970; Harvey 1925). Until recently, similar strategies were adopted toward UN human rights envoys. Burmese monarchs were particularly sensitive to being belittled by envoys themselves, for example, by being sent representatives of trading companies or governors rather than direct monarch-to-monarch contact. Accepting such lower-ranked envoys willingly would have diminished their legitimacy. "Isolation and a desire to find solutions to local problems from within the Burmese tradition" are one of the more significant continuing features of Burmese politics (Silverstein 1977, 4).

Labels of "isolationism" and "xenophobia" seem, however, a slight overstatement. Rulers were more concerned about being nondependent on external powers. A more appropriate term would be "autarky," economic (and political) self-sufficiency (Taylor 2001a). Burma's consistent efforts at political neutrality and nonalignment, both before and particularly after colonialism, stand out. Ne Win's isolationism was as much a practical response to the superpower rivalry in the region as anything else. Dependency on external powers, economically or politically, would undermine any claim to *kammaraja* legitimacy.

Impact on Development Programming

Residues of these ancient political values reverberate within contemporary Burmese politics. While they are most readily observable in the actions of the various juntas, they are also often evident in the positions and actions taken within the current reform, including those not only of former military leaders but also by opposition groups, local officials, ethnic minority leaders, civil society, and business and even academic institutions, religious institutions, and families (Steinberg 2010b). The persistence of traditional values has implications for international development and suggests some approaches are more likely to be resisted while others may gain ready acceptance.

For example, traditionally the creation of alternative centers of power has delegitimized the state. Advocacy and capacity building toward modern state institutions like an independent judiciary, democratic opposition, free press, civil society, trade unions, property rights, and even a middle or business class with independent security in private wealth challenges traditional ideas regarding the nature of power and means to retain rulership. To the extent these ideas continue to motivate members of the political elite, these ideas will continue to attract opposition. At the same time, though, these values do suggest that even senior regime officials may not be solely motivated by rent-seeking and personal power but have an intrinsic political and personal motivation toward providing welfare, poverty alleviation, and development to their people, provided higher-order concerns about order and security are not threatened. This may imply the possibility of success for a well-thought-through constructive engagement strategy, even with those holding to traditional zero-sum perceptions of power.

Finally, these perceptions have major implications for community-level participation and empowerment. On the one hand, if villagers do not expect assistance from their rulers, assume they must own the responsibility for their own futures, and have had minimal contact with the international development industry, dependency is less likely to be an immediate issue. On the other hand, a long history of compliance in a highly hierarchical social structure, where their religion has taught them not to question authority, may raise additional challenges to achieving participation, equity, and empowerment. These ideas will be picked up again in later chapters discussing the fieldwork research results.

Second Narrative: Interaction With the West and the Colonial Experience

Traditional ideology alone, however, does not fully explain the behavior of Myanmar's postindependence military rulers and the persistence of authoritarian rule. Myanmar's current condition is the culmination of a number of interconnected pathways (Taylor 2005), another of which is the Burmese experience of colonialism and the longer history of interaction with the West. The preeminence of the military, for example, has much to do with the British use of warfare as the means of state building (Callahan 2004). This is another major historical narrative shaping the contemporary context.

Early Impressions: Precolonial Interaction With the West
For many Myanmar elite, the history of interaction with the West has been predominantly negative. The first recorded European visitor to Burma was a Venetian merchant in 1435, and most Europeans who arrived over the following two centuries were Portuguese merchants, missionaries, or adventurers (Donnison 1970). A considerable number of these adventurers served in the

armed forces of Arakan, Pegu, and Siam against the Burman kings, the Burmans themselves being much slower in incorporating mercenaries into their armies.

In 1600 the Portuguese adventurer Filipe de Brito set up a trade monopoly at Syriam, across the river from modern Yangon. Having served as a mercenary with the Arakanese, he now converted rebel Mon groups to Catholicism and set up his own kingdom. Using ships to control sea trade and levy import duties, he raided Buddhist pagodas for precious stones and gold, accumulating massive wealth before the Burmese eventually defeated him at a cost of 30,000 lives. In a gesture of goodwill, survivors (both Mon and Portuguese) were spared and settled up-country in their own villages (Donnison 1970; Hall 1956; Harvey 1925; Maung Htin Aung 1967).

This experience left deep suspicion of Europeans in the minds of the Burmese, and as Donnison (1970) argues, its impact on subsequent history should not be underestimated. Burman interest in trade was dampened such that when silting in the Pegu River and peace with Siam suggested relocating the capital, the Burmans moved their capital 600 kilometers inland in 1635 (Hall 1956). As the Dutch, French, and then English arrived intermittently over the following years to open trading posts and shipyards, Burmese rulers variously showed little interest, obstructed their activities, or attempted to create their own trade monopolies.

> It is not without significance that Siam, which, when forced in the next century to evacuate its capital built one at a seaport rather than further inland, managed to survive as an independent state, while Burma succumbed to foreign conquest. The chief ingredient in the failure of the Burmese kingdom was supplied not by "Western Imperialism," but by the intransigence and xenophobia which radiated from the Court of Ava. (Hall 1956, 66)

In 1742, during the bitter rivalry between the Mon and the Burmans that eventually brought down the Second Burmese Empire, Burman forces sacked the foreign settlements among the Mon at Syriam (Hall 1956). This incident similarly colored European perceptions of the Burmese. Just a decade later the incident retold at the beginning of this chapter occurred, in which the British invaded Negrais to preempt a perceived French incursion, and Alaungpaya wrote that now famous gold letter to King George II, offering recognition in exchange for trade and arms (Hall 1956). The British lack of reply followed by a withdrawal was seen to confirm Burman suspicions, culminating in another massacre of foreigners in 1759, this time of the British at Negrais. Burman–Western relations just never seemed to get off on the right foot. The French tried one more time, obtaining permission for a shipyard in Rangoon; however, their support for a failed Mon rebellion in 1768 led to a further massacre. The Burmans became convinced that both the French and the English were arming and supporting rebels to overthrow their rule.

There can be little doubt that these incidents colored views on both sides, resulting in deep distrust and strengthening the autarkic, isolationist, and non-dependence tendencies in Burmese polity, distrust that has not been fully overcome to this day. By the time the British sent their first genuinely political (not commercial) envoy, Captain Symes, on a diplomatic mission in 1795, "the British encountered little but hostility and deliberately imposed humiliation" (Donnison 1970, 58; also Harvey 1925). The Burmese felt insulted at being sent envoys from British viceroys rather than the king, given Burmese governors had very little real power (Harvey 1925). For their part, British delegations were accompanied by escorts designed to intimidate, and from 1799 they pressed for a treaty of "subsidiary alliance" (Hall 1956, 99–100), something impossible for Burmese kings to concede without losing substantial political legitimacy.

Three Anglo-Burmese Wars

The inability of both sides to find grounds for trust and to negotiate effectively exploded into three Anglo-Burmese wars, culminating in full annexation of Burma. The first war (1824–26) has been called the "worst-managed war in British military history" (Hall 1956, 103–5). Despite the British eventual victory, 45 percent of the 40,000 British troops, including most of the Europeans, died when troops were cut off from supplies. While Arakan and Tenasserim were lost, the war gave hope to the Burmese that the British lacked real military might.

A blockade of Rangoon less than thirty years later triggered a second war (1852–53). The British annexed Lower Burma quickly and decisively, leaving the Burmese in shock (Hall 1956). When the British did not withdraw after a brief show of force, as anticipated, the Burmese feared a full takeover. The annexed territory responded with a grassroots rebellion that required 10,000 additional troops and three years to pacify. The British were surprised that even after defeat, the Burmese were neither submissive nor inclined to conduct trade negotiations. Envoys "had to encounter all the arts of subterfuge, evasion and studied rudeness, with which earlier envoys had had to contend" (Hall 1956, 115).

A tense, three-decade standoff resulted, culminating in a third war (1885–86). It has been argued that the decision to invade Upper Burma was ultimately dictated by powerful British capitalists eager to expand their personal financial interests, the trigger being a trade dispute over teak logged in Burmese territory (Webster 2000). Defeating the main Burmese army in just months, the British anticipated they would be welcomed as liberators from the despotic King Thibaw. Having boasted that they could take Mandalay with as few as 500 men, they were unprepared for the resulting rebellion that required 40,500 additional troops and five years to quell (Hall 1956; Taylor 2009).

The brutal pacification of this popular rebellion contributed seriously to the Burmese experience of colonialism. Geary, a journalist with the *Bombay Gazette*, arrived in Mandalay in less than a month after the initial victory to report on the conquest. He found the Burmese "stunned and terror-stricken" at the British "subjection by terror" (Geary 1886, 236). The rice crop had failed in 1884, and a severe food crisis erupted as the British invasion interrupted the poor 1885 harvests. In the confusion as the British swept away the old royal administration, villages sent out men to scavenge food, and most armed themselves. Colonial literature speaks of *dacoits*, armed gangs of robbers, roaming the country, but today many scholars also see a rapidly organized grassroots rebellion targeted against the British (e.g., Maung Htin Aung and Aung-Thwin 2008). Foreshadowing the serious ethnic politics of today, ethnic Karen troops recruited in Lower Burma were used in this suppression, as they had been guides for the British Army in the two preceding wars, and they were even described as "positively enthusiastic" contributors (Smith 1999, 45).

Geary (1886, 248) concluded that the main cause of the quick spread of what he called a resistance movement was the "promiscuous shooting of so-called dacoits" by British forces.

> Dacoits are shot without trial . . . [officers] regard every armed Burmese as a dacoit, and the villagers found near the scene of a raid are in considerable peril. . . . They will be shot as dacoits if they have arms; if they have none, they will be robbed and possibly murdered by the dacoits. (Geary 1886, 45)

A key rationale for the war had been the alleged brutality of King Thibaw. Before the invasion, given the food crisis, armed robbers caught by Thibaw were imprisoned briefly, tattooed as a warning, and then sent home for a second chance (Geary 1886). Many expressed horror at the British cruelty in direct contrast:

> British military officers acted as both judge and jury. . . . British troops carried out mass executions and committed other atrocities. As the guerrillas fought on, the British adopted a "strategic-hamlet" strategy: villages were burned, and families who had supplied villages with their headmen were uprooted from their homes and sent away to Lower Burma. (Maung Htin Aung and Aung-Thwin 2008)

Such an account echoes Western outcries over the infamous Four Cuts Strategy of Ne Win and subsequent army commanders against ethnic insurgents—but this action was first perpetrated by the British against Burmese communities seeking food and defending their homeland against foreign invasion.

The Colonial Experience

The subsequent Burmese experience of colonialism differed substantially from that of the rest of British India. Central to Burma's particularly negative experience were direct rule rather than rule through local hierarchies, integration of Burma into British India despite little shared culture or history, and importation of large numbers of Indians for the administration and economic development of Burma. Many Burmese view direct rule as the result of Burmese nonacquiescence to Britain's commercial and strategic desires (Thant Myint-U 2001). Because of Britain's harshness and lack of consideration of Burmese culture, history, and identity, "The Burmese regarded British government as an even greater evil than Burmese monarchy had been, with most of its vices but few of its virtues" (Taylor 2009, 117). Distrust of the West by many political elite today is in part a continuation of such nationalistic sentiment.

To be fair, not all Burmese resented the British presence, as illustrated, for example, by the large number who migrated to Lower Burma between the second and third wars. The city of Pegu, for example, doubled in size with economic migrants from Upper Burma during the ten years (1852–62; Donnison 1970). Nonetheless, twenty-five years after the pacification there was both a serious growth in violent crime and the emergence of a nationalist resistance movement, "as a new generation who did not remember the harshness of annexation" grew up, now deprived economically and of self-respect (Donnison 1970, 91–92).

Indian Migration and Domination

Burma was administered as a province of British India until 1937, when it became an independent colony. Until then, seeing the Burmese as unmotivated workers, the colonial administration heavily promoted Indian migration, sub-sidizing travel costs (Taylor 2009). Rangoon soon had the world's highest rate of migration, even outstripping New York (Charney 2009). By 1921 some 55 percent of Rangoon was Indian (Charney 2009), with 480,000 new Indian migrants arriving in 1927 alone (Hall 1956). Indians had a disproportion-ate influence in government and trade, were the largest landowners in Lower Burma, provided most of the finance for agricultural development, and had a virtual monopoly in key areas of the civil service (Donnison 1970; Taylor 2009). Most stayed only two to four years, taking their earnings with them when they returned home (Taylor 2009). By the time the first steps were be-ing taken toward self-rule in the 1920s and 1930s, the majority of Burmese in Lower Burma were landless laborers occupying the lowest rung of the social hierarchy in their own country (Hall 1956). The economy was built on mi-grant workers who lacked social bonding to Burma, did not intend to settle in the country, and felt no motivation for self-sacrifice for the good of the com-munity (Taylor 2009).

> The stark contrasts between the prosperity of the foreigners (in-cluding Asian migrants) in Rangoon and the rural Burmese masses lent weight to the impression that any prosperity which the British brought was not for the benefit of the Burmese. (Charney 2009, 20)

Imported Indian labor drove Burman workers away and bypassed the need for the British and Burmans to learn to work together (Furnivall [1939] 1991). It "erected a barrier between Burmans and the modern world that has never been broken down" (Taylor 1995, 52, quoting Furnivall 1941, 46). Few British spoke more than marketplace Burmese (Donnison 1970). Highlight-ing Burmese marginalization, Europeans wanting to work in the *Indian* Civil Service in Burma had to pass exams in Hindustani, not Burmese (Charney 2009). The British colonial presence in Burma was thus "much more superfi-cial, at least as far as political culture is concerned" than that of the rest of the subcontinent (Perry 2007, 21). The Burmese, an ethnic minority in the major cities of their own country, gained little or none of the benefits of the booming economy (Donnison 1970; Charney 2009).

Ethnic Policies

The British classified the ethnic Burman majority as a "martial race," a threat to order and stability, concluding prior to the third war that the ethnic minorities needed protection (Thant Myint-U 2001; Taylor 2005). They thus created two Burmas: "Ministerial Burma," covering lowland areas dominated by the Burman majority, was placed under direct rule and subject to British legal, administrative, and educational oversight, while "Frontier Areas" in mountainous areas populated by ethnic minorities were left under the control of traditional rulers (Smith 1994). Smith (1999) argues that most of the ethnic minorities incorporated into the Frontier areas of Burma had previously been little affected by precolonial governments on the central plains of Burma. Now thrust together, both sides had grievances against the other over this arrangement. While the British quickly developed agriculture and industry in Ministerial Burma, the Frontier Areas, Karen, Kachin, and Chin minorities were actively recruited into the army and police to control Ministerial Burma, alongside Indian forces. Burmans were not admitted until WWI (Smith 1994; Taylor 2005)—and even by 1940 just 12 percent of the army were Burman (despite constituting two-thirds of the population), while Karen, Chin, and Kachin (10 percent of the population) made up over 75 percent of the army (Steinberg 1982). Making things worse, many Karen, Kachin, and Chin converted to Christianity, increasing Burman antagonism toward both the British and the minorities who closely aligned with them.

Some scholars argue that race was not a significant issue in Burma prior to colonialism and that wars before that time were about political and personal power politics rather than race (e.g., Houtman 1999; Steinberg 2006). The SLORC regime argued that all ethnic groups were peacefully united prior to colonialism, even sharing a common ancestry, and that the British are responsible for creating all of the current ethnic tension (Minye Kaungbon 1994; Rozenberg 2009). This is clearly an overstatement, although "the colonial authorities' insistence upon racial distinctiveness gave ethnicity a greater centrality in political thought than it had previously had" (Taylor 2009, 150). Ethnic divisions today "have become the major political factor facing the society" (Steinberg 2006, 25) and a major issue for INGO equity and empowerment initiatives.

Colonial Administration

British administration had negative implications on local representation and empowerment. For example, it replaced locally appointed township headmen, *myothugyi*, whose role had included representing the interests of the township, with salaried officials acting merely as instruments through which central government policy was implemented (Taylor 2009; Donnison 1970; Furnivall [1939] 1991). Furnivall, a public official who arrived in Burma around the

turn of the twentieth century, remarked that the object of the colonial administration was not for the good of the people but for increased production for
the British (Furnivall [1939] 1991). The need for increased coercion to rule,
demonstrated by the rapid rise in the need for police and prisons, has long
been linked to this loss of local voice (Taylor 2009; Furnivall [1939] 1991).
The British administration was

> incomparably more authoritative and effective than any other that
> Burma has ever known. . . . It was a highly centralized and pa-
> ternalistic system, not at all unlike that imposed by the Burmese
> kings—except that it was vastly more effective (and to that extent
> more burdensome) and of course, that it was imposed by foreign-
> ers. (Donnison 1970, 77, 83)

Rather than reconstructing Burmese political values in the more liberal
and modern ideas prevalent in Europe during that time, the colonial administration largely reinforced traditional ideas about political power being legiti-
mized through centralized control, while demonstrating a far more efficient
means to exert that control down to the village level (Steinberg 2006). Despite
local representation being reintroduced shortly before independence, the very
short and limited experience of democracy under colonialism gave little time
for new values to take root. For most of the colonial period, the British ruled
by decree and maintained control by retaining the right to arbitrarily suspend
the law and declare a state of exception (Silverstein 1977). They maintained
control, as Duffield expresses it, "through holding self-reliant populations on
the threshold of emergency" and keeping them independent of the state in
terms of their welfare and social survival (Duffield 2008, 8). It could be argued
that subsequent Burmese military regimes have largely perpetuated these patterns demonstrated by the British.

The YMBA, Nationalism, and the Hsaya San Rebellion

Burmese nationalism and opposition to British rule simmered continually. The
Young Men's Buddhist Association (YMBA) was formed in 1906 among newly
educated young urban Burmese to promote Buddhism and Burmese culture.
By 1917, fewer than thirty years after the end of the third war, they had taken
on the function of a political party advocating self-rule, leading mass strikes
and street protests in 1920, which enlisted large numbers of monks in scenes
reminiscent of the mass demonstrations of 1988 and 2007. Maung Maung
Gyi's (1983) opinion is that had Burma been given independence at this point

in time, a complete reversion to monarchical rule would not have been unlikely.

In their struggle for independence, the nationalists attracted people to their cause by fanning into folklore stories of the splendor and order under Burman Buddhist monarchs (Maung Maung Gyi 1983). When an earthquake nearly destroyed Pegu in 1930, the astrologer-monk, Hsaya San, became convinced that this disaster reflected the diminished *hpoun* of the British and hence was an omen of the end of colonial rule. Raising a following among poor villagers, Hsaya San was declared king and launched a two-year rebellion. One cause of this rebellion was the severe crash in rice prices during the Great Depression; another was simmering anti-British sentiment. The untrained rebels had very few weapons, but the British response was harsh. By 1932 some 10,000 rebels had been killed and 9,000 captured, with mass executions and burning of villages. Photos of decapitated heads were posted at police stations across the country as a deterrent, inadvertently evoking further nationalist sentiment. The British marveled at their superstition without recognizing the alienation and depth of feeling the peasants had against foreign rule (Maung Htin Aung 1967; Charney 2009).

Residues in the Contemporary Context

This history of interaction with the West is therefore another major historical narrative shaping the contemporary political context. While colonialism did bring benefits, such as a modern education and health system, these experiences also underscored the fierce Burmese priority on independence from foreign domination and exploitation. For many, they also demonstrated the effectiveness of a modern military in ensuring the security and control that traditional ideology called for, together with the means to exercise direct control over the entire state. Without doubt, they also fanned ethnic differences into one of the largest issues facing the country. Despite the passage of time, these feelings all still resonate strongly in contemporary polity and are of direct relevance to the sensitivity INGOs need to display in their interaction with local stakeholders.

Third Narrative: Independence, Postcolonialism, and Military Rule

Just as precolonial political ideology and the colonial experience are narratives continuing to inform contemporary politics, the more recent history of WWII, independence, and the crises that followed form a third major narrative, with many continuities impacting both contemporary politics and the economy.

Nationalism, War, and the BIA

The rallying cry of the Burmese during the Indo-Burmese riots of 1930 was "Do Bama," literally "We Burmese" or "Our Burma." The racial aspiration unleashed by the ensuing movement led to mass strikes, eventuating in separation from India and limited self-rule. The *Thakin* (master) Party, formed by university students and recent graduates to contest the 1937 elections, was strongly nationalist, demanding total economic and political freedom from Indian and British dominance. Boycotting the 1937 elections and calling the new constitution a sham, they quickly grew to become a major political force. The *Thakin* described themselves as anti-imperialistic and democratic, adopting leftist ideas because of their anti-imperialism (Suu Kyi 1995b; Taylor 1987). Many described them at that time as being authoritarian. For example, Donnison suggested they were

> fanatical idealists . . . very socialist . . . hostile to all that could be considered foreign . . . [who] would accept nothing less than complete independence for Burma and [were] perfectly prepared to use violence to attain this end. (Donnison 1970, 118)

The *Thakin* Party was proscribed in 1941 because of its hostility to the government (Donnison 1970). Mass arrests followed when the *Thakin* and some other politicians began forming private armies (Maung Htin Aung 1967). In the midst of this unrest, and as a demonstration of just how strong the anticolonial sentiment was, the Thirty Comrades were smuggled out of Burma for military training in Japan. Among these were not only Aung San but also future democratic-era Prime Minister U Nu and the military strongman Senior General Ne Win. The intention was to use the Japanese as a means to liberate Burma from the British, believing a Japanese invasion would be countered at the border by the British, allowing an uprising by the Burmese to secure an independent Burma under the Japanese domain (Naw 2001).

The Thirty Comrades followed the Japanese forces into Burma in 1942, recruiting 50,000 men into the Burma Independence Army (BIA) in their two months en route to Rangoon—almost as many troops as the Japanese had in their entire invasion force (Charney 2009). One reason the British were so quickly defeated in Burma was the lack of an army with incentive to defend the country.

The Burmese army was thus birthed with political motivations, commencing with driving the British out of Burma but extending well beyond this in both political and economic spheres.

> Unlike the Indian Army from which it sprang, Burma's army had no tradition of political neutrality or detachment. It saw its role as defender of national integrity in political as well as military terms. (Perry 2007, 22)

As Taylor notes, going into the war and then at independence,

> Very few expected to return to monarchy, but many sought to guide the state along familiar paths, and looked forward (nostalgically and inaccurately) to a new version of the alleged order of the pre-colonial state. (Taylor 2009, 236)

Preeminent among these familiar paths, the army felt it necessary to be involved in politics "in order to achieve the officer corps' notions of a correct social and political order" (Taylor 2009, 236).

The BIA emerged after independence as the premier national institution (Haacke 2006; Callahan 2004) and was almost exclusively Burman. With most ethnic minorities excluded from its ranks, and with a majority of the former colonial soldiers and remaining civil servants coming from ethnic minorities, the BIA was birthed steeped in ethnic tension (Taylor 2009). Progress in ethnic relations was shattered when the BIA fought with the Japanese against minority regiments who remained loyal to the British (Smith 1994). Tens of thousands died in bloody clashes and retaliatory killings that seriously inflamed tensions. The Karen, in particular, maintained contact with the British throughout the war and regarded the *Thakin* as enemies (Naw 2001). Ethnic minority leaders have frequently said these war massacres led to their resolve to take up arms after independence if their political demands were not met.

Much of the ethnic hostility that erupted in Burma at independence can thus be attributed to the disparity in colonial treatment, exacerbated by the events of the war. The level of trust Aung San was able to generate among the minorities in the lead-up to independence shows this might have been able to be overcome, had the postindependence government treated ethnic minorities as equals and built a truly plural or federal state, as promised. Nonetheless, the quick recourse to violence by so many ethnic groups only highlights the depth of fear and distrust that the new government inherited, making rapprochement highly problematic.

The *Thakin* soon found the Japanese worse than the British, treating Burma as an occupied enemy territory and imposing "a reign of terror" (Maung Htin Aung 1967, 301). Aung San made contact with the British and set up an underground movement, arranging to mutiny and help liberate Burma from the Japanese on condition of complete independence from Britain. Connecting with the *Thakin* like this left ethnic minorities still loyal to the British feeling betrayed, and as Donnison (1970) observes, effectively sidelined the moderates opposing the autocratic and radical tendencies of the younger nationalists, instead setting these more radical *Thakin* up as national heroes.

> To welcome with open arms the army which had fought against the British on the side of the Japanese for just so long as it had suited them, all of whose members were technically guilty of treason, was a poor way in which to reward and put heart into those Burmans who had remained loyal to the British connection or who, without necessarily wanting the continuance of this connection, nevertheless were opposed to the communistic ideas and dictatorial attitudes of the *Thakin*. (Donnison 1970, 127)

While Aung San himself grew into a true statesman during the independence negotiations, his assassination with seven cabinet members just six months before independence reignited ethnic fears and allowed the more radical authoritarian, socialist, and ethno-nationalist views to resurface among many of the remaining, competing *Thakin*. Likewise, Japanese administration of Karenni and parts of Shan States independent of the rest of Burma during WWII fueled the aspirations of these ethnic groups for autonomy and set the stage for multiple political and ethnic rebellions.

Chaos at Independence

Civil war was an almost natural consequence of ethnic minority fears and the rivalries between the surviving *Thakin*. Aung San had managed to overcome enough ethnic tension to engineer a fragile trust with many minority leaders. This concord was badly damaged by his assassination, which also created a leadership vacuum. Fueled by traditional ideas of personalized power, those elite unwilling to accept their exclusion from power plunged the country into a plethora of disunified armed rebellions remarkably similar to those in many earlier periods of political contestation (Taylor 1987, 2009). The Red Flag (hard line) communists rebelled before independence (Donnison 1970), and within three months of independence the well-organized Communist Party of Burma launched an all-out offensive (Smith 1999). Within one year at least ten other rebel groups including the Karen, Mon, Karenni, Pai, and Arakanese followed suit (ICG 2003), making the task of political integration at independence formidable indeed.

During the democratic era, the *tatmadaw*, the Burmese army, slowly regained control of the country under the firm leadership of General Ne Win. In the process the army became further entrenched as the preeminent national institution. Chin and Kachin units initially sided with the Burma army but also later rebelled. Ethnic animosity and rebellion was further heightened by Ne Win's 1962 coup, prompted in part by Shan efforts to draw up a more federal constitution and his subsequent ruthless suppression of rebel groups, forcibly relocating tens of thousands in order to cut off food, funds, intelligence, and recruits (ICG 2003).

Significant to contemporary international relations, most of the leaders and ethnic minorities vying for power were able to find foreign allies, with the Chinese backing the Community Party of Burma (CPB), Islamic mujahedeen backing groups in Arakan, and the United States, Britain, and Thailand supporting anticommunist ethnic minorities such as the Karen (Thant Myint-U 2009a; Callahan 2004; Selth 2002). Both the powerful CPB and the Kuomingtang Chinese Nationalist (KMT) armies inside Burma offered arms and training. By the 1970s two major alliances had emerged, another proxy frontline in the cold war: the CPB and allied groups controlled nearly the entire Chinese border, while the National Democratic Front (NDF) maintained a pro-West/anticommunist policy along the Thai border and were supported by the United States as a buffer against the perceived communist threat (Kramer 2009).

This foreign support inflamed Burman fears of foreign intervention and created a siege mentality whereby foreign powers of all persuasion appeared intent on exerting their political will over the struggling Burmese state, and the army was the only force capable of ensuring the survival of the Burmese state. Callahan argues that the sort of institutional reforms toward more inclusionary politics that most other postcolonial states were able to achieve were swept off the agenda

> when "the Cold War threatened to swallow Burma"—in particular, when the United States began training Chinese Kuomingtang (KMT) soldiers in Burmese territory [without Burmese approval] for their eventual counterattack. (Callahan 2004, 5)

A large part of Ne Win's success in regaining control over most of the country was the priority given to building the size, professionalism, and re-sourcing of the military (Taylor 2009), a priority Burmese leaders have felt a need to maintain in the face of perceived internal and external threats. Thus the early rejection of Western alliances based on the colonial experience was reinforced over time by Western support for ethnic insurgents, and this reaction has been further accentuated since 1988 by the Western push for regime change.

Economic Collapse

One commonly expressed view is that at the time of independence from Britain in 1948, Burma was a prosperous country with every reason to expect a bright future. Prominent modernization scholar Pye, for example, argued,

> In terms of objective considerations, it would be difficult to find any serious reasons for Burma's not being able to develop its economy rapidly . . . there are so few objective handicaps to economic development in Burma. . . . In a ranking based on eleven indices of economic development Burmese stood as the 26th out of 46 countries. . . . Burma belongs to a middle category of countries in most aspects. (Pye 1962, 60)

It is beyond dispute that many policies and practices of military governments since 1962 have been disastrous, but it would be wrong to simply blame the subsequent economic collapse on "The Burmese Way to Socialism" or military rule, as many do (e.g., Clark 1999). Some 400,000 British and Indians left Burma as the Japanese WWII invasion became imminent, most never to return (Taylor 1987). The resulting drain of capital plus economic and administrative expertise set Burma up for difficulties even before the war, despite Britain forgiving all financial debt at independence. The massive infrastructure damage of the war only compounded the problem, with Burma possibly being the most war-damaged country in Asia (Charney 2009; Taylor 1987).

> The Japanese occupation of Burma wrecked the country's economic system. Burma suffered more from the war than any other Asiatic country save possibly Japan herself. Many of her towns were reduced to ashes . . . works, mines equipment and river transport were destroyed . . . air-raids kept her railways out of action. The Japanese systematically looted the country. (Hall 1956, 172)

Even before the war, colonial prosperity "lay only in the national statistics" (Taylor 1995, 49), and little wealth was in Burmese hands. The civil war added to WWII damage, eroded tax revenue, and consumed a great deal of the funds required for reconstruction and development (Donnison 1970). "Burma was devastated as the armies of two colonial powers trampled across its soil" (Smith 1999, 60). The democratic civilian government's decision in 1951 to make education free for all was admirable but served to further impoverish the state. Thus, while socialist policies, nationalization, corruption, and incompetence all subsequently seriously compounded the situation, the idea that at independence Burma had every reason to expect economic prosperity, and therefore by implication that the policies and practices of the military government are primarily to blame for today's economic miseries, is a myth.

Military Rule and Bankruptcy

Ne Win justified his 1962 coup as being necessary to maintain national unity, prevent the breakup of the union along ethnic lines, and protect state sovereignty against outside control, all the while defending Buddhism (Steinberg 2001). Breakup of the ruling coalition in 1958 led to heated parliamentary debate that appeared stuck in a quagmire. Negotiations to resolve the ethnic conflicts were being contemplated, without preconditions ruling out secession. Rather than see this as an opportunity for democracy, with the possibility of federalism and a loyal democratic opposition emerging, Ne Win interpreted this as chaos that had to be brought under control (Maung Maung Gyi 1983).

> Overnight Burma slid back to the rule pattern of the days of the Burmese monarchs . . . the general public is as submissive as ever to whoever is in power. . . . The military elite led the Burmese masses back into their old familiar ground of pre-democratic life style and values. . . . Despite its facade of constitutional apparatus and formal rules, Burma is ruled by Ne Win in the role of absolute monarch. (Maung Maung Gyi 1983, 125, 192, 199, 225)

The subsequent isolationism, autarky, socialism, military-bureaucratic rule, and zero-sum personal politics all resonate with precolonial ideology and postcolonial sensitivities. These traits have been subsequently reinforced by the challenge of state building in the face of numerous internal and external threats.

Twenty-six years later repression, economic mismanagement, and failed socialist policies brought Ne Win's rule to an end. Economic crisis triggered mass demonstrations, which dislodged him from power. Stagnant agricultural production, overvalued currency, uncompetitive public companies, high inflation, a booming black market, and massive debt led to the virtual bankruptcy of the state (Taylor 1995; Steinberg 2001). Foreign reserves are estimated to have fallen to just US$10 million in 1987–88 (Rüland 2001), in what Steinberg (2001, 42) declares the "nadir of economic decay." The government lobbied the United Nations for least developed country (LDC) status, to gain debt relief and lower interest rates, and has remained on the list ever since.

Under pressure, General Ne Win resigned in mid-1988, recommending liberal economic reform and a referendum on multiparty democracy. His replacement, Sein Lwin, was implicated in several earlier crackdowns and lasted only seventeen days. Mass demonstrations rapidly escalated until the infamous 8.8.88 massacre, in which up to 3,000 demonstrators were killed. Sein Lwin was replaced by Dr. Maung Maung, who agreed to economic reform and multiparty elections with a strictly neutral military. However, despite announcing such sweeping reform and being extremely restrained toward demonstrators, Dr. Maung Maung was perceived to be too close to Ne Win; mass demonstrations continued until the commander in chief of the armed forces, General Saw Maung, assumed power and formed the State Law and Order Restoration Council (SLORC; Charney 2009).

In its own words, SLORC ostensibly stepped in to save the country from chaos, disintegration, and foreign subjugation, the same old recurring themes.

> At a time when the mother land Union was on the brink of being burnt down to ashes by hellfires in the 1988 disturbances, the State Law and Order Restoration Council (Tatmadaw) saved it in the nick of time. It then endeavoured to avert the terrible fate in store for the nation and build it up into a mountain of gold. (Skidmore 2004, 79)

SLORC quickly pledged to follow through on Ne Win's agenda by liberalizing the economy, opening international trade, and turning power over to a multiparty democratic parliament; they embarked on a reform agenda "with dynamism and enthusiasm" (Taylor 2001b, 9). However, many saw the council as too closely associated with the previous regime's failure and violent suppression of dissent, and international outrage continued. Together with SLORC's immense fear of foreign manipulation behind the hugely popular Aung San Suu Kyi, it quickly began feeling "surrounded, beleaguered and under siege" (Steinberg 2001, 43). With old memories and fear provoked, attitudes hardened, and Suu Kyi was arrested in 1989 as a risk to state security. When her National League for Democracy (NLD) unexpectedly won 392 of 485 seats in the 1990 elections, the SLORC regime quickly adopted the position that it could not relinquish power until a new constitution was instituted that could ensure continued unity and sovereignty (SLORC 1990). Instead of power transfer, the offices of the NLD were closed with mass arrests of members and supporters (Fink 2001; Oehlers 2004). Subsequent demonstrations were met with force, leading to the impasse of the last two decades, which will be examined in the next chapter.

Narratives in Perspective

Despite the very welcome political reform of 2011–12, the relevance of these three narratives on the contemporary sociopolitical context within which INGOs operate can hardly be overstated. As previously noted, most development mistakes in fragile and conflict-affected states result from insufficiently detailed analysis of the sociocultural, institutional, historical, and political dynamics and the assumption that democracy would of itself promote peace (World Bank 2006). This in-depth contextual history has illuminated many of the contemporary tensions, fears, and sensitivities out of which many within the ruling elite operate, and the reasons behind their belligerence toward the West, ethnic minorities, and the democratic opposition.

These narratives suggest that some development approaches, such as public confrontational forms of advocacy or a strongly rights-based approach, particularly if led by agencies perceived to be Western, may yet provoke strongly reactionary responses—reactions not entirely based out of self-preservation by authoritarian despots, as many outside advocates of political change in Myanmar imply. Indeed, these narratives suggest a measure of humility is called for by the international community, particularly by Western donors, INGOs, and civil society, for our part in the creation of disorder and destitution. These narratives likewise suggest that many military and political elite, as well as government officials, have long held altruistic motivations around which constructive international engagement on poverty alleviation and development priorities may proceed.

4

Myanmar Times: Contemporary Economic and Sociopolitical Context

For the past 20 years Burma has been portrayed in the media as primarily a democracy issue: the military regime and its repression of the democracy movement led by Aung San Suu Kyi dominates what little coverage there is. It's a compelling story, and Aung San Suu Kyi has emerged as an iconic global figure. But it's also a story that's been frozen in time since the early 1990s—almost all the news about Burma is about this long standoff between her and the generals—and it's very one dimensional. (Thant Myint-U 2009a)

It was the middle of the rainy season, and we were caught in a heavy monsoonal downpour. I shuffled into the middle of the backseat of the taxi to try to stay dry as the heavy rain splashed in from both sides, through windows open a couple of inches to allow some air circulation and prevent the windows from completely fogging up. Winding the windows up and turning on the fan would solve both problems, but the fan and air conditioner did not work, and there were no window wipers in this thirty-five-year-old shell of a car, just as there was no floor covering or trim on one of the doors. I was damp from the rain, the airless humidity was stifling, and it was almost impossible to see through the windows. Stationary in the Yangon traffic as water flooded the road, I tried to engage the driver in conversation. I quickly pieced together his story despite his broken English and my very limited Burmese.

Htin (not his real name) graduated from Rangoon University with a law degree eight years previously. However, as a devout Buddhist he quickly became deeply concerned about the level of corruption in the legal profession in his country and could no longer rationalize such behavior to himself. As he explained this to me, he pointed to a sticker on the dashboard that translated roughly as "avoid evil, keep your thoughts pure, and live an honest life." Htin explained that he had resolved not to practice law so long as cases were decided by bribery more often than by rule of law. Instead, he turned to taxi driving. An orphan with no siblings, he was now thirty-three years old and married, with a two-year-old daughter. They live in a small, wooden, rented dwelling in Okkalapa district, near the airport. His wife had worked before the baby was born, but for the past two years, Htin has been supporting his family as the sole breadwinner. So I quizzed Htin about his income and expenses. He averaged US$30–35 a day in fares, he claimed, but had to pay US$10 a day to rent the car plus an average US$9 a day in fuel. He is also responsible for half of all maintenance costs on the taxi, meaning his family of three live on around US$10 per day. And this is for a taxi driver working in the economic capital of the country!

Moving again, slowly through the rain and traffic, Htin made a point of observing we were driving past "The Lady's" house. Not that it was my first time down University Avenue. But it was June 2009, and the nation was waiting impatiently for the verdict in Aung San Suu Kyi's trial, after the American, John Yettaw, foolishly swam the lake to her house. Crowds had filled the street, in front of this gate, every Sunday during her campaign two decades ago, waiting hours to be inspired by her words, with truckloads of security forces standing by to intimidate or barricading the street. Today it was wet, and Suu Kyi was being housed in the prison complex. Just two armed soldiers guarded the gate. The political impasse has long held the nation captive.

My taxi driver's reminder as we drove past took me back to my first trip to the country in 1992, when my wife and I visited to explore the possibility of commencing some sort of small projects in the country. That was during the height of the tensions over the military not handing over power to the National League for Democracy after its decisive win in the 1990 elections. I had stepped out of the antiquated airport terminal into an unmarked, equally dilapidated taxi, and the moment the door shut, the driver had earnestly begun ensuring I was properly informed about the military regime and Aung San Suu Kyi. It was an interesting experience, hearing this activist's passion as we drove past the many soldiers on the streets, with parks and streets barricaded from the public, and soldiers with guns in their hands and ammunition straps across their chests.

Much has changed over the past two decades, and while the tension is less intense, and taxi drivers no longer volunteer such animated political commentary, there is as much hope as ever. While the political impasse continues to hold the nation captive, and the nation remains almost as economically stagnant and internationally isolated as ever, the people still exude an air of expectation of a more promising future.

I think it would be fair to say that winds of change are clearly blowing through Burma. The extent of it is still unclear, but everyone who's gone there recognizes that there are changes. (Kurt Campbell, US Assistant Secretary of State for East Asian and Pacific Affairs, September 2011)

It is increasingly clear that we are witnessing significant reform in Myanmar. It is now over a year and a half since the November 2010 elections that were widely criticized as being neither free nor fair (e.g., ICG 2011b; Farrelly 2010; Zarni 2011). However, a growing number of indications suggest that major political and economic reform is underway, despite the country remaining a "military dominated ersatz democracy" (Holliday 2011a, 10).

This chapter builds on the historical analysis of the previous chapter, examining the contemporary political, economic, and humanitarian setting to which INGOs contextualize their development activities. The historical narratives discussed in chapter 3 highlight political values, fears, and strategic concerns that are held by many members of the political elite and suggest that for those who hold such values more strongly, reform will need to continue to evolve incrementally. The contemporary sociopolitical context is analyzed in this chapter through the perspectives, values, and strategic concerns of the four major competing actors: the armed forces (and those who have recently resigned from the armed forces to take up politics), the democratic opposition, the ethnic minorities, and the international community. Despite difficulties of poor data, the economic context is then considered, followed by an exploration of the humanitarian situation and extent of poverty in the country. This chapter, therefore, offers vivid analysis of the contemporary political, economic, and humanitarian context INGOs work within in Myanmar.

Winds of Change

The resignation of Senior General Than Shwe and dissolution of the State Peace and Development Council (SPDC) in March 2011, making way for the inauguration of President Thein Sein and the convening of Parliament, could be seen as no more than cosmetic change. General Thein Sein was prime minister in the old regime, and he simply removed his uniform to become president. This transition has proven, however, to be a real change of personnel in effective control over the country, and significant policy change does appear to be occurring as a result (ICG 2011b).

Thein Sein's presidential inauguration speech called for sweeping political and economic reform, including things like national reconciliation, an end to corruption, a market-oriented economy, foreign investment, development of the health and education sectors, and work to alleviate poverty in cooperation with international and local organizations (NLM 2011b). Many feared this was mere rhetoric. Certainly, in the same address Thein Sein also declared that Myanmar needs to continue to build a strong, modern military to prevent bullying by other nations, and his oath to office involved pledging to uphold the Three Main National Causes of "non-disintegration of the Union, non-disintegration of national solidarity, and perpetuation of sovereignty," the mantra used by the former regime to justify the 1988 coup and the dominant role of the military over the past two decades (Minye Kaungbon 1994). These factors, together with the dominance of the military and regime-backed Union Solidarity Development Party (USDP) in Parliament, are troubling. Nonetheless continuity, especially at the rhetorical level, is to be expected, and there is a growing number of encouraging indications that he is in fact instituting much of this agenda as real reform.

> One year into the new semi-civilian government, Myanmar has implemented a wide-ranging set of reforms as it embarks on a remarkable top-down transition from five decades of authoritarian rule. . . . This ambitious agenda includes further democratic reform, healing bitter wounds of the past, rebuilding the economy and ensuring the rule of law, as well as respecting ethnic diversity and equality. The changes are real, but the challenges are complex and numerous. (ICG 2012, 1)

> The president has made clear that he intends to do much more to accelerate democratic reform, rebuild the economy, promote ethnic peace, improve rule of law and heal the bitter wounds of the past. . . . There is a broad consensus among the political elite on the need for fundamental reform. This makes the risk of a reversal relatively low. (ICG 2012, 16)

This past year has seen many changes. For example, Thein Sein moved quickly after his inauguration to appoint a number of well-respected nonmilitary advisors on political, economic, and social affairs. One of these is U Myint, longtime economic advisor to Aung San Suu Kyi and the NLD, now chief of the Economic Advisory Unit. U Myint has long championed the needs of the rural poor and moved quickly to hold a *Rural Poverty Alleviation Workshop* in May, with a raft of recommendations apparently gaining presidential approval. These include acknowledgment of the extent of poverty, preparation of a *Poverty Reduction Strategy Paper* (PRSP), land and tax reform, pro-poor macroeconomic policies, and improvement of government transparency and accountability while tackling corruption and the vested interests of elites (U Myint 2011). This was followed by a broader *National Workshop on Reforms for National Economic Development* in August, with a number of reforms proposed by nonmilitary participants being adopted into policy (NLM 2011d).

Surprising many, there was a level of democratic debate inside the new parliament from the outset, with quite lively discussions on issues like political prisoners, taxation, mobile phone costs, and registration of LNGOs, all published in the *New Light of Myanmar*. The fact that relevant ministers have been required to answer questions is significant, and there have been some improvements as a direct result. Likewise, censorship of foreign news websites and car importation restrictions were relaxed in September—the latter breaking the monopoly held by the top generals and their cronies. Market-rate money changers have been legalized, as have trade unions who have been guaranteed the right to strike, and laws allowing peaceful demonstrations have been passed. Legislation has even been passed to introduce election of local officials at the village tract level. These are all major changes.

At the end of September 2011, Thein Sein suspended the controversial Myitsone Dam project, a move that was welcomed by Suu Kyi but that provoked the ire of the Chinese, who have invested much of the US$3.6 billion into the project (Hseng 2011; Ba Kaung 2011). This was a defining, and risky, decision, which went well beyond what activists were calling for and would not have been taken for reasons of popular pressure alone. Personal concerns, internal regime rivalry, and strategic calculations of Myanmar's position between China, the West, and its regional neighbors undoubtedly had more to do with the decision than mere civil advocacy. Nonetheless, coinciding with popular demands, this move further legitimized civil advocacy and the sense of reform among the Myanmar people.

More significant is the formation of a *Myanmar National Human Rights Commission* in September 2011, followed by the release of 6,359 prisoners (including some 200 of the estimated 1,000 political prisoners). The UN special rapporteur on human rights in Myanmar declared this "a key moment in Myanmar's history" and a real opportunity to deepen the commitment to democracy. At the same time, he expressed concern that "gross and systematic violations of human rights" still exist in Myanmar and that the new government's express commitments to other human rights have largely not yet materialized as concrete action (Quintana 2011).

However, the most significant change has been the political reconciliation that has facilitated Aung San Suu Kyi's election and the return of the NLD to the political process (ICG 2012), as well as an invitation for exiles to return home and rapid progress in reaching preliminary ceasefire agreements with almost all the armed ethnic minorities in the country (ICG 2011c). The president met directly with Suu Kyi in August 2011, who came away from the meeting optimistically saying, "We have reached a point where there is an opportunity for change" (*Irrawaddy* 2011). By January 2012 the NLD was legally registered, and Suu Kyi and forty-two other party members won seats in the national or state parliaments in by-elections held in April 2012. By April, ceasefire agreements had also been signed with the 11th Army Group, the only major group outstanding being the Kachin Independence Organisation.

Any one of these changes would have been unimaginable a year ago. Whether the key motivation is achieving removal of international sanctions and the chairmanship of ASEAN in 2014, or domestic ambitions for securing long-term sovereignty and economic development, they still justify raised expectations of significant political and economic reform over the coming years. In 2011 the former ILO representative to Myanmar Richard Horsey argues,

> What we are witnessing now is more-or-less what we should expect to see if in the early stages of evolution away from authoritarian rule. This does not mean that is what is happening, but that we should not jump to the opposite conclusion. (Horsey 2011)

A year later, and despite vested interests and the inertia of postcolonial sensitivities, reform continued to evolve quickly. To this point, reform remains too superficial to have made much tangible difference to the daily lives of most of the population, apart from the clear air of expectation and changed attitudes by officials. But reform is definitely becoming more grounded and difficult to unwind. Recent US official comment reflects a tension over Myanmar policy. The US Department of State's special representative for Burma, Derek

Mitchell, commented recently on the sense of expectation that "something is happening" in Myanmar during a visit in September (Mitchell 2011), and the Department of State recently called the new government "reformist" and "open-minded" (State Dept. 2011). However, a key demand remains the release of all political prisoners, and without that the US Congress renewed sanctions for another year in September 2011. At the time the Senate committee chairman commented,

> Over the last year the Burmese regime has "severely restricted and frequently violated freedoms of assembly, expression, association, movement and religion." And in furthering its hold over Burmese society, the regime has committed crimes of murder, abduction, rape, torture, recruitment of child soldiers and forced labor—all with impunity. In recent months, however, we have seen some encouraging steps. . . . But it is far too soon to think that the walk to freedom has succeeded. (Baucus 2011)

Reform to this point has had minimal direct impact on the operation and projects of INGOs in Myanmar. Based on recent history, international responses that engage constructively with this reform while demanding accountability, and that allay rather than provoke fears of loss of sovereignty or disorder, will be crucial for the continued momentum of reform. Increased development cooperation, particularly focused around rural poverty alleviation, appears to offer great potential for such constructive engagement.

To achieve this, detailed understanding of the major sociopolitical actors and their strategic interests is required. This following section analyzes the competing perspectives, values, and strategic concerns of the four key political actors: the *tatmadaw* (armed forces) and ruling elite, Aung San Suu Kyi and the democracy opposition, the ethnic minorities, and the international community.

Competing Political Actors and Interests

The dominant characterization of Myanmar in the Western imagination over the past two decades is of a nation of gentle, peace-loving, and long-suffering people abused and terrorized by a brutal, authoritarian, and rapacious clique of generals (Tegenfeldt, *Hope* 2009). This depiction is presented as a stark contest between good and evil, democracy and totalitarianism, human security and violent suppression, and economic development and cronyism and poverty. It is of a once prosperous nation now in abject poverty because of the ineptitude, rent-seeking, and callousness of these ruling elite, violators of human rights who have been challenged patiently over decades by a united mass democratic movement led by the eloquent Aung San Suu Kyi. As with most characterizations, this is very oversimplified, as the current reforms are showing. Those who have not seen past this characterization, however, find themselves unable to believe the current reform.

The Tatmadaw (Armed Forces)

> In the contemporary world, there is probably no other country of significant size or regional influence in which the military has as much and as pervasive power, and has held it for such an extended period. . . . Its influence is comprehensive, pervading the society to a degree essentially unknown even in other countries where the army is a coercive force with a greater total number of troops. (Steinberg in Selth 2002, xxv)

The 2008 constitution guarantees a leading role to the *tatmadaw*, Myanmar's "premier institution since Independence, with no serious institutional competitor" (Haacke 2006, 13; see also Callahan 2004). Guaranteeing 25 percent of parliamentary seats to appointees of the military ensures its role in politics continues. The only other institution of similar size is the *sangha* (monkhood), whose nature and societal role are very different; however, the degree of separation beginning to emerge between the military-appointed bloc in Parliament and the former-regime-backed USDP has interesting implications for a possible divergence within what was previously a singular military position on issues.

Popular characterizations of the SLORC/SPDC military regimes portrayed them as irrational and self-seeking, and some scholars were inclined to dismiss the official discourse as "nothing more than primitive propaganda without any substantial content" (Rozenberg 2009, 15). Too little is firmly known even now to make hard-and-fast judgments about the inner workings of what was a most secretive clique (Taylor 2009). Nonetheless, the regime does appear to have been operating out of a considerably coherent ideology (Houtman 1999), discernible through pronouncements of their political objectives.

A decade ago Selth (2002, 3) noted, "The armed forces of a particular country are shaped almost as much by that country's geostrategic position and modern history, as by any features of the contemporary strategic environment." This is certainly true in Myanmar. The *tatmadaw* has long seen itself as the protector of sovereignty and national unity. Without dismissing the seriousness of the human rights allegations leveled against the *tatmadaw*, it is worth noting that it has been engaged in active, armed civil conflict continually since WWII, in one of the longest running civil conflicts in the contemporary world. "We see how war and especially counter-insurgency operations can brutalize an army after just a few years—imagine what it does after six decades" (Thant Myint-U 2009a). This conflict has claimed an estimated million casualties on all sides since independence, around 30 percent of all civil conflict casualties in Southeast Asia during that time (Steinberg 2010b). Likewise, the diverse foreign backing for these insurgencies has "had a profound impact on the thinking of modern Burma's rulers, including those military officers holding power in Naypyidaw [prior to the 2010 elections]" (Selth 2008a, 4), in terms of both international relations and the way they default to seeing their own people as a real or potential threat (Callahan 2004).

In its own eyes, SLORC stepped in during the chaos of 1988 to save the country from disintegration or foreign subjugation, as the *tatmadaw* had done many times before (Taylor 2009). Two presidents had fallen in less than two months, and despite promised economic and political reform, demonstrators controlled the streets, and the situation headed toward anarchy. While the offer of multiparty elections in which the military was to remain strictly neutral ran counter to many vested interests and raised the specter of reprisals by a new administration, it seems fair to concede that its conscious motivation was as much the restoration of law and order and the protection of national unity and sovereignty.

Quickly embarking on liberal economic and democratic reform, the military may have initially genuinely intended to hold unelected power only briefly, although it almost certainly expected to continue to play an ongoing role in parliamentary politics. Unfortunately, its mode of restoring order resulted in many casualties, provoking an unexpected domestic and international backlash. Any genuine reform plans were sidetracked by paranoia over the perceived threat of disintegration of the union and subjugation to the West. "The underlying problem was that the SLORC viewed civilian party politics as necessarily chaotic and contributory to national disunity" (Charney 2009, 165).

Fears, Values, and Strategic Interests
SLORC declared *Our Three Main National Causes* in mid-1989 to justify its coup and explain the role the military saw for itself (Minye Kaungbon 1994),

slogans retained by the SPDC and still summarizing official policy. These slogans were continually repeated in government newspapers until early 2012, as shown in Figure 4.1, and incorporated into the oath of office for the president.

Having taken control, SLORC set out to restore order, reunite the country, and reconstruct the economy. The regime's early claims to legitimacy rested on success against ethnic separatists, then, later, in response to Suu Kyi's ongoing challenge by appeal to other traditional symbols of political legitimacy (Selth 2010a, 2). These objectives were thus expanded in 1992 into *Twelve National Objectives*, slogans required to be reproduced in most newspapers, magazines, and books published from that time until a relaxation on state propaganda in August 2011, as shown in Figure 4.2.

These objectives clearly outline the SLORC/SPDC agenda and reveal much about values of many *tatmadaw* elite, being expressed very paternalistically in terms of the state needing to closely oversee the economy, morals, culture, and patriotism and protect a gullible people from foreign domination. They bespeak the belief that *tatmadaw* (or former military leaders) alone can offer the sociopolitical leadership required to bring unity out of chaos and usher in a new era of prosperity. Foremost among the priorities expressed in these objectives are to forge a strong, unified nation out of competing groups and to safeguard national sovereignty against neocolonialism.

The problem of social unity is one of the greatest problems that have plagued both democratic and authoritarian governments since independence (Silverstein 1977). Nation building requires creation of a single national identity out of the diverse ethnic peoples, and Burma's fractured ethnic history has made nation building a mammoth task (Smith 1999). The difficulty of this is highlighted in by the fact that the Burmese state "has been continually at war with the population mapped into its territorial claim" since the arrival of British colonial authority in Burma, almost two centuries ago (Callahan 2004, 13). SLORC/SPDC argued that ethnic conflict was the result of suspicion

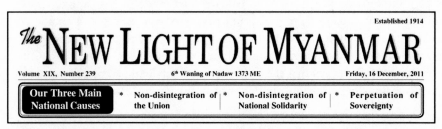

Figure 4.1 The *Three Main National Causes* in the government-run *The New Light of Myanmar* newspaper, December 2011.

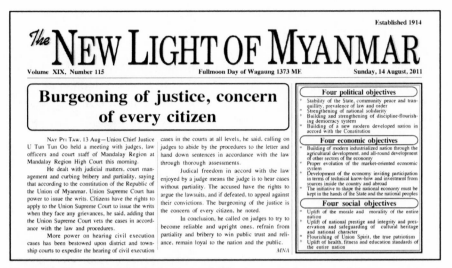

Figure 4.2 The SLORC/SPDC *Twelve National Objectives* on the front page of the government-run *The New Light of Myanmar* newspaper, August 2011.

and division deliberately sown by the British to facilitate colonial rule (Minye Kaungbon 1994), and a central motivation of the military has been to (re-) unite these diverse ethnic groups, militarily if necessary, thereby ending the insurgency that has prevented stability, peace, and the building of a modern, developed nation.

Fortunately, negotiated rather than military means are now being adopted to bring about peace. However, the issue of nation building out of diverse ethnic identities remains. Central to the *tatmadaw's* long-standing agenda has been to establish a single national culture, a goal expressed in the second of the social objectives mentioned previously, what Houtman refers to as "Myanmarification," "the search for a single dominant Myanmar national culture that could be respected both internally and externally" (Houtman 1999, 91). It is noteworthy, however, that SLORC/SPDC sought to achieve this through "reconsolidation," not reconciliation, a distinction in terms that reflects the Burmese words chosen by the *tatmadaw* to describe their peace.

The second priority observed in the SLORC/SPDC objectives is to safeguard national sovereignty against neocolonial imperialism.

If there is one clear message that Myanmar's government broadcasts consistently, then this is that the country will resist what it perceives as "attempts to subjugate Myanmar" or "neo-colonial politics." (Haacke 2006, 19)

This is brought out even more clearly through another extremely common set of slogans also required to be printed in newspapers and periodicals prior to August 2011, the *People's Desire*, shown in Figure 4.3. In the eyes of SLORC/SPDC, the West's strong support for Suu Kyi only

[reinforced their] suspicion that she is, in fact, a stooge of "neocolonialists" in "big Western nations" hell-bent on imposing their will and advancing their own national interests, ideological or otherwise, in Myanmar. (Zarni 2007, 204)

Badgley (2004a) concludes that the strategic interests of the military regime were (1) attaining unity and cohesion between Myanmar's diverse ethnic populations, (2) acculturating the population to a unified Burman language and culture, (3) managing the military hierarchy structures and military–monkhood codependency by which its power is maintained, and (4) attempting to navigate foreign policy away from isolation to increasing interaction with at least its Asian neighbors, if not the wider international community.

Burmese leaders have lived in fear of invasion or foreign control since independence (Selth 2008a). Ne Win was primarily concerned about China; SLORC/SPDC feared invasion by the West.

The regime's fears of armed intervention have been dismissed as the paranoid delusions of an isolated group of poorly educated and xenophobic soldiers, jealous of their privileges and afraid of being held to account for their crimes against the Burmese people. . . .

People's Desire
* Oppose those relying on external elements, acting as stooges, holding negative views
* Oppose those trying to jeopardize stability of the State and progress of the nation
* Oppose foreign nations interfering in internal affairs of the State
* Crush all internal and external destructive elements as the common enemy

Figure 4.3 The SLORC/SPDC slogans, in the *People's Desire* in a recent edition of *The New Light of Myanmar* newspaper, August 2011.

[This is a] rather simplistic and self-serving explanation. (Selth
2008a, 4)

While there may never have been any real likelihood of invasion, the
regime remained convinced that the United States and its allies were determined to force regime change (Selth 2008a, 2008b). Fears were heightened,
for example, when the United States tried to have Myanmar discussed in the
UN Security Council, and then in 2006 when President Bush, in his State
of the Union speech, listed Myanmar (Burma) alongside Syria, Iran, and
North Korea immediately after references to the US invasions of Iraq and
Afghanistan. Prime Minister Blair of the United Kingdom then subsequently
labeled the SPDC as a "loathsome regime" that he "would love to destroy"
(Selth 2008a, 16). One official regime publication offered the theory that the
United States wants regime change in Myanmar because it is the weakest link
in America's containment policy toward Chinese expansionism in the Bay of
Bengal region (Hla Min 2000). "The SPDC effectively [saw] US sanctions
and its support for the NLD and [Suu Kyi] as a form of low-intensity warfare" (Haacke 2006, 64).

Armed interventions in Panama (1989), Somalia (1992), Haiti
(1994), Kosovo (1999), Afghanistan (2001) and Iraq (1991 and
2003) are all viewed by the Burmese leadership as examples of the
US's determination, unilaterally if necessary, to intervene in the
affairs of other states—including the overthrow of governments
whose policies are inimical to Washington. (Selth 2008a, 16)

It is hardly surprising, therefore, that the Burmese reacted when the
United States, the United Kingdom, and France dispatched a joint naval task
force after Cyclone Nargis in May 2008. As if confirming their fears, while the
Burmese hesitated, numerous Western politicians and activists called for an
armed incursion into Burmese sovereign territory to deliver aid. The French
minister for Foreign and European Affairs, Bernard Kouchner, for example,
issued a statement that Paris could not wait any longer for UN approval and
would send a naval vessel to deliver aid directly to the Burmese (Selth 2008a,
2008b). They did not, but Joint Task Force Caring Response had a combined
capacity of up to eighty-two helicopters together with landing craft and over
4,000 assault troops. While the ships were laden with aid, not troops, the sense
of confrontation only hardened the military leadership's conviction that it still
faced the serious possibility of attack.

One reason the regime showed suspicion toward humanitarian agencies is that aid has been provided by numerous governments to a wide range of domestic opposition and activist groups (Selth 2008a). Donors speak in terms of "promoting political capacity building" and "strengthening civil society," yet funding was given to organizations directly promoting regime change. Unsurprisingly, this was seen by both SLORC and SPDC as part of clandestine foreign operations, bringing suspicion on the work of all humanitarian agencies inside the country.

To ensure the regime's ability to end the civil conflicts and to ensure sovereignty against perceived outside threat, the *tatmadaw* was dramatically increased in size and military capability to now be the second-largest army in Southeast Asia (Selth 2009). Some of the military-political leaders see themselves as still engaged in a patriotic anticolonial struggle, which makes the current reform by recently retired military leaders all the more remarkable. Military leaders have long shown a genuine desire to move toward increasing regional and global interaction, although not at the expense of security (Haacke 2006). From the more conservative military (and recently ex-military) perspective, if security can be maintained and military (or recently ex-military) leaders are allowed to continue to guide, then reform and development fit very well within the *tatmadaw* elite's thinking and philosophy.

Within this context then, the reform agenda of Thein Sein and some of the other new key leaders seems to be far-reaching, and a challenge to traditional ideology and rhetoric.

Aung San Suu Kyi, the Democracy Movement, and the People

The political values and strategic objectives of Aung San Suu Kyi and the democracy movement are far more readily understood in the West, since they are far closer to our own. A reluctant leader who stepped forward during the chaos of 1988 (Suu Kyi 1995b, 193), Suu Kyi allowed herself to be a unifying figure for popular opposition because of the "aura of legitimacy" bequeathed by her father's reputation (Charney 2009, 154–55). Aung San, her father, is *the* Burmese national hero (Wintle 2007), accredited as founder of the *tatmadaw* and both leader of the resistance against the Japanese and architect of independence from Britain (Suu Kyi 1991; Naw 2001). His legacy and ideology have been continually appealed to by all sides of Myanmar's political divide ever since his assassination (e.g., Suu Kyi 1991, 1995b; Callahan 2000; Fink 2001; Skidmore 2004). Suu Kyi presents herself as continuing that struggle for freedom.

Suu Kyi was just two years old when her father was assassinated. She grew up largely in India, where her mother served as ambassador, later being educated in England and marrying Oxford scholar Michael Aris. She thus lived most of her life abroad, returning to Burma in 1987 to nurse her sick mother. It is not surprising, therefore, to find her ideas laden with values of democracy and human rights (e.g., Suu Kyi 1995a, 1995b, 1996). She remains, nonetheless, very Burmese. Her guiding principles clearly derive from those of Aung San (Selth 2002), and she eloquently draws on both traditional Burmese and Buddhist ideas to express these political values.

Suu Kyi's philosophy connects an alternative set of traditional Buddhist political values with ideas about freedom developed under colonial repression (Silverstein 1996). Traditionally, Burmese Buddhists did not make the intellectual leap from religious liberty into ideas of political freedom, traditionally linking a strong state with absolute monarchy. Suu Kyi and the NLD, instead, have appropriated alternative Buddhist visions of moral authority (Schober 2011, 3), espousing "traditional Theravada Buddhist beliefs and values within a modern democratic political ideology" (Philp 2004, 11).

Suu Kyi frequently frames her critique of the regime in terms of a Buddhist advocacy for democratic and human rights, a Buddhist ethic reminiscent of that of Thich Nhat Hanh and the Dalai Lama. In this she draws on the legacy of kings like Mindon (1853–78), renowned for their kind, peace-loving, humane, magnanimous, and pious nature. She likewise critiques the regime by reminding the people that in Buddhist mythology, the first king was elected by unanimous consent of the people to restore peace and justice after society fell from its original purity (Suu Kyi 1995b). Suu Kyi argues that even the traditional Buddhist view of kingship

> does not invest the ruler with the divine right to govern the realm as he pleases. He is expected to observe the Ten Duties of Kings, the Seven Safeguards against Decline, the Four Assistances to the People, and to be guided by numerous other codes of conduct such as the Twelve Practices of Rulers, the Six Attributes of Leaders, the Eight Virtues of Kings and the Four Ways to Overcome Peril. (Suu Kyi 1995b, 173)

These *Ten Duties of Kings*, for example, include *dana* (liberality), which Suu Kyi equates with provision for the welfare of the people and thus that Buddhist values require the provision of basic needs such as livelihood, health, and education (Suu Kyi 1996). She likewise argues that the duty of *avirodha* means "non-opposition to the will of the people" and thus is a Buddhist endorsement of democracy.

Suu Kyi is dismissive of SLORC/SPDC's statements about their security concerns:

> There is nothing new in Third World governments seeking to justify and perpetuate authoritarian rule by denouncing liberal democratic principles as alien. By implication they claim for themselves the official and sole right to decide what does or does not conform to indigenous cultural norms. Such conventional propaganda aimed at consolidating the powers of the establishment has been studied, analysed and disproved by political scientists, jurists and sociologists. (Suu Kyi 1995b, 167)

By presenting herself and the NLD as an alternative government ready for office, some argue that the military perceived her in traditional terms as a contender to the throne (Mya Maung 1999). Her more conciliatory tone and willingness to work within a political system she still regards as flawed has been a major key to the ability of the national reform agenda to progress this far.

Suu Kyi and the NLD have always in theory supported the idea of a professional, apolitical military that has a significant role in the country but is clearly answerable to an elected civilian government (Selth 2002). She and the NLD are thus vocal opponents of the constitutional allocation of one-quarter of parliamentary seats to military appointees. However, in her galvanizing public address of 1989, while she ruled out a mutiny by the army and called on them to be apolitical, Suu Kyi simultaneously publicly challenged the army to support democracy. Many interpreted this as a call for soldiers to disobey orders.

> When my father founded the army, it was not for the purpose of interfering in politics. Rather it was for the purpose of supporting the people in their political struggle. I address all the people in the Army and saw that because of your love of your country it is your duty and responsibility to provide backup and support to fulfil [*sic*] the wishes and desires of the people. (Suu Kyi 1988 speech, cited in Selth 2002, 278)

It is poignant that she addressed this to "all the people in the *tatmadaw*" rather than to the senior generals. This, of course, only fueled regime fears of disunity leading to potential disintegration of the state or control by foreign powers.

Her position toward the military hierarchy appears to have hardened after she was imprisoned, ignored, and attacked. Thus while Suu Kyi's stance on democracy and human rights resonates very strongly within the West, and she is hugely inspirational, several respected interview respondents commented anonymously during the research for this book that her stand has often been as equally hard-line as that of the former generals. Her biographer, Justin Wintle, commented on her release in November 2010,

> If the army is principally responsible for the stasis, it is arguable that Ms Suu Kyi's principled commitment to full democracy, and her unwillingness, or inability, to make meaningful compromises, has been a significant contributor. (Wintle 2010)

Some even suggest that Suu Kyi and the NLD in the past pursued a confrontational, all-or-nothing agenda derived from "zero-sum" ideas about power (Pedersen 2008, 256). Upon her two earlier releases from house arrest, in 1995 and then again 2002, Suu Kyi repeatedly resorted to acts of political provocation (Haacke 2006). For example, she held rallies drawing huge crowds, looking very much like she was campaigning for office, and likened the regime's Union Solidarity Development Association (USDA) to the Nazi Brown Shirts, while the NLD compared the regime to Japanese fascist occupation (Skidmore 2004). These are very strong, emotive, and confrontational characterizations, and her much more conciliatory tone since her 2010 release is possibly as much a factor in the current change as is Thein Sein's remarkable reform agenda.

Democracy activist turned scholar Zarni (2007) observes that while the public respects and loves Suu Kyi, scenes of her addressing massive audiences are misleading in that they give the impression that the NLD and "the masses" are one and the same. Rather, as Suu Kyi herself has noted, what the masses most desire is security and freedom from fear (Suu Kyi 1995b). The masses primarily seek more than just governance and are less concerned about revolutionary change in the form of government than they are about the personal nature of those in power. Min Zin (2010, 96) similarly argues that at the height of demonstrations in 1988 and again in 2007, the NLD itself showed a "tendency to seek to centralise control, a symptom of political culture in Burma." In 1988 the opposition failed to seize on promises of reform, instead continuing to press for a complete abdication by the ruling party to an interim government. Their failure to compromise then has been said to have "allowed the hardliners within the ruling body to make a justification and preparatory time to shift from their indecisive wait-and-see approach to a swift crackdown on the protests" (Min Zin 2010, 90).

For most Burmese, the *tatmadaw* is not a totally corrupted institution, and most families in central Burma rely on some relative in the military for access to products and services they could not otherwise access (Callahan 2000). The army, publicly credited with winning independence from Britain, is the largest patron–client structure in the country has, and in Callahan's words, it has acted as a benefactor for many as well as an oppressor. The *tatmadaw* and regime-sponsored organizations such as the former USDA (now the ruling USDP) are institutions that redistribute resources to the general population—not fairly or efficiently but to such an extent that even the most sincere admirers of Suu Kyi also rely on their family connections with the *tatmadaw* (Seekins 2005).

It is also important to observe that many public servants and members of the military are torn between the two sides. Many are convinced that the generals honestly believe they are doing the right thing for the people and believe that they are making Burma a better place (Skidmore 2004). However, many also support Suu Kyi and the NLD, as demonstrated by the fact that all four parliamentary seats up for election in the administrative capital of Naypyidaw in the April by-elections were won by the NLD representatives (although only by the narrowest of margins).

Ethnic Minorities

The third major competing domestic political actor is actually a varied assortment of ethnic minorities. Myanmar is one of the most ethnically diverse countries in the world, with ethnic minorities making up about one-third of the population and occupying roughly half of the land area (ICG 2003). Despite SLORC/SPDC contentions that ethnic conflict is a remnant of British divide-and-rule tactics, Myanmar's diverse ethnic groups have never shared a common set of values, identity, or sense of loyalty (Silverstein 1977).

> Myanmar seems like a country of ill-fitting ethnic nationalities crammed into one state united only by a long-gone colonial power . . . sharing little common memory and only a vague vision of integration into one society. (Badgley 2004a, 17–18)

Myanmar has been afflicted with some of the longest running armed civil conflicts in the world, being described by its former military rulers as the "Yugoslavia of Asia" (Smith 1997, 10). While international attention has focused on the struggle for democratic reform, ethnic division "has long been the most important issue facing the country" (Holliday 2010b, 125), requiring at least as much effort to resolve. "Ethnic conflict perhaps represents an even more fundamental and intractable obstacle to peace, development and democracy" (ICG 2003, 1). The previous chapter outlined this conflict and its background. Smith (1994) and South (2008b) offer the most comprehensive histories of the conflict. Continued democratic and economic reform are unlikely without a political settlement that addresses ethnic minority concerns (Kramer 2009). The current round of ceasefires is an optimistic first step, but a temporary end to violent struggle is a long way from a long-term negotiated solution. There are some very long-standing grievances.

Grievances and Strategic Objectives
The minority peoples felt the deprivation of political and economic power during the military era even more acutely than the majority Burman population, as both the government and the officer corps are overwhelmingly Burman and widely perceived as a foreign force within minority communities (ICG 2003). The leadership of the *tatmadaw* is ethnically Burman (Selth 2002).

The main grievances of the ethnic minority groups are their lack of influence in political decision making, the lack of economic and social development in their areas, and the repression of their ethnic cultural identities and religious freedoms by the government's nation-building agenda (ICG 2003; Kramer 2009). While most ethnic political leaders and civilians favor democratic rule, they are concerned that a simple transition to democracy will not lead to a resolution of their political problems; they fear a democratic agreement that leaves ethnic issues unresolved. Smith (1999, 439) quotes one Kachin leader, commenting, "Even if Aung San Suu Kyi was prime minister, we would still have the Burmese army in the Kachin State." Most ethnic political leaders today reject separatism and favor limited autonomy within a democratic federal state (Kramer 2009). The key words for ethnic minority aspirations are "self-determination" and "equality," although as Zarni (2007) notes, the overwhelming majority of civilians would now be happy to simply have fundamental security in their lives and an end to conflict.

> Given the scale of conflict and bloodshed in the past five decades, it needs to be recognised that reform and social transformation are long term processes and will undoubtedly be a challenge for any government that comes to power in Rangoon in the coming years. (Smith 1997, 8)

Cease-Fire Agreements and the Future

Over twenty armed insurgencies were active at the time of the 1988 uprising and controlled large areas of territory (Smith 1994). The dramatic collapse of the Community Party of Burma (CPB) in 1989, precipitated by ethnic minority leaders turning against the CPB's Burman leadership, led to a range of truces between ex-CPB-aligned forces and SLORC (Kramer 2009). This placed increased pressure on the remaining armed groups, resulting in a second set of cease-fires with NDF members in the mid-1990s. By 1997, there were twenty-two cease-fire groups (ICG 2003), and by 2003 the only significant groups continuing armed struggle were the Karen National Union, the Karenni National Progressive Party, and the Shan State Army (South) (ICG 2003). The Kachin Independence Army has recently returned to open conflict with army forces while the Karen and Shan are in very promising talks with the new government.

These cease-fire accords offered a cessation of hostilities, with the ethnic armed organizations providing a transitional administration but with access to territory by Burmese forces and bureaucrats. Any political solution was deferred to the writing of the 2008 constitution. Given the key demand of ethnic minority leaders is to be on the inside of the political process (Smith 1997), the inclusion of state assemblies in the new constitution with some decentralization of power represents possibly the greatest success of the 2008 constitution, a document otherwise very heavily criticized. It constitutes something of a win for the ethnic delegates to the Constitutional Commission who continued negotiating after the NLD withdrew from the process, although with state assemblies now dominated by *tatmadaw* appointees and the USDP, they have so far failed to deliver on their potential.

The greatest positive outcome of the cease-fires, apart from the minimization of bloodshed and destruction, has been the facilitation of development in these areas (ICG 2003). In negotiating these cease-fires, the military government promised support to develop these regions, and following the cease-fires most groups were given business opportunities or resource concessions by the government (Kramer 2009). This has increased access for INGOs into these regions and facilitated the development of LNGOs. Some officials openly encouraged religious groups, as the major nonpolitical organizations in these regions, to engage in community development, resulting in the formation of what are effectively local faith-based development NGOs (ICG 2003). The two largest such LNGOs, Metta (formed October 1998) and Shalom (formed early 2000), both arose from the Kachin cease-fire movement and quickly became umbrella organizations for many other smaller and unregistered groups, able to work effectively into these restricted areas.

The conclusion of these cease-fire agreements was seen by the SPDC as one of its major accomplishments (Kramer 2009). However, while the cease-fires have brought many ethnic groups into the reform process, several are still fighting, and peace remains fragile, with most groups still armed. Long-standing grievances remain largely unaddressed (Kramer 2009; Holliday 2010b), as evidenced by the recent return to armed conflict in Kachin State. Not all actors are prepared to negotiate on the regime's terms of "reconsolida-tion," not reconciliation. Some identify the government as *the* problem and will not be happy with anything less than regime change (South 2008b). On the propaganda side, the regime has convinced many Burmans that ethnic leaders are no more than criminals, drug dealers, and warlords who must be "annihilated" (Smith 1997, 12; Fink 2000). It will be interesting to see whether the current negotiations can reconcile these conflicting interests and smooth over the past extreme rhetoric.

> Solutions will not be found by trying to rewrite the past but by facing up to long-standing grievances and sufferings in a new spirit of understanding and reconciliation. (Smith 1994, 14)

The International Community

> Myanmar today is embroiled in a battle of ideas, identities and values which is as much global as it is local. (Duffield 2008, 6)

For at least the past two decades, there has been a fourth significant actor in this drama, namely, the international community. As with the ethnic minorities, referring to the international community as a single actor is a gross oversimplification. The various states, international bodies, regional groupings, and international organizations each have their own perspectives, strategic concerns, and agendas in relation to Myanmar. Pedersen (2010) succinctly sums up the various international responses. Western countries, he observes, shunned the military regime and imposed a variety of sanctions aimed at forcing the regime to relinquish power to a democratic government. Myanmar's neighbors sought to normalize relations, particularly around trade, arguing that economic cooperation provides the best path to a more stable, prosperous, and rights-abiding country. And international organizations took a middle path, working with the government as necessary for the explicit purpose of advancing the country's political, economic, and human development.

None of these approaches have produced major successes, in part because of the enormity of the task at hand, in part because they have tended to work at cross-purposes with each other. (Pedersen 2010, 114)

The gravity of international concerns over human rights violations has already been noted. Myanmar is a strong state in terms of maintaining "control, coercive power, and the willingness to employ such power" (Steinberg 2006, 20). To highlight the comparatively strong state apparatus, as well as the authoritarian domestic and recalcitrant international position of the government, some, particularly the United States, have referred to Myanmar with such emotionally laden terms as "pariah state" and even "rogue state" and "outpost of tyranny" (Haacke 2006; Steinberg 2006). Various Western leaders have labeled the regime as "thugs," "grotesque," "wicked," and a "loathsome regime" they would "love to destroy" (Selth 2008a, 16). Such emotive rhetoric has only antagonized without pointing to solutions, painted overly simplistic pictures, and strengthened the hand of more hard-line elements within Myanmar (Badgley et al. 2004).

The implication is that the state's administration is irrational, when in fact it may be quite rational given different premises and in its own terms . . . the use of such terms are insulting to the target, and in turn makes any possible negotiates at a later date more difficult. (Steinberg 2006, 211)

Holliday (2011a) makes the observation that international assistance to Burma increased twentyfold during the 1970s, despite being a military-led authoritarian state during that period and that it is only in the post–cold war era that Myanmar has become labeled a pariah state, with greatly restricted humanitarian aid by the West. "It can be argued that such a strong and sustained policy position would have been less likely if the Cold War had not ended, and Burma's importance in the local competition between the superpowers had not significantly diminished" (Selth 2002, 16).

Strategic Interests of the West

"Throughout modern history, the importance of Burma's geostrategic position has been recognised by the world's most powerful countries," including Britain, France, India, China, Japan, and, more recently, the United States (Selth 2002, 13). Major powers have therefore maintained a strategic interest in Myanmar. Nonetheless, to speak of Western strategic interests and a Western response implies an alignment of views and interests that does not exist. The United States, Europe, and Australia, for example, have each developed somewhat different perspectives and policies toward Myanmar and have very different strategic concerns (Steinberg 2007).

The United States speaks predominantly about human rights and democracy, being particularly incensed over the denial of the democratic will of the people expressed in the 1990 election and the subsequent treatment of Aung San Suu Kyi and the NLD (Steinberg 2007, 2010b). US focus has been on the release of Suu Kyi and democratic transition (Haacke 2006), and to that end the United States has imposed the most restrictive sanctions against Myanmar of any country. It has also used its position on international bodies to block IMF, World Bank, and ADB involvement in Myanmar and apply pressure via the General Assembly and the Human Rights Council (Haacke 2006).

While US policy toward Myanmar has largely been value driven, at a broader level the United States has also held concerns about Myanmar being a possible risk to global order and its projection of power into the region. It has therefore been concerned that Myanmar does not pursue weapons of mass destruction and is not involved in narcotics, that ethnic fighting is at least contained, and that economic and particularly security ties with China do not become too close (Haacke 2006). In 2005, while attempting to escalate discussion of Myanmar to the UN Security Council, the US permanent representative to the United Nations John Bolton spoke in terms of

> threats to international peace and security caused by actions of the Burmese government that have resulted in things like ethnic cleansing, refugee flows, international narcotics trafficking, trafficking in persons, failure to act adequately on threats like HIV/AIDS or avian flu. (Bolton 2005)

These claims are largely based on the report to the United Nations commissioned by Vacláv Havel and Archbishop Desmond Tutu (Cary 2005). However, these US-led attempts to put Myanmar on the Security Council agenda failed because Myanmar's regional neighbors disagreed with the regional security threat assessment (Steinberg 2007; Haacke 2006), but it does highlight US concerns. In 2010, the United States began pushing for a UN commission of inquiry into human rights abuses (Pomfret 2010; Lynch 2010), another move that attracted little other foreign support.

European Union concerns have been similar but not always as vocal. Focus has been primarily on achieving respect for human rights, "and a transition to democracy would be acceptable" (Haacke 2006, 62). The sanctions under the EU Common Position on Burma/Myanmar, which have now been largely suspended, were not as comprehensive as US sanctions but still included an arms embargo, a visa ban on senior officials, a ban on nonhumanitarian aid, and a limited ban on investment. Many of these elements are considered "largely symbolic" (Howse and Genser 2008, 175), as, for example, Europe stepped in to replace lost humanitarian funding after the Global Fund pulled out of Myanmar (Steinberg 2007).

For Australia, Myanmar holds a more regional security concern, and as such Australia has taken a somewhat different line (Steinberg 2007). Of Western donor countries, Australia places the highest value on humanitarian assistance (Asia Society 2010b) and is the only Western country to have given any aid to projects involving civil service capacity building during the SPDC military period (ICG 2002). Consistent with Australia's broader foreign policy orientation, Australia has maintained diplomatic contact and offered benchmarks for greater official engagement (Steinberg 2007). Australian sanctions have also now been fully suspended, but even at its high the policy was tightly targeted on only named individuals connected to its ruling military regime and thus was the least stringent of the Western sanctions regimes (Asia Society 2010b).

Strategic Interests and Responses From Regional Neighbors

There is equally no agreed Asian or even unified ASEAN position on Myanmar. Instead, there is a range of strategic concerns and interests held by each regional neighbor, who respond to the needs and concerns from its own perspectives. The interests of China, India, ASEAN, and Japan differ substantially (Asia Society 2010b).

China is Myanmar's largest neighbor and shares its longest border. After the reaction of the West to the events of 1988–90, SLORC turned to Beijing for political support, purchase of military equipment, and trade (Haacke 2006). "Political, commercial, and military relations between China and Myanmar have grown as their interests have become aligned" (Asia Society 2010b, 31), and Jagan (2010) contends that Myanmar became China's most strategic ally in Southeast Asia. China engaged directly with the regime, becoming a major investor in infrastructure and the development of energy and gas reserves and a major supplier of consumer and capital goods. More than 90 percent of direct foreign investment in Myanmar in 2008 was Chinese (Jagan

2010), and Myanmar could have suffered shortages of commodities without the massive influx of Chinese products (Kudo 2007, 102). Strong economic ties with China were instrumental in the survival of the regime in the face of Western sanctions. China's primary strategic concerns are firstly stability along its border and secondarily access to energy (ICG 2010a; Yohome 2010). Other strategic concerns are containment of the rise of India, and road, rail, and air access to the Indian Ocean (Li and Fook 2010).

China claims it "respects Myanmar's sovereignty, does not interfere in the country's internal affairs, and encourages the country to engage with the international community" (Asia Society 2010b, 31). China never had any interest in or appetite for sanctions (Holliday 2010a) and called on the international community to offer more constructive assistance toward Myanmar while calling on Myanmar to speed up political settlement of ethnic disputes and become more democratic (Haacke 2006). In recent years, the Burmese looked to China for diplomatic support; however, Myanmar was very keen to avoid undue military, political, or economic dependence on China, something that motivated the regime to develop counterbalancing relations with ASEAN, India, and Thailand. Claims of China's influence in Myanmar policymaking over the past fifteen years, as well as ideas such as the Chinese having military bases in Myanmar, "have been greatly exaggerated" (Selth 2007b, 22), something probably borne out in the decision to suspend the Myitsone Dam project. The Chinese argue that US and EU sanctions "have adversely affected the country, especially the common people" (Asia Society 2010b, 26), although their own investment and engagement behavior in Myanmar belie the genuine priority of such concerns beyond rhetoric.

India, like most Asian governments, "believe[s] that sanctions and isolation imposed on the regime have been the two largest impediments to change . . . [and are] hurting the people of Myanmar progressively harder" (Asia Society 2010b, 42). India has accorded Myanmar the lowest priority of all of its immediate neighbors in regard to international relations, being primarily concerned to contain China's increasing power in the region (Egreteau 2008). It has also had a strong strategic interest in developing markets into Southeast Asia, prompting a move to closer engagement (Kanwal 2010). However, India has been urging a radical change in Western policy toward Myanmar, arguing,

> If there is anything that could be done, it can only be accomplished through interface with the government. . . . Any measures to help the people of Myanmar will be a slow, tedious, and laborious

process, concentrating initially on humanitarian work and consciously avoiding raising suspicions about any political agenda.
(Asia Society 2010b, 42)

ASEAN's policy over the past two decades has claimed to be been one
of "constructive engagement," and it has been argued that Myanmar's admis-
sion into ASEAN membership was allowed in large part to counterbalance
expanding Chinese influence and power in the region (Rüland 2001). Ne Win
refrained from joining ASEAN when it was established in 1967, arguing that
US bases in Thailand and the Philippines demonstrated ASEAN was not non-
aligned (Haacke 2006). The more pragmatic SLORC expressed interest in
joining ASEAN in the early 1990s, a move opposed by the United States and
European Union. For Myanmar, ASEAN membership has offered increased
legitimacy and a constructive engagement policy that has opened regional
markets and access to institutional capacity building. For ASEAN, Myanmar's
membership has enhanced its claim to truly represent Southeast Asia.

There has largely been little "constructive" about the engagement of
Myanmar's regional neighbors, who have generally pursued national economic
interests over reform. Nonetheless, calls by ASEAN for the release of Suu Kyi
have made it harder for the regime to sideline her and the NLD, and it was a
Thai "road map to democracy" proposal that prompted the Myanmar counter-
proposal that has led to this current point of reform. It might, therefore, be said
that the ASEAN constructive engagement policy has had the greatest impact of
all in achieving reform. Certainly, ASEAN involvement was very influential in
breaking the deadlock in aid delivery after Cyclone Nargis. It might, therefore,
be said that the ASEAN constructive engagement policy has possibly had the
marginally greatest impact of all in achieving reform, although international
organizations, notably NGOs, are really the only international actors who can
reasonably claim to have engaged constructively.

Japan's position, too, is quite opposite to that of the United States, seeking to promote human rights and democratization but seeing this as best done
through engagement and dialogue, particularly through development aid and
technical assistance (Haacke 2006). Japan has been a major donor, and as a
regional power with strong links into the country and region, Japan feels it
has "a special responsibility" to address the situation in Myanmar (Asia Society 2010b). It argues, "Rather than isolate Myanmar, the country should be
integrated into the region economically, and assistance should be provided to
encourage economic reform and to promote democracy and human rights"
(Asia Society 2010b, 58).

Japan has been the biggest donor to Myanmar both prior to 1988 and since. Japan sees building ASEAN nations bordering China as a means to balancing China's power and thus has a strategic objective for humanitarian aid, political engagement, and trade expansion (Shihong 2010). It has led the way in stepping up humanitarian assistance and offering government and civil society capacity building, rather than only providing aid through UN agencies and NGOs (ICG 2002). Japan also has provided grant and technical assistance to government departments, mainly in the health and education sectors, and technical assistance in structural reform of the economy (Asia Society 2010b). Japan sees itself as situated in between the Western prosanctions camp and the Asian constructive engagement philosophy.

This, then, briefly summarizes the complex political context of Myanmar, dominated by competing strategic interests between domestic actors and clouded by the diversity of strategic interests and responses of the international community. As the OECD (2007b) report on development in fragile states discussed earlier noted, as important as historically informed analyses of the context are, the most important factor to successful state building is a process of negotiation among all contending interests. Significant political progress in Myanmar will require the military (and ex-military) elite, the democratic opposition, the ethnic minorities, and the international community to all achieve progress toward mutual goals through negotiation. Such negotiation is progressing but is still in its infancy. This suggests that extreme sensitivity to the strategic concerns of all political actors will continue to be a requirement of effective INGO humanitarian poverty alleviation efforts for some time to come.

Poverty and Humanitarian Need

The Economy

Myanmar is a rich agricultural country with abundant natural resources, the land itself offering the hope of a prosperous future. The economy has been built on agriculture, which is now being surpassed by exports from substantial natural gas reserves. The country is the world's largest exporter of teak; is one of the world's principal sources of rubies, sapphires, jade, and pearls; and is known for its tin, tungsten, and silver production. The country possesses extensive regions with rich soil and good rainfall, suitable for highly productive agriculture, with major river systems allowing irrigation in many other regions. With a population density considerably lower than that of most of its regional neighbors, agricultural prosperity is definitely possible. Indeed, during its colonial heyday in the 1920s and 1930s, Burma was the world's leading source of rice, earning it the nickname "the rice bowl of Asia" (Perry 2007, 51) and making it home to "some of the most productive and prosperous paddy farmers in the world" (Asia Society 2010a, 14).

Yet, despite this potential prosperity, Myanmar today is impoverished by conflict, inept policies, and international isolation. Politics and the economic circumstances of the poor are interlinked; politics is a significant causal factor behind the poverty and poor economy, while international attempts to engineer political change have aggravated both the conflict and the economic underdevelopment for several decades.

According to official data, the Myanmar economy has enjoyed sustained double-digit growth every year since 1999–2000. Official government statistics claim most sectors of the economy are booming, with exports rising 33 percent over the past two years, rice exports up 128 percent, tax revenue up 28 percent, tourism up 27 percent, domestic savings up 116 percent, and vehicle registrations up 16 percent (CSO 2011). Officials have begun talking about Myanmar catching up economically with its neighbors by 2015 and with the West by 2030 (in U Myint 2010).

Rather than having an economic boom, however, "Burma is still one of the poorest countries in the world and the poorest state in Southeast Asia" (Turnell 2010b, 7–8). Most sectors of the Myanmar economy appear to be languishing, although accurate data are scarce. Perhaps Burmese economist Khin Maung Nyo is correct in asserting,

> No one understands the Myanmar economy. If someone says they understand the Myanmar economy, they don't understand anything. If they say they understand the Myanmar economy, they don't have a clue. (Khin Maung Nyo 2011)

Myanmar's new chief economic adviser, U Myint, has repeatedly highlighted the dubious nature of the official statistics (U Myint 2007, 2010). He points out, for example, that the government's economic figures claim economic growth rates double that of neighboring countries, yet with just half the investment. He also notes that the ratio of exports to gross domestic product (GDP) does not correlate with other states and that the structure of the economy has changed little in the past seventy years. Agriculture accounted for 47.9 percent of GDP in 1938–39 and is still 43.4 percent of GDP in 2007–8. These facts, he argues, make claims of sustained high economic growth most unlikely.

The public data are largely ignored and are probably thought not fit to be printed, so do not appear in the major regional and world economic reviews and reports. (U Myint 2007, 56)

Most internal and external observers believe economic activity in Myanmar to be much lower than reported. Estimates for the 2007–8 financial year by the IMF, the UN Economic and Social Commission for Asia and the Pacific (ESCAP), and the Economist Intelligence Unit (EIU) of the London *Economist* magazine place GDP growth in the range of 3.4 to 5.5 percent before the impact of Cyclone Nargis and the global financial crisis (U Myint 2010). On the basis of anecdotal evidence, U Myint speculates that the economy may have actually been stagnant prior to the 2010 elections and reform.

Turnell et al. are of similar mind:

These [double-digit growth] claims are without foundation and are greatly at odds with other proxy measures (such as electricity generation, fertilizer use, and so on) of national output. Revised GDP growth estimates for Burma over the last few years would suggest rates of around 3 percent per annum as more likely, the principal driver of which has been Burma's rapidly increasing export of natural gas [something that] masks an economy that is otherwise essentially stagnant. (Turnell, Bradford, and Vicary 2009, 633)

Elsewhere, Turnell (2010b) estimates GDP growth at 2 to 3 percent and goes so far as to claim that, apart from the windfall from natural gas, Myanmar's economy is actually "regressing in every important respect" (2008, 1). Collignon (2001) estimates the long-term trend of economic growth to be just 1 percent.

Best estimates place annual GDP at just US$280 per capita in 2008, or a little under US$0.77 per day (Turnell, Bradford, and Vicary 2009). Attempting to adjust this for relative cost of living, by calculating purchasing-power parity (PPP), is extraordinarily difficult, given the dearth of reliable data, and Bradford (2004) argues that most calculations for Myanmar significantly overestimate real income and production figures. Nonetheless, UNDP estimates for GDP-PPP per capita were just US$1,027 between 2002 and 2005 (UNDP 2004, 2007), falling to US$904 in 2007 (i.e., US$2.48 per day; UNDP 2009). The IMF (2009) put the figure at a little over US$3 per day. Any of these estimates suggest Myanmar is a long way from catching up with its neighbors. Bradford concludes,

For Burma to reach the level of GDP per capita that Thailand experienced in 2000 within 50 years, it would require real growth in per capita output in Burma of 3.6 percent per annum. In terms of world growth history, this is an extremely high sustained rate of growth. (Bradford 2004, 10)

U Myint draws a similar conclusion, calculating that even if double-digit GDP growth were real and could be sustained, "it would take 39 years to catch. up with the level of per capita GDP that Malaysia hopes to attain by 2020" (U Myint 2010, 22).

Inflation is one of the greatest concerns in the Myanmar economy, running at an annual average of 24.9 percent between 2000 and 2008 (U Myint 2010). Reports suggest it hit 35 percent in 2007 (EIU 2008) and 50 percent in 2008 (Turnell 2008), with 40 to 45 percent figures also reported a decade ago (Collignon 2001). Whether or not these latter figures are accurate, only Zimbabwe, Congo, and Angola have worse inflation figures in recent UNDP reports (UNDP 2010). Official Myanmar data claim inflation is running at just 7.5 percent (CSO 2011).

The most common reason ascribed to such high inflation has been the printing of money to fund budget deficits (Mya Than and Thein 2007; U Myint 2010; Sein Htay 2006; Turnell 2007a, 2008; Turnell, Bradford, and Vicary 2009). Indeed, money supply grew at an average 28.5 percent per annum between 2000 and 2008 (Turnell, Bradford, and Vicary 2009). Other recent significant inflationary pressures have included dramatic rises in public sector salaries and official fuel prices, the shift of the capital city, and the impact of Cyclone Nargis (U Myint 2010). One major implication of such high inflation is that savings and investments have not been held in the local currency (Collignon 2001; Steinberg 2010b), given interest rates are well below the inflation rate. This added significant domestic savings and investment weaknesses to the economy. One of Myanmar's key problems was a lack of monetized capital in the country (Collignon 2001).

A reversal of this problem over 2011–12 has caused significant pressure on the Myanmar economy, as large foreign currency savings have been repatriated in the hope of a brighter economic future, driving down the exchange rate and driving up property prices and inflation.

Agriculture, the largest sector of the economy by employment, is neither maximized nor efficient. It is estimated that 9.3 percent of Myanmar's land area is currently "wasteland suitable for cultivation," neither forested nor utilized (EIU 2008), while most agriculture is done by hand or animal-drawn equipment. Just 15.9 percent of agricultural households own any form of motorized or mechanical agricultural equipment (IHLCA 2007). The inability of most farmers to access finance imposes heavy costs on productivity and inhibits cultivators from moving to more capital-intensive modes of production (Turnell 2008). Even fertilizer is beyond the reach of most farmers. New aid and legislative initiatives around microfinance aim at addressing this major structural weakness of the economy but are yet to make an impact on livelihoods.

Myanmar's major exports are, in order of dollar value, natural gas, then timber, pulses and beans (for which Myanmar is now the second-largest exporter in the world), garments, and rice (CSO 2011; Turnell 2008). Natural gas is now by far the country's largest export earner, comprising almost 40 percent of exports by value over the past four years (CSO 2011) and responsible for much of the recent growth in the economy. The Yadana and Yetagun fields in the Gulf of Martaban came on stream in 1998 and 2000, respectively, and the Shwe field in the Bay of Bengal, which connects to China's Yunnan province via a 2,400-kilometer pipeline, may begin producing in 2013 (Asia Society 2010a; Turnell 2007b). Combined, it is estimated that these fields could bring in US$3–4 billion annually in export earnings over the next twenty to thirty years. This natural resource discovery brings with it the possibility of either transforming the national economy or only further accentuating inequality through a "resource curse."

There were persistent allegations under the SPDC that vast amounts of revenue from these natural gas exports were unaccounted for, because of account keeping at the official exchange rate that overvalues the currency by more than 150 times its market value (Asia Society 2010a; Turnell 2007b). Turnell (2008) observed that natural gas earnings for 2006–7, recorded at the official rate, amounted to a mere 0.6 percent of budget receipts, while the 2010–11 budget documents only US$33 million of the US$4.7 billion in revenue received, based on what neighboring states claim to be spending on these resources (Turnell 2011). Some allege the total accumulated unaccounted funds to 2009 was US$5 billion and that this had been either misappropriated into offshore accounts (EarthRights 2009) or used to fund certain military or national priority expenditure off-budget (Turnell 2010a, 2011).

One recent positive change made by the Myanmar government is that since January 2011, it has began publishing the national budget again (Turnell 2011), after almost a decade of not publishing these vital data (ICG 2009). The Myanmar budget has long had a disproportionate allocation toward items that do not contribute directly to production, such as defense, religious ceremonies and rituals, and new cities and physical infrastructure (U Myint 2010). While infrastructure may in time contribute to production, funding for the *tatmadaw* is by far the largest budgetary component. The *tatmadaw* is the largest armed force in Southeast Asia, numbering around 350,000 to 400,000 personnel (Turnell 2008; U Myint 2010), and it is widely claimed that Myanmar has one of the world's highest rates of military spending as a proportion of government revenue (Dapice 2003). The SPDC government long argued that military expenditure averages just 9 percent of the budget (Sein Htay 2006), but the official 2010–11 budget figure showed 51 percent spent on defense (Turnell 2011).

Since the 1988 coup, the regime has undertaken an ambitious modernization and expansion of the armed forces. Myanmar thus has the highest military spending and is the second-largest importer of arms among the least developed countries (LDCs; Alamgir 1997). Selth (2008a) puts the defense budget at an average 35 percent of the annual national budget since then. Sein Htay (2006) argues that with expenditure easily disguised via the multiple exchange rate system, actual military spending could be as high as 60 percent. Either way, "Burma now boasts a very large, reasonably well-integrated, well-armed, tri-service defense force" (Selth 2007a, 14). To protect its interests during the move to a semicivilian government, the previous regime introduced legislation preventing the new parliament from discussing changes to military spending (Turnell 2011). This places a significant limitation on addressing disproportionate military expenditure, and it will be interesting to watch whether the new parliament can revisit the question of military expenditure over the next year or two.

Hopefully, the more objective and reformist economic views of U Myint and others recently appointed to advise the new president will lead to major changes in economic management in coming years. The recent announcement of relaxation of car import restrictions is one such very small but positive move (NLM 2011a, 2011c). U Myint (2007, 2010) has acted on his previous recommendations of exchange rate unification, and he continues to call for publication of accurate and detailed economic data, further liberalization of the export market, improvements in quality and production of agricultural commodities, development of labor-intensive industries, financial services, telecommunications and information technology, and preparations for greater regional integration. It is hoped such policies will emerge in the near future. Sustainable macroeconomic growth, Turnell (2008, 2010b) suggests, will also need effective property rights, rule of law, rational and consistent policymaking, an efficient civil service, privatization of government monopolies, recapitalization of rural finance, and liberalization of agriculture, foreign trade, investment, and interest rates.

Income Poverty

Beyond an economic crisis largely caused by mismanagement, inordinate military expenditure, and an emerging "resource curse," the people of Myanmar have faced a long and very real humanitarian crisis. Callahan (2010) suggests this need has often been overstated by those advocating political change, while Inwood (2008) argues that internal political processes mean most publicly available data understate the gravity of the need, particularly in geographic locations where assistance is not being provided. The severity of poverty needs to be clearly determined, and it is welcome to see U Myint forming a Myanmar Development Resources Institute in part to clarify such issues and provide appropriate policy advice.

The most recent and thoroughly researched poverty data come from the *Integrated Household Living Conditions Survey in Myanmar (2009–2010)* (IHLCA 2011), which was undertaken jointly by the Myanmar Central Statistics Office and the UNDP. The survey estimates the proportion of the Myanmar population who live in absolute poverty to be 26 percent (IHLCA 2011). The poverty line was calculated to reflect the minimum food and non-food expenditure required to meet a basic calorie intake while continuing to subsist, accounting for Myanmar food consumption patterns and prices. It was set at 376,151 Kyat annually per adult equivalent, or 1,030 Kyat per day—almost exactly US$1 per day at the informal economy exchange rate for mid-2010 (Shwe Rooms 2011). According to this survey, almost one-third of the rural population live below this subsistence level. There are, however, huge regional variations. For example, 73 percent of the population in the Chin State live below this absolute poverty line.

This survey reports an apparent fall in absolute poverty over the past five years, since the previous survey, with the incidence of reported poverty falling from 32 percent (IHLCA 2007) to 26 percent (IHLCA 2011). This is despite the impact of Cyclone Nargis and the global financial crisis. The authors do, however, urge considerable caution in interpreting this trend, given other data conflict significantly. For example, while the survey suggests that the poorer segments of the population have experienced faster income growth than the wealthy, resulting in increased caloric intake and small asset holdings, moderate and severe malnutrition levels have remained constant (at 32 percent and 9 percent of the population, respectively). Likewise, the food share of consumption and the rate of landlessness have both increased since their last survey.

Regardless of any possible improvement, both the rate and the level of poverty reported are alarming. More than one-quarter of the population live on less than US$1 per day, with over 10 percent of the population experiencing this level of poverty as a chronic condition. The food component of this measure suggests that the average family spends almost three-quarters of its income on food, with just one-quarter of this meager subsistence income available for nonfood expenditure on clothing, accommodation, transportation, education, health, and other essentials combined (Thant Myint-U 2009b). Still, this is an improvement from 1997, when the average family income could meet only three-quarters of the family's total food and nonfood consumption needs (U Myint 2010). "In no other country in the Asian region does an average family devote such a high share of household consumption expenditure to food" (U Myint 2010, 26).

One of the many ways many Burmese households have survived such scant economic circumstances has been through remittances sent home by family members working abroad, both legally and illegally (Asia Society 2010a). Surveys of remittances to Burma from workers in Thailand suggest that the average annual payments per sender are more than Burma's per capita GDP and that well over US$300 million was being sent home annually by Burmese living in Thailand a decade ago (Turnell, Vicary, and Bradford 2007). With more than two million Burmese estimated to live abroad in Southeast Asia, China, India, and the developed world (ICG 2009), remittances are a significant economic lifeline for many otherwise impoverished families.

This survey also does not capture the large proportion of the Myanmar population who are only marginally above the poverty line. These people's proximity to absolute poverty and their vulnerability, however, is illustrated by an estimation from the UN resident coordinator in Yangon that an increase in food prices of just 15 to 20 percent could push the number of people in absolute poverty to "well over 50 percent" (Pedersen 2008, 10). This goes a long way to explaining previous estimates of poverty in the country, which ranged from "half the population" (e.g., Steinberg 2006, xxxvi) to 90 percent living on less than US$1 a day (WHO 2008).

Multidimensional Poverty

Poverty, of course, is not primarily a lack of money but, as Sen (1993, 1999a) argues, is deprivation in any of a multitude of dimensions, resulting in people being unable to satisfy crucially important functions. Poverty is the result of deprivation that leads to a lack of well-being, as well as exclusion, lack of opportunity, and lack of freedom to choose how to live. There are thus multiple dimensions of possible deprivation.

The UNDP's *Human Development Index* (HDI) seeks to measure poverty on a broader range of indicators than just income. While classifying the country as having low human development, this index places Myanmar at number 149 out of 197 countries ranked (UNDP 2011). This is, however, based on government-supplied data that are widely held to be too high. Nonetheless, this HDI data suggest there has been a significant overall increase in development over recent years, with an improving HDI score, and offers examples such as mortality rates for those younger than five years old falling from 147 deaths per 1,000 live births in 1996 to 98 per 1,000 in 2008. This is solid progress, although a comparison with Australia's rate of mortality for those younger than five years of age, at just 6 per 1,000 live births in 2008, shows how large the gap remains.

The UNDP's (2011) new *Multidimensional Poverty Index* seeks to measure the number of people experiencing multidimensional deprivation, as well as the intensity of that deprivation across ten indicators, within the health, education, and standard of living dimensions of poverty. The report suggests that 31.8 percent of the Myanmar population are multidimensionally poor, and another 13.4 percent of the population are poor in one dimension and facing significant risk of multidimensional poverty. The report also finds that those who are multidimensionally poor in Myanmar typically suffer a particularly high intensity of multidimensional deprivation, with 9.4 percent of the population living in "severe poverty."

This is not surprising. The percentage of the national budget spent on health and education fell steadily during the 1990s (Suu Kyi 1996), and while spending has increased somewhat in the past decade, nonmilitary services are still grossly underfunded. "Burma is the only country in the region whose defense budget is greater than that of health and education combined" (Selth 2002, 135). Turnell (2008) estimates Myanmar spends a mere 1.4 percent of its GDP on health and education, less than half that spent by the next poorest member of ASEAN (Laos). Purcell (1997) found that in the mid-1990s, the government's education and health budget was consumed almost entirely by salaries, with bodies such as UNICEF providing the bulk of program funding and with little or nothing left for maintenance and program development.

Table 4.1 offers a comparison between Myanmar and regional and LDC reference countries in terms of government spending on health and education. Estimates of military spending are not provided in comparative reports.

Table 4.1
Government Spending on Health and Education
in Myanmar and Reference Countries

	Health		Education
	2005 (PPP US$)[a]	**2007 (% GDP)**[b]	**2007 (% GDP)**[b]
Singapore	301	2.8	1.0
Thailand	63	2.7	4.9
Indonesia	12	1.2	3.5
Vietnam	10	2.8	5.3
Cambodia	7	2.8	5.3
Laos	4	0.8	2.3
Myanmar	<1	**0.2**	**1.3**
Sudan	11	1.3	—
Zimbabwe	9	4.1	4.6
Congo	2	1.7	1.8
Ethiopia	4	2.2	5.5

a. *WHO Statistical Information System (WHOSIS) Core Health Indicators* (WHO 2009).
b. *Human Development Report 2010: The Real Wealth of Nations—Pathways to Development* (UNDP 2010).

Government investment in education fell to just 0.3 percent of GDP in 1999–2000, placing it among the lowest in the world (UNICEF 2003). It has since increased to 1.3 percent in 2007 (UNDP 2010), but this still leaves it very poorly funded. Myanmar's education system has thus now degraded to such an extent that the national average years of schooling is just 4.0 years, and less than 17 percent of the population over twenty-five years of age have had any secondary education (UNDP 2010). Myanmar thus claims one of the highest primary school enrollment rates in the Asia-Pacific region but has one of the lowest secondary school enrollment rates (ESCAP 2008; IHLCA 2011). And while Myanmar claims an adult literacy rate of over 90 percent (UNDP 2010), a 1999 UN survey found functional literacy to be only 53 percent nationally and as low as 10 percent in some remote areas (Pedersen 2008). Myanmar "is one of the few places in the world where the present generation of children will be worse educated than their grandparents" (Turnell 2010b, 22).

Myanmar likewise had the lowest per capita government expenditure on health care in ASEAN (Vicary 2007). Government figures show Myanmar spent just US$0.66 per capita on public health in 2006–7 (MoH 2008),[1] almost double the amount spent the year before and up substantially from previous years but still exceptionally low even for a poor developing nation. Because of low government spending on health, and despite the high rates of poverty, 89 percent of all health expenditure in Myanmar is private expenditure (ESCAP 2008). Turnell quotes an unnamed UNICEF source as suggesting the Myanmar health system has become the second worst in the world, after Sierra Leone, and is now "a hub from which communicable diseases such as HIV/AIDS, elephantiasis and avian influenza spread though the region" (Turnell 2008, 3).

Chronic underfunding has resulted in a wide range of significant health needs. Life expectancy at birth for women is just sixty-five years, while for men it is well under sixty (ESCAP 2008). Infant mortality and mortality rates for those younger than age five years are now the third and second highest in the Asia-Pacific region, respectively (ESCAP 2008), and the rate of death from AIDS is now equal to the highest in Asia, equal with Thailand. One in five people have not been vaccinated against measles, and the same percentage do not have access to basic health care, while 30 percent do not have access to safe drinking water (IHLCA 2011). Malaria threatens 70 percent of the population and is the leading cause of morbidity and mortality (WHO 2008), with one-third of all malaria-related deaths in the entire Asia-Pacific region now occurring in Myanmar (ESCAP 2008). Pregnancy-related deaths are the leading cause of mortality among women of reproductive age and are mostly preventable, while nationwide 32 percent of children younger than age five years are moderately to severely underweight, another 32 percent are stunted, and 8.6 percent are wasted from poor nutrition (WHO 2008). Anemia is put at 71 percent among pregnant women and 75 percent for schoolchildren (WHO 2008), while only 37 percent of households consume a recommended daily requirement of calories, and only 56 percent consume sufficient protein (EC 2007).

Similar deprivations occur beyond health and education, as a smattering of the available data shows. A low 2.0 percent of the population has telephones, either fixed or mobile (UNDP 2010). There is just one registered vehicle of any description for every twenty-two people in the country (CSO 2011). Almost half the population has access to nothing better than leaves or thatch as roofing material, while over half do not have electricity (IHLCA 2011). Landlessness is a significant problem, at 24 percent of those who derive their primary income from agriculture, the largest employment sector (IHLCA 2011). And less than one-third of those engaged in agriculture can access any form of credit, as can just 11 percent of the remainder of the population (IHLCA 2011).

In short, while there are hopeful signs of improvement, and of positive policy change, "the daily life of the average person in Myanmar is characterised by grinding poverty and unrelenting struggle for survival" (Asia Society 2010a, 21–22).

Concluding Picture: The Sociopolitical Context

This, then, is the complex political and humanitarian context INGOs face as they approach poverty alleviation in Myanmar.

Residues of precolonial Burmese-Buddhist political ideology remain, particularly in some of the perceptions about power and statecraft. These are not all negative, as Aung San Suu Kyi's discourse about traditional ideas of the duties of rulers, provision for the welfare, and respecting the will of the people has shown. However, traditionally these values were linked to political legitimacy with ideas of *hpoun* and the demonstration of accumulated *kamma*. Merit, while demonstrated through Buddhist patronage and charity, was also demonstrated through order and control, resulting in authority being seen as highly personalized and hierarchical, and nondependence on others being an important value.

These traditional values are echoed in contemporary politics, certainly under Than Shwe but also now under Thein Sein. For example, while also reflecting more contemporary political thinking, the emphases on nation building, achieving order and control over ethnic minority territory, and having a slowly guided, orderly transition to democratic rule and a market economy are all loaded with traditional political values. Change in these values is only likely to be gradual, as is the full transfer of power to a fully civilian government, even if the pace of reform remains rapid.

A postcolonial narrative is also clearly evident in the Myanmar sociopolitical context. Centuries of suspicion, conflict, and tension between Myanmar governments and the West have only been accentuated since independence, first through foreign support for ethnic insurgency, then through more direct pressure for regime change. Oddly, the largely positive experience by both sides of temporary expansion of international assistance in the wake of Cyclone Nargis, after a thorny first few weeks, may have done more to reduce suspicion and tension on both sides than six decades of independence combined. International rapprochement and internal reform may therefore trace their roots, in part, to the context-sensitive work of INGOs and other development agencies, as documented in the following chapters.

A final major issue within the sociopolitical context of Myanmar is that of the ethnic tension, with its long, deep history. The important task of nation building is grossly complicated by serious tension, distrust, and violence, as well as fears of being marginalized economically and politically and of being assimilated culturally. Brokering solutions is also complicated by the fact that the international community, particularly the West, is so complicit in the origins, complexity, and perpetuation of the issue.

Great economic and humanitarian need, particularly in health, education, and livelihood, are complicated by the vested interests of the regime, traditional political values, postcolonial sensitivities, and ethnic security concerns. The opposition's democratic and human rights positions, as well as its perseverance, are inspirational, but its approach until the past year has only succeeded in increasing political tension and heightening security. The seemingly intractable ethnic divisions continue to result in deep-rooted social conflict, even to the village level, driving marginalization and exclusion. The West's confrontational sanctions approach has repeatedly provoked reactions and empowered hard-liners in their defense of national sovereignty, while significantly restricting humanitarian aid funding and mandates. Meanwhile, Asian neighbors have achieved some, limited, humanitarian and political gains but largely committed minimal resources themselves to these ends.

However, the outlook for improvement is very positive. The new government has overcome significant security and postcolonial concerns to place a genuine priority on addressing poverty and weaknesses in the economy. The opposition has likewise softened its democratic and human rights demands sufficiently to engage within the political process, as it too demands a priority is placed on meeting these needs. The seemingly intractable ethnic divisions are at a critical juncture, with cease-fires and negotiations in most areas. And the European Union and Australia have lifted sanctions and increased aid, reducing the risk of Western political confrontation empowering hard-liners. All these factors bode well for the future.

Nonetheless, the persistence of traditional values, historical grievances, and postcolonial sensitivities and the domestic and international political context have implications for international development and suggest certain approaches are more likely to be resisted while others may gain ready acceptance. Traditional values suggest some development approaches may be easily interpreted as a threat to personal power, even where they are not intended as such. Postcolonial sensitivities and fears of neocolonial motives suggest the need for Western donors and agencies to deliberately focus on trust building and suggest the humanitarian approach to development of many INGOs in Myanmar may be a means of facilitating progress. Ethnic fears, violence, and marginalization have huge implications for equity and participation in development, as well as advocacy and other aspects of INGO development. Peace-building and conflict-sensitive development approaches are clearly called for.

How INGOs respond sensitively to this context will therefore be documented and analyzed in detail over the next three chapters.

Note

1. Converted from Kyat into US$ at the exchange rate quoted by *The Irrawaddy* (see irrawaddy.org) for February 2007. Vicary (2007) puts the figure at US$0.09 before PPP calculations. The WHO (2009) online statistical database simply lists this figure as less than US$1 in PPP terms.

Part 3

Context-Sensitivity in INGO Development Practice

Part 3 of this book moves past the literature and the analysis of politics and economics to detail and analyze the ways in which INGO field-workers adapt their organizational mandate and international development approaches to be sensitive to the sociopolitical context of Myanmar, as described in the previous sections. This section is based largely on interviews with key INGO managers and development professionals working inside Myanmar and adopts a phenomenological approach that articulates their perspectives, primarily in their own words, before engaging in analysis. To clearly distinguish interview responses, quotations from the interviews are shown in italic text and quotations from the literature in roman text.

5

Doing Context-Sensitive Development in Communities

Sociopolitical and economic contextual factors have a major impact on the manner in which INGOs approach working in local communities. Even at this point in the political reform processes, much of the INGO work in Myanmar is directed at extreme poverty alleviation in rural villages rather than broader development objectives. Research shows that effective INGO development work in communities contextualizes approaches at each stage of the intervention or program.

Over a coffee in the offices of the Hope International Development Agency, Yangon, David Tegenfeldt told many stories. This is one of them relayed during my interview with him in June 2009:

> There is a village up in the north of the country that I visited a little over ten years ago now. As we drove into that village in kind of a remote area in a truck, there was a bunch of villagers doing roadwork. My immediate assumption was that it was forced labor. My wife and I, we rode in, and I said, "Urgh, seeing this out so remote is discouraging." We turned the corner and came into the village, and the village was laid out on a grid, with crowned roads, grass growing beside the road, and a drainage ditch on each side of the road. Every house had a cactus and bamboo lattice woven fence, with houses set back, up on poles, and with a latrine out back, a place to keep their draught animals, and a pig sty/pen rather than just running around wild, citrus trees, a garden patch . . . and I said, "Wow, this is amazing!"

> *I went and started asking them typical questions, and it soon became clear. When they had an issue, either the whole community or representatives they had chosen and respect came together. What they said is, they keep talking about it until they come to an agreement, and then they follow it through and people are committed to it. Here is this one community I ran into up there, and they developed this on their own with no foreign input (no international agencies came in or anything).*
>
> *Their leader was killed about 10 to 15 years ago, and they are continuing on. Sustainability! . . . When I ask them, "What percentage of your primary-age children are in school?" They said, "A hundred percent, of course." I said, "Why do you say, 'of course'?" They said, "Because education is important." This was a village in Burma that came up with this on its own. It looks like a relatively wealthy community. Why? Because they worked together. They don't allow alcohol to be produced or sold in their villages. Most other Kachin villages have a problem with alcohol abuse. . . . Participation is one thing. But it is this kind of deeper, spiritual level of how people see each other, how they relate to each other that really makes a difference.*

This chapter analyzes ways in which INGOs contextualize empowerment of local communities under ideas of participation, equity, sustainability, active citizenship, and sensitivity to culture, religion, and language. Broadly speaking, effective INGO programs place additional emphasis on highly participatory development, often with the goal of building the capacity of participatory committees to the point they become long-term sustainable community-based organizations that can continue to work for the good of communities without the same need for outside facilitation or funding. This is highly suited to the Myanmar context, yet takes significant time and a clear process to overcome the tangible sociopolitical barriers. In such a politically and ethnically divided society, however, equity in participation is a major concern, with emphasis required on equity for those of different ethnicity, religion, political persuasion, and age, as much as on gender equity. At least until the recent political reform, to do no harm most organizations have felt the need to take on most advocacy roles on behalf of communities and limit active citizenship, elsewhere widely seen as the logical conclusion of highly participatory development. Sensitivity to the local context involves efforts at peace building, such as facilitating negotiation skills, consensus decision making, and respect for individual difference, as well as work to strengthen both bonding and bridging social capital. Given the large role religious belief plays for most of Burmese society, cultural sensitivity also involves working with this and thus often partnering with religious organizations. Finally, use of local language is highlighted as a means of enhancing understanding of culture and facilitating partnerships and collaboration with stakeholders in work in local communities.

Participation

Participation is a central concept in development theory, having "become widely accepted as the minimum requirement for successful and sustained development outcomes" (Clarke 2009, 1065; Chambers 2005). The UNDP, for example, has long argued that participatory approaches are crucial to any successful human development (e.g., UNDP 1990). "Empowerment happens when individuals and groups are able to imagine their world differently, and are enabled to take action to change their circumstances" (Eyben et al. 2008, 3). Diokno (1978) argues that development requires people's participation in decision making and that denying participation is the nature of authoritarianism and repression.

The participatory development model was discussed in some detail in chapter 2 and revolves around concepts of empowerment, ownership, and partnership (Chambers 2005). These are all ideas involving power within relationships, and in that sense participation has a political dimension. Øyen (2002) argues that an implicit assumption in much of the ideology behind shared decision making in participatory development is that participation will, over time, lead to increased political participation by the marginalized poor and further democratization of the country. Stiglitz (1999) and Sen (1999b) both echo similar ideas, linking participation with democratization. Øyen contends that this assumption is ideological and rooted in Western culture rather than empirically based and conveys a political dimension on the implantation of participatory development practices and possible political restrictions in more politically restrictive contexts. Oakley (1991) concurs that political power can be a fundamental obstacle to participatory development. It has already been noted that Alston, the former chair of the UN Committee on Economic, Social, and Cultural Rights, considers it quite unrealistic to expect fully participatory development to succeed in a country that is fundamentally authoritarian in nature (Alston 1995).

These perspectives raise many questions about the possibility of implementing fully participatory development approaches in a politically restrictive space, such as Myanmar has long been. This question was therefore directly raised and explored in some depth with interview participants, out of concern that highly participatory development may either be restricted by the political context or result in some form of unwanted consequences. The following responses were somewhat surprising and demonstrate the experience of the more highly respected and effective agencies.

What Level of Participation in Myanmar?

Participation is not always implemented well in Myanmar. While this may be true anywhere, political limitations, access issues for personnel, local and regional conflict issues, restricted and short-term funding, and concerns about restrictive official attitudes mean some agencies' participatory programming has been less well constructed in Myanmar than it would be elsewhere. One Burmese former manager for a UN agency complained that participatory committees set up for most projects *"are just user groups that stop at the end of the project, leaving again a vacuum"* (Source 41 2009). Another, a bilateral donor, complained about the projection of INGO identity and will, something that compromises genuinely participatory processes:

> *[INGOs] say participation and ownership but like to label the school or well with the agency's brand logo . . . the INGO have their perceived idea on politics, and that becomes dangerous for the community.* (Source 2 2009)

Nonetheless, most agencies still do adopt a participatory approach, and throughout the interviews it was found that those INGO leaders and agencies who self-assessed their work as more effective and who were most highly recommended by other respondents all implement highly participatory, "process-led," "human-centered," or "integrated" development, programs that create ownership by empowering communities to assess their needs, prioritize, and design the mechanisms and solutions to address those needs, often utilizing strength-based or asset-based approaches and resulting in the emergence of genuine community-based organizations (CBOs) in the longer term.

This finding, that highly participatory development works well in Myanmar, reflects global thinking about best practice development. Yet it is counterintuitive given the strongly authoritarian government. One respondent commented,

I found myself, in my early time here, amazed that we had the flexibil-
ity to do what we were doing with so much of this community empow-
erment work. It puzzled me immensely as to why there was never any
kickback on this. (Allan, *Spectrum* 2009)

Obstacles to Highly Participatory Development

Anthropological research by Skidmore (2003, 2005) and Fink (2000, 2001) into the psychological impact of military rule on the people in Myanmar, as observed in chapter 4, demonstrated that under military rule the population largely developed an aversion to risk (trying new things) and was disempowered in decision making. This conclusion is mirrored in Aung San Suu Kyi's (1995a) writing. One journalist interviewed, who had long-term experience in the country, fully concurred: "*People here are not willing to try things outside areas that are safe*" (Goddard, *MT* 2009).

The enormous groundswell of hope and expectation created by the political reform of 2011–12 has gone partway to addressing this fear. Nonetheless, oppressive control did tend to cause the disempowered poor to refrain from active involvement in participatory processes or to abstain from expressing their voice, and this refrain from participation has only partially been restored to this point. Power still opens the possibility of decision making being dominated by those connected to the governing party or military.

Respondents bore out this concern in communities. Certainly, "*fear is a significant component of the landscape here . . . it is very real*" (Tegenfeldt, *Hope* 2009). There is

a lot of fear of doing new things, or of being seen to be taking the lead
on things or pushing things forward . . . there is kind of a status quo
culture. You don't ever stop doing anything, but you don't do anything
new either. . . . There is a real fear of being clamped down on, with a
really strong self-reliance. (Wells, *Paung Ku* 2009)

At the same time the "*chronic resource shortage of grinding poverty has a very disabling effect*" (Allan, *Spectrum* 2009). Combined with "*a kind of cultural-religious kammaic view, [these factors have] quite an impact on how people perceive the possibility of change and their personal role in it*" (Dorning, *Burnet* 2009).

People will come together, but they're not used to making decisions for
themselves . . . some of that is due to political repression, and some of it
is due to the people just being really poor. (Agland, *Care* 2009)

Thus, in this context, invitations to participatory development are

often met with skepticism from village leaders . . . worried what this will mean for their relationship with local authorities . . . if the local authorities do not agree. . . . For the population that is then the same thing . . . skeptical . . . wondering what it means for them, if they are really going to have a say in the development of the community . . . skepticism that you will really be able to provide that for them. (Source 20 2009)

Nonetheless, even before the 2010 elections, a majority of interview respondents felt Skidmore's, Fink's, and even Suu Kyi's conclusions about the debilitating impact of fear immobilizing people, resulting in a breakdown in collective community action and demotivation for action, apply more in the political space than in development and poverty alleviation—and perhaps more in urban and periurban areas than in rural communities. They thus believe that fear and skepticism can be overcome and that highly participatory development is thus not only possible but even strongly applicable in Myanmar. However, they emphasized process as important.

Generating This Participation in Myanmar
In many parts of the country, community-level participatory committees are already in existence. Commencing in 1992–93, the UNDP initiated human development programs in townships and have since tried to develop participatory projects in many areas. The result is there is some form of development committee widely in place in townships. However, "*they are at village-tract level, which is really too big to allow [meaningful] participation*" (Lancelot, *MDM* 2009). The first stage in generating a high level of participation in community-level projects, for many INGOs, is therefore to establish village- or community-level participatory committees. There are now an increasing number of such committees at the village level, particularly throughout the region targeted in the post–Cyclone Nargis reconstruction and recovery efforts, but many communities remain who still do not yet have such a committee.

Gaining approval and building a relationship with local officials is a crucial first step.

[Forming] a village committee is, of course, a very sensitive thing here in this country, more sensitive than in other countries. But once we

have got agreement with the local authorities to start it, then it is quite similar to other countries. (Feindt, *Welthungerhilfe* 2009)

A process involving sufficient time, a considered approach, and the demonstrated involvement or approval of key people is then critical to overcome this fear and skepticism. The process is greatly helped if formal or informal community leaders in the village commit their support early:

An individual who is able to motivate and inspire others, and that's usually someone in the village themselves . . . that may be a headman or former headman. . . . They need to be confident in their position. So whether that means they've got high-level relationships or they formerly occupied a good position . . . [they] have to be fairly confident in their position. (Griffiths, *TLMI* 2009)

Most people also require a demonstration that the development intervention has approval from local officials.

They need the door opened for them by local senior authorities, to give them permission before they're willing to move forward . . . they would need to make sure that the link is there . . . they need to be reassured that what they are doing is acceptable. Here it is more than in other places. . . . Here it needs to happen. (Agland, *Care* 2009)

Gaining the initial approval and a good level of cooperation from local officials is most often undertaken by local partner organizations, who indicate they can spend "*a lot of time talking to local officials to convince them this is good for the community and not a threat*" (Source 20 2009). In other instances this is a learned skill undertaken by key community formal or informal leaders who have the confidence to approach authorities and who have learned that "*if you don't liaise with the authorities, then the authorities will follow up what you have been doing anyway, so you might as well try to do the right thing*" (Allan, *Spectrum* 2009).

Liaison with officials is often not a role undertaken directly by the INGO though, which may be attributed in part to the misgivings many officials have about any Western-based organization, connected to Western governments or not. It also reflects Western-donor policies restricting the use of development assistance funds. This partner and community leadership at this point demonstrates why strong buy-in from the right key community leaders and partnership with the right local organizations are often essential for INGOs to establish strong participatory processes. Local communities and partners are generally far more aware of the need for gaining cooperation of local officials than INGOs and more confident of the means and approach.

Where possible, including officials in projects in such a way that they can consider they helped the work and take some credit for the results can be fruitful, although this can result in pressure for infrastructure projects, which is a predominant focus of many local authorities because such projects provide the most tangible outcomes they can readily report to their chain of command (Allan, *Spectrum* 2009).

Recent reform has impacted this approach, though. One of the consequences of moves to replace personal power with process has been an increased reticence by local officials to make personal, unsanctioned judgment decisions. Hopefully this is a temporary setback on the road to more transparent and fairer governance. However, for now partial decentralization of decision making, announcement of new rules without clear guidelines, and an increasing separation of state from military administration have in many instances resulted in greater confusion about who has authority to make decisions and how decisions are made. Personal approaches are not always as productive as they often previously were. Yet, at the same time there has been a general increase in responsiveness by officials and an increase in their display of willingness to assist. This highlights an increasing (not decreasing) benefit of constructive engagement with local officials.

Nonetheless, even with this sort of process in place, "*getting people to talk and contribute takes time—two years in my experience*" (Source 41 2009), one Burmese national former manager with a UN agency noted. Another INGO leader explained they regularly spend two years just building the relationships in a village by doing isolated sectorial projects before they attempt to commence an integrated participatory project with a new community (Tumbian, *WV* 2009). Developing highly participatory processes in Myanmar takes considerable time and focus. The pressures created by a lack of resources and short funding cycles for projects mean that "*it needs more time than we normally get from donors*" (Feindt, *Welthungerhilfe* 2009).

Reasons Participation Is Emphasized in Myanmar

One final observation from the fieldwork research is that many INGOs indicate that, if anything, they emphasize generating a high level of participation even more strongly in Myanmar than their organizations do elsewhere. Many indicate that they prioritize participation both because it is highly suitable to the Myanmar context and because it is highly necessary for democratization.

Many informants pointed to high levels of volunteerism, self-reliance, self-motivation, and independence within the culture as making highly participatory programs particularly suitable in Myanmar (Source 24 2009; Tegenfeldt, *Hope* 2009; Tumbian, *WV* 2009; Wells, *Paung Ku* 2009). These very positive attributes of the Myanmar people are demonstrated, for example, by the spontaneous and extensive civil society response to Cyclone Nargis (CPCS 2008). Certainly, as previously noted, a very long-term traditional Burmese perception of governmental authority is that it is one of the five evils people must endure, thus that self-reliance is a far more common attitude than dependence on government or other outside assistance. The Western adviser to one unregistered LNGO noted,

> *We've found that communities, unlike so many countries where they have so much Western support and INGOs and all, that people here do things for themselves. In the communities you'll find them thinking in terms of doing things for themselves.* (Source 37 2009)

Despite the poverty, this allows strength-based or asset-based approaches (Mathie and Cunningham 2003) to be highly successful in Myanmar. One good example of this is the *Fellows* program of ActionAid, in partnership with Shalom, Metta, and several other organizations. The *Fellows* program gives young people intensive training in development and empowerment and places them in local communities for two years with little additional project funding (Allen, *Spectrum* 2011; O'Leary, *ActionAid* 2009; Saboi Jum, *Shalom* 2009). Their role is to act as catalysts of locally sustainable change, with their youth assisting communities seeing them as facilitators rather than leaders of projects (Ahamad, *ActionAid* 2012). By 2010 this program had fellows working in over 400 local communities, with a very impressive track record of health, education, and livelihood outcomes with only minimal external funding (ActionAid 2010; Ferretti 2010; Löfving 2011).

A couple of informants went further, explicitly stating that participation was a deliberate effort on their part to build highly democratic grassroots practices, preparation for a more democratic national future (Source 24 2009; Source 41 2009; Source 28 2009). One respondent expressed the sentiment that while the international pressure for top-down democratic change resulted in a two-decade stalemate, opportunity for democratic change continued to exist throughout this time at the community and small local organization level, and therefore this is where the resources had to be directed. Interestingly, several respondents advocating high levels of participation as a means of democratization identified themselves with a rights-based approach to development and saw participation as part of a process of educating people about rights and developing active citizenship, but doing so safely from within the process of providing other assistance programs.

This is consistent with other studies; South (2004, 2008a), for example, argues that while the development of civil society is not in itself sufficient to bring about national-level political transition, promoting grassroots social mobilization builds networks of independent, community-level participation that can address underlying inequality and undermine the ideological and practical basis of military rule. Promotion of participation at a community level has thereby helped form a base of broad-based democratic political participation and active citizenship, which hopefully can now support sustained political transition. Almost a decade ago South argued that empowered, participatory civil society "will be essential to any process of sustained democratization" (South 2004, 234). Given the restricted humanitarian space INGOs have worked within, focus on grassroots, bottom-up, community-based approaches to development has possibly had the greatest effect on national-level sociopolitical change. Bottom-up approaches have the ability to support national democratic development, although it is less likely they can be the principal driver of democratic reform.

Equity

Equity is a fundamental element of effective participatory development and requires that the disempowered be given input into decision-making processes, that equal opportunity be afforded to all, and that inequalities be redressed (Klasen 2006). Equity in development is usually emphasized in terms of gender issues, to address the serious gender disparity in most societies and even within development organizations. Nussbaum (2000, 1), for example, observes that "women in much of the world lack support for fundamental functions of human life," identifying a range of social and political inequalities that commonly lead to women working harder while being less well nourished, less healthy, more vulnerable to violence and abuse, less literate and educated, more discriminated against, and facing greater obstacles than men, without effective legal recourse or guaranteed human rights.

More broadly, equity speaks of addressing all forms of social and political inequality that lead to marginalization, exclusion, and discrimination, acting as drivers of poverty for individuals and groups of people. Addressing equity issues is essential to poverty alleviation and sustainable development (World Bank 2005). Equity "requires the voices of women, the young, the old, and landless, disabled, and other marginalized groups [to be heard alongside] the voices of traditional leaders, religious leaders, and landowners" (Clarke 2009, 1066). It requires the removal of barriers and disadvantages faced by marginalized groups in society (Klasen 2006). Equitable development therefore also needs to be sensitive to conflict and seek to mitigate fault lines within society and communities that drive exclusion and marginalization (Carment and Schnabel 2001; Conflict Sensitivity 2004).

Equity is a significant issue in Myanmar. Unlike participation, equity was not an issue that was directly inquired about during the fieldwork but was rather a topic raised extensively by respondents themselves. The extent to which equity is crucial for context-sensitive development in such a "*deeply fractured society*" (Wells, *Paung Ku* 2009) quickly became apparent. Building equity and genuine participation in the face of exclusion and marginalization requires time and deliberate effort to empower the voices and opportunities of women, minorities, and other marginalized groups. The deep ethnic, religious, and political divisions in Myanmar society have been examined in detail in the previous chapters, divisions with a long history of serious grievances and competing strategic goals. Overcoming these barriers to ensure equitable participation and program involvement is a major concern.

"*The result of living under such a system of strict hierarchy, is that [most] are not used to being able to have a say in the development of their own village*" (Source 20 2009). Equity in such a context needs concentrated effort to mitigate fault lines and marginalization within society and build conflict-prevention measures into communities (Conflict Sensitivity 2004; Carment and Schnabel 2001). Peace building is an extremely significant component in ensuring equity: "*Without peace we cannot have sustained development*" (Saboi Jum, *Shalom* 2009).

Hope International Development Agency is possibly the agency most directly and extensively targeting social exclusion in development within Myanmar. David Tegenfeldt, senior advisor to the organization, argues,

> *[Westerners] characterize this country as a peace-loving Buddhist people who have the misfortune to be ruled by some military thugs. . . .*
> *I see this, in contrast, as a country that has a long, deep, and broad history of violence, and the use of violence and the threat of violence to maintain social control. And those methods of social control . . . go*

throughout the institutions of this country. It is in the family, it is in the community organizations, it is in the religious organizations, and of course it is in the military. So, in fact, the way I would describe this country is: It is a resource-rich country with a very poor population that has a problem with relationships. So if, in fact, the problem is relationships, we cannot just focus on the removal of the military hierarchy . . . we need to work on ways of relating to each other that use more dialogic methods of negotiating our differences . . . so that the diversity of this society does not continue to tear it apart. (Tegenfeldt, *Hope* 2009)

Perry (2007) agrees in his analysis of the development failure in Burma, contesting,

The popular western view of Buddhism as gentle and non-violent [is not correct] . . . this [authoritarian violence] is no Burman peculiarity—recall Kampuchea. . . . In practice Burma is a violent place on which violence religion is a weak restraint. (Perry 2007, 41)

Equity issues are thus of fundamental importance.

Gender remains a significant equity issue in Myanmar (Feindt, *Welthungerhilfe* 2009). When asked about the reported reduction in household-level poverty over the past five years (see IHLCA 2011), Tegenfeldt commented, "*Yes, but if the men still control the budget and eat well while the women and children are undernourished, then how much benefit is there?*" (Tegenfeldt, *Hope* 2011). However, women have enjoyed a social position and respect in Myanmar that may be a little less inequitable than in many other traditional societies. For example, women in Burma traditionally "enjoyed great freedom in marriage, divorce, inheritance and property ownership rights" (Silverstein 1996, 214) and have long been accepted in business, money lending, and the gem trade (Perry 2007). Myanmar has, likewise, already achieved gender equity in the education enrollment indicators of the Millennium Development Goals (MDGs) (ESCAP 2010). Thus, focusing equity solely on gender issues, Perry (2007, 6) argues, simply demonstrates the "blinkered character of some development discourse."

Several respondents made this point, emphasizing that religious and ethnic background and things like political view or affiliation and age are equally important factors, requiring similar equity mainstreaming across programming to overcome discrimination and ensure equity. For example, one Burmese respondent commented, "*Religion is very important . . . like gender*" (Salai, *SWISSAID* 2009).

> *We oftentimes come in with a Western perspective . . . our proposal documents all say we are being sensitive to gender issues. There is no box saying we have to be sensitive to ageism issues—but quite frankly ageism is probably more an issue here than gender is . . . and gender is a big issue. The hierarchy here is differentiated on a number of issues, of which gender is only one. But from a Western perspective, we only ask about gender.* (Tegenfeldt, *Hope* 2009)

As well as addressing gender disparity, equity must reduce suspicion between groups and build social cohesion. Participatory practices must demonstrate development is not just for one ethnic, religious, or political group. One INGO reported coming under pressure several years ago to exclude known supporters of the NLD from eligibility for its microfinance program (Source 31 2009). Likewise, the Myanmar Red Cross came under pressure at one point to exclude NLD supporters from even giving blood donations (Tha Hla Shwe, *MRC* 2011).

> *This is a very authoritarian, very hierarchical culture, and we must change those relational dynamics before we can hope to change issues like corruption and vested interests at the national level.* (Tegenfeldt, *Hope* 2011)

Other research has corroborated the fact that one of the difficulties of working in partnerships in the Myanmar context is the extent to which local civil society shares the cultural tradition of hierarchical relationships (LRC and Oxfam 2010).

However, political discrimination is not only unidirectional or perpetrated by those aligned with the Myanmar regime. Local informants argue that Western INGOs sometimes equally discriminate against local people perceived to have overly strong connections to the regime (Salai, *SWISSAID* 2009). The serious concern of many international agencies is the extent to which most poor people defer to village leaders, military officers, or those connected with the regime. Agencies report that it is not uncommon for villages to choose local members of what was the regime-backed Union Solidarity Development Association (USDA), which has now been converted into the Union Solidarity Development Party, the new ruling party in Myanmar, to serve on village development committees. Clearly, where their election was due to deference by community members out of a sense of hierarchy, power, or patron-clientism or where their presence on committees was shown to stifle the voice of more marginalized groups, this would be reason for serious concern. Out of such concerns some INGOs have, therefore, discriminated against USDA/USDP members, preventing their election to committees. This, however, should be seen as a positive move, as a sign of broad representation, provided genuinely participatory processes facilitate all members of the community having a voice. Concern was expressed by local informants that too many INGOs have their own idea on politics and use these to discriminate against some community members.

There is evidence in the literature that unequal power distribution within villages must be carefully monitored (Labonne and Chase 2009; Platteau and Gaspart 2003). However, there is also evidence that accountability processes and highly democratic decision-making processes are significant factors safeguarding against elite capture of community-driven development (Fritzen 2007). While INGOs should strive to ensure committees include women and some of the poorest and most vulnerable, equity also means USDA members must not be excluded simply because of political affiliation (Win, *Oxfam* 2009). Equity means village and religious leaders are also included in participatory processes, not completely sidelined (Tumbian, *WV* 2009).

Dealing with the root causes of authoritarianism and marginalization that seek to deny voice and opportunity to women and minorities is essential to equity in development. Empowerment should facilitate personal transformation that results in people coming to see one another in more mutually respectful relationships. It must help groups develop good communication, negotiation, mediation, and consensus decision-making skills. It must build inclusiveness and encourage decision-making skills based on equity and fairness at every level of society.

Building equitable processes is possible in Myanmar; however, agencies do not find it easy: "*We have found that the process has been a real struggle*" (Agland, *Care* 2009). Oxfam speaks of the significant time and very deliberate awareness raising that must take place before equity concerns can begin to be addressed (Win, *Oxfam* 2009).

Sustainability

The concept of sustainable human development was developed by Anand and Sen (1996, 2000) and is an application of the idea of sustainable development to the UNDP's human development concept. The World Commission on Environment and Development defined sustainable development as "development that meets the needs of the present without compromising the ability of future generations to meet their own needs" (WCED 1987) and highlighted that the concept contains within it the two key concerns: that needs of the world's poor must be given overriding priority, and that the environment has only a limited ability to meet present and future needs. Sustainable development builds on the idea that society needs to manage three types of capital: economic, social, and ecological (McKenzie 2004), and thus sustainability requires appropriate utilization of all three systems (Fowler 2000b).

The political and economic restrictions in Myanmar mean that the economic and social dimensions of sustainability require equal attention, whereas the ecological dimension is often the primary focus of sustainability in many other parts of the developing world. Sustainable human development explores these ideas of economic and social aspects in particular, while keeping environmental and resource sustainability issues in mind. Sustainable human development is therefore defined as "expanding and sustaining the choices for all people in society" (UNDP 1996) or as "the enlargement of people's choices and capabilities through the formation of social capital so as to meet as equitably as possible the needs of current generations without compromising the needs of future ones" (Banuri et al. 1994).

The *Human Development Report 1996* spoke of the need to sustain short-term advances in human development, and concurs that "issues of sustainability go beyond the environment" to include the need for economic and social sustainability of human development (UNDP 1996, 63). The UNDP suggests that sustainable human development requires sustaining poverty elimination, supporting livelihoods, and ensuring equity in a socially and ecologically sustainable way. Social sustainability of development interventions requires participation, organization, and sufficient skill and process development for communities to collectively identify their strengths and needs and cooperatively take responsibility for them (McKenzie 2004). Thus, capacity building and governance are essential components for social sustainability of development interventions (UNDP 1997). At a minimum, sustainability of the impact of development interventions requires ongoing support from community networks, civil society, and local authorities.

Social sustainability thus obviously has been a significant concern in Myanmar where the capacity of and partnership with local authorities has been limited. Concerns over the potential negative impact on sustainability of authoritarian rule, abuse by authorities, and governance failures led to many questions about INGO approaches to sustainability being put to informants in the fieldwork interviews. Sustainability of the results of development interventions needs to be carefully planned.

Local and regional authorities, even when they are fully supportive, have very limited resources and capability. In an environment where international agencies are restricted in building the capacity of even township officials, it is difficult to empower such officials to provide systems of support for village-level development. In most parts of the country, there is also a low baseline of capacity in surrounding communities and civil society, limiting the support that might come from community and civil society networks. Social sustainability therefore requires communities themselves be able to maintain their own development achievements beyond the project life cycle.

A number of INGOs interviewed have implemented a very deliberate goal of capacity building equitable, participatory committees within local communities into well-functioning CBOs. The goal is CBOs that are able to maintain, if not advance, the process of community empowerment and community-led sustainable development without the requirement for ongoing outside facilitation and funding, by either the international agency or the local agency. The *Fellows* program by ActionAid and others have already been noted, but such strength-based or asset-based approaches are not uncommon. This resonates well with Fowler (2000), who argues that real sustainability depends on building community capacity to the point CBOs emerge, capable of continuing to plan and direct their futures without dependence on either the NGO or the government. A large number of informants assess this approach as effective in Myanmar:

> *We have proven on the ground [in Myanmar] that the poor, if given opportunity, can fully participate in prioritizing their needs and to work together with the project in shaping their lives. . . . If these groups are given proper support, guidance and training can be a springboard to the emergence of community-based organizations.* (Source 41 2009)

Part of the reason for this appears to be that, rather than a learned dependency, "*it is just the complete opposite: most people are not expecting any help from anybody and assume they are just going to have to do it themselves*" (Wells, *Paung Ku* 2009). This attitude reflects the traditional Burmese proverbs and attitudes toward kings and authorities dating to precolonial and colonial times, as discussed in chapter 3, in which most people attempt to avoid official contact and assume they cannot rely on assistance from the government. Self-help and community cooperation are also very traditional Buddhist ideals.

However, given the fear-impact of authoritarianism on the people, this level of community capacity development takes time. While the approach and program of agencies differ, the agencies involved suggested that from their experience it takes between seven (Source 41 2009) and fifteen years (Tumbian, *WV* 2009) to develop a functioning CBO in a village community. Agencies like ActionAid and Shalom believe it can be achieved in as little three years if it is made a deliberate and intensive central focus of an intervention, with a facilitator living in the community much or all of the time (Allan 2011; Ahamad 2012). It was also noted that success in such a venture "*depends largely on whether committee members are assigned by the village, or whether people with a real heart, spirit, and genuine leadership character are brought into the committee*" (Source 41 2009).

Funding restrictions and short project-cycle time frames undermine the development of social sustainability:

> *I think this is really the main issue. If we could take more time on these processes . . . what we would start is a kind of social transformation, and I wish we would have more time for this, but we don't. This is maybe one of the reasons why sustainability is always the question, whether the committees are really sustainable even beyond the project period.* (Feindt, *Welthungerhilfe* 2009)

Active Citizenry

Active citizenship is widely seen as the logical conclusion of highly participatory development, when communities and local NGOs take ownership of development initiatives that they naturally advocate and hold authorities to account to sustain the development (Clarke 2009). Given the surprising finding that, despite the high degree of authoritarianism in the country, the most effective development programs in Myanmar are strongly participatory and inclusive initiatives, one might anticipate effective programs also incorporate a high degree of active citizenship. Bray (2009) describes active citizenship in terms of public accountability, involving

> strengthening the voice and capacity of citizens (especially poor citizens) to participate in exacting greater accountability and responsiveness from public officials and service providers . . . [to ensure]

that those with the power to affect our lives are held to account for their actions. (Bray 2009, 42)

However, effectiveness of such accountability is highly dependent on the political climate and cultural context. Newell (2002) argues that success in such public accountability is limited to places where the state tolerates protest and criticism, where a free media exists, and where an accessible and functioning legal system operates under rule of law.

Respondents were very conscious that empowerment and awareness raising of rights must "do no harm" and not put people or communities at risk. They are also very aware that *"most Burmese are very reluctant to challenge authorities at any level"* (Goddard, *MT* 2009) or even to talk about issues they perceive as relating to higher levels of authority (Wells, *Paung Ku* 2009), although this has been changing noticeably over the past year or more. One respondent candidly noted that prior to the current turn of events, *"there is a lot of evidence that the government views the people as the enemy, that they fear the public, and fear the public doing too much"* (Long, *MT* 2009).

In the midst of a discussion about local NGO and CBO networks, Dorning lamented, *"What we can't do here, but would be possible in other countries is . . . they could become political in themselves, they could lobby for their own constituency"* (Dorning, *Burnet* 2009). That is definitely changing a year after the new parliament was convened, but most INGOs still discourage the politicization of their work in villages or of their local partners, engagement that would otherwise see them lobby local, regional, or national officials for their own needs, cause, or constituency. For example, debate has recently resurfaced as to whether local and international NGOs should even ban their staff from participating in the peaceful candlelight demonstrations in Yangon calling for reliable electricity supply. Apart from actively seeking cooperation from officials at a township level through lines of relationship, INGOs have largely assumed the role of advocacy on behalf of local communities. Some INGOs have even avoided even using the word "empowerment" in communication with the government (Source 6 2009).

This finding is consistent with research on places where active citizenship may put people in danger. Clarke (2009, 1065), for example, notes that participation has become "fetishised to some degree," such that it is considered the overriding factor in all development interventions and that consequently active citizenship is also widely assumed to be optimal in all circumstances. Instead, using the example of illegal Burmese workers in Thailand, Clarke argues for realistic expectations. Questioning whether active citizenship should always be a goal of community development, he concludes that active citizenship may not be possible (or optimal) where public participation could endanger lives and where people do not have the supporting legal and political mechanisms for such a role. He concludes that in such situations, INGOs should assume an advocacy role on behalf of such vulnerable people, as in fact INGOs have in Myanmar.

Nonetheless, the space for active citizenship does appear to be expanding quickly in Myanmar. Over the past few years a number of local NGOs have become adept at using the government's own language to open public political debate and build political capital, such as Myanmar Egress, who publish *The Voice* journal discussing democracy and democratic values while maintaining a good relationship with the government (Wells, *Paung Ku* 2009). And there does appear to have been a further decided change in the space for active citizenship since the recent elections and the inauguration of the new president and parliament.

Local NGOs have become far bolder in using the public civil space to engage in public debate of policy issues, something previously heavily restricted. For example, local advocacy so raised the profile of the controversial Myitsone Dam hydroelectricity project in Kachin State that it became a common discussion topic even on the streets of Yangon, leading to the project's suspension in September 2011. Similarly, local groups are organizing regular seminars in Dawei calling for corporate social responsibility in relation to the deep-sea port, and an Ayeyawaddy River awareness campaign by a local Yangon-based foundation is using media and art to raise issues of watershed and environmental management within the Ayeyawaddy basin (Wells, *Paung Ku* 2011).

Successful change through active citizenship by community association is also becoming more possible. One good example of this is the work of the Network Advocacy Group (NAG), formed in 2009 to assist with recovery efforts after Cyclone Nargis. Recognizing the possibility of legally forming associations now and mobilizing interest groups, it has redirected its focus to address food and livelihood security through active citizenship. One of NAG's projects involves the formation of fisher-folk associations in impoverished fishing villages in Pya Pon. Traditional village common fishing rights have been progressively allocated to business interests through licensing systems introduced over the past two decades, stripping local fisher folk of their livelihoods. The new associations have begun to advocate for fishing rights and to protect their interests in the fisheries supply chain. Over the first three months of 2012 alone, advocacy to local and regional authorities saw community commons fishing rights restored to six villages, demonstrating an entirely new ability for active citizenship by the poor to address systemic injustice.

This is a new level of locally led active citizenship being permitted by the new authorities, and something most INGOs have yet to significantly engage with. It also highlights that context-sensitivity is not static but requires continual repositioning of a development approach as sociopolitical context itself continually changes.

Sensitivity to Culture and Language

Language and Culture

One final comment from several agencies regards the insights gained into the culture through learning the language and staying in country long enough. Since trust in relationships appears so central to effective development in Myanmar, longer terms for international staff remaining in the country, and learning the language, are useful tools.

Language learning is not an expectation for most agencies in Burma, unlike, say, Thailand, where it was more often considered a necessity. The Burmese have a stronger heritage of English speaking than the Thais do, because of their colonial history, and a lot of officials want to speak English as a matter of pride (Griffiths, *TLMI* 2009). Nonetheless, one of the best ways to gain insight into culture is through language, and many key people in the country including many connected with senior government officials do not have strong English skills. Those who are fluent in Myanmar speak highly of the advantage speaking the language creates:

> *Being able to speak Burmese language . . . when we meet with officials, it's relaxed . . . there's no need for translation . . . they are less afraid of miscommunication. . . . By understanding language and culture, you understand a way of thinking . . . even if you don't agree with the perspective, by understanding it you understand why a decision is made . . . [it] really helps you to be more confident in building relationships with local communities, government officials, and authorities. . . . When you [speak the language], it's got a very high value here.* (Griffiths, *TLMI* 2009)

Conclusions on Context-Sensitive Development in Communities

INGOs clearly find the need to contextualize their development approaches toward local communities in Myanmar in order to ensure and enhance effectiveness, because of the domestic-international political nexus embroiling the country and other contextual factors. Within communities this largely involves intensifying efforts to generate genuine participation, ensure equity and effective empowerment, and offer the best chance of sustaining the results of development interventions, rather than limiting or restricting these activities because of the authoritarian context. These findings both highlight the need for context-sensitivity in the application of development principles and demonstrate that the popular idea that Myanmar is too restrictive an environment for effective poverty alleviation is based on a lack of understanding of the actual situation inside the country. While effective long-term sustainability of development requires engagement at more than merely the community level, this research demonstrates that relief can be delivered from the immediate impacts of poverty inside Myanmar even where broader development partnerships and capacity building are not in place. However, it also demonstrates that advocacy, active citizenship, and local capacity building have new levels of effectiveness only now becoming apparent a year after the reform agenda of the new president, Thein Sein.

Effective INGO community development in Myanmar places particular emphasis on high levels of participation in development, with a clear process and sufficient timeline needed to elicit genuine involvement and overcome the obstacles of fear. In such a divided and hierarchical society, capture of community-led development by powerful interest groups is likely unless power imbalances based on gender, age, ethnicity, religion, and political affiliation are directly addressed. This makes addressing equity concerns a significant issue. Equity in Myanmar embraces gender inequality but also extends into many other arenas of discrimination and marginalization. Sensitivity to the local context involves efforts at building peace, building social capital, and remaining conflict-sensitive in all development programming.

The goal of community participatory development is long-term sustainability of results. In light of the restrictions most organizations face preventing them from engaging in local government capacity building, many of the more effective INGOs deliberately plan from the outset to develop village CBOs as a means of facilitating social sustainability beyond the direct involvement of the agency. However, to do no harm most INGOs have been cautious to empower local communities and partners for advocacy and active citizenship, taking on this role for themselves out of concern that until now empowering communities to advocate with authorities beyond the local level may be neither possible nor desirable. New possibilities, of course, are now emerging.

INGO leaders who are more fluent in the Burmese language and who have been in the country longer also highlight the importance a personal understanding of the Burmese language provides to understanding the culture and to building effective trust relationships with authorities and thus advocate much longer terms for senior appointments by INGOs to the country, with a budget to become fluent in the language before taking on their role. These examples, therefore, demonstrate many of the context-sensitive adaptations INGOs need to make to global INGO development approaches in order to enhance development effectiveness.

6

Context-Sensitivity
in Stakeholder Relations

The unique history of Burma/Myanmar . . . calls for unique solutions to rather common international problems that many states
share, although those in Myanmar are exacerbated. (Steinberg
2010b, xxx)

David just loved telling stories. He continued,

> In those days [1991–92], when I was traveling in here and when we first
> started working up in Kachin State . . . we were only the fifth organization
> to sign an agreement at that time, and the international agencies were
> only working in the satellite townships around Mandalay and Yangon
> and in northern Rakhine with the Rohinga—the rest of the country was
> untouched. . . .
>
> The very first official trip I took after we signed our MOU was a
> project trip down the river from Myitkyina. We had a small team, an ini-
> tial team we had hired, maybe four or five people on the trip. We were
> going to meet village leaders down the river. They sent a special branch
> police officer with us—a fairly seasoned guy. My initial reaction was,
> "Why is he along? This is an intrusion. He is going to make us look like
> we are with the government or with the police. And we don't want to
> have that identity." But my national colleagues treated him like he was
> a member of our team, sharing their food with him. By the time we were
> not even done sharing with leaders and our health worker and midwife

about our health education messages, he became so excited that he began delivering the messages himself directly to the villagers, saying to the villagers, "You really need to listen to these ladies, because you see those big goiters you have, well that means that the brain development of your children is being stunted. It is not just the goiters." He was giving the whole message! "You really need to get iodized salt. This is something that is really important for your young people and the future of your village." He was delivering our message.

The long and the short of it is that by the time we finished our two- or three-day trip, he explained to me that we were doing exceedingly good work that the government would very much welcome, and in his required report directly to the northern commander he would give us a very positive recommendation. He said we would have nothing to worry about from the government. The next time, a few weeks later, I came up to Myitkyina, probably within twenty to thirty minutes he showed up. He had told the staff they had to inform him the moment I showed up, but the reason he came was not to monitor me; he came to report to me about his meeting with the commander. He told me how well the meeting with the commander had gone, how happy the commander was, how relieved, that we were actually a good organization, and that he was not going to have to worry about us. And he told me, you will have no problems going forward. You will be fine.

Now, I could never have convinced the commander myself that we were an okay organization, but a trusted emissary of his who had monitored us for a few days and become convinced we were doing good work—he opens the door wider for us. And that—I learned that from our national staff. It wasn't my natural inclination. My inclination was to stay as far away from this guy as much as possible and give him as little opportunity to intrude on our visit to these villages as possible.

This is an excerpt from an interview with David Tegenfeldt, senior advisor with Hope International Development Agency, June 29, 2009, Yangon.

One of the greatest issues complicating the work of INGOs in Myanmar has been the strained relationships between the Myanmar government and the Myanmar people, and between the Myanmar government and the international community. The complex domestic and international political context therefore impacts INGO stakeholder relationships even more solidly than it impacts INGO development work in communities.

This chapter explores how INGOs manage these relationships with other stakeholders, considering relationships with local civil society, LNGOs, government officials, other agencies, and the international community. It explores context-sensitivity in relations with domestic stakeholders under the ideas of partnerships and capacity building, advocacy, rights-based approaches to development, and accountability. Again responses are presented phenomenologically from the INGO point of view, with analysis interspersed. INGOs approach working with civil society, local NGOs, and officials quite differently in Myanmar than they would in most other countries, having found the need to limit and adapt many of their approaches in what has been a highly politicized context.

The next chapter, chapter 7, will then explore how INGOs negotiate to create and enlarge the humanitarian space in Myanmar, both with the Myanmar government and particularly with the international community.

Partnerships and Capacity-Building Civil Society, LNGOs, and Newer INGOs

Civil Society and LNGOs

It has long been recognized that INGOs need to move from being service providers to equal partners with civil society in facilitating development (Paldron 1987). Strengthening civil society is essential to promoting self-help and overcoming both paternalism and dependency (Frantz 1987). As a result, capacity building and local organizational development are primary objectives for many development agencies globally; "Instead of local organizations being the means for sustaining projects, projects are now seen as means for strengthening local organizations" (Pettit 2000, 57).

The capacity and development of civil society in Myanmar was, however, long constrained by government policy and action restricting basic freedoms (Liddell 1997; Steinberg 1997; ICG 2001). A decade ago Steinberg wrote, "The military have destroyed whatever remnants of civil society . . . existed in the country. The private groups that continue are controlled or authorized by the state" (Steinberg 2001, 53). Skidmore described it as the "strangulation of civil society through censorship, propaganda, self-censorship, informers, and the surveillance and regulation of the public space" (Skidmore 2003, 9).

Because civil society was a restricted space in Myanmar, this was an aspect respondents were directly interviewed about at some depth. What almost all agencies clearly agree on is that over the past decade or so, a very active civil society has begun to reemerge, often not registered and usually not large but very active. One respondent described much of it as attempting to operate "*below-the-radar*" (Lancelot, *MDM* 2009; Lorch 2007) until very recently. The response to Cyclone Nargis clearly demonstrated both the resurgence of this "informal" civil society and also how robust this sector has become in such a short space of time (CPCS 2008). A large number of these groups are now beginning to seek registration.

This civil response to Cyclone Nargis is entirely consistent with traditional perceptions of authority and rulership, as discussed in chapter 3. Despite the military's perception of itself as being the only effective protector and provider of development for the people, the local response to the disaster was to organize self-help, leading to the reestablishment of scores of civil society groups and community networks.

Since Nargis there has thus been a large push to develop partnerships between local and international NGOs (Dorning, *Burnet* 2009). Complicating this, however, has been the politically constrained operating environment that creates the perception of high levels of risk for civil society actors, as well as most LNGOs being very limited in their capacity given their early formation stage (LRC and Oxfam 2010). In reality, few welfare-oriented civil society groups have actually got into serious trouble except in the immediate aftermath of Cyclone Naris; however, the fear remains very real.

"*There is a widespread recognition from the international community that they don't have enough interaction with local groups*" (Dorning, *Burnet* 2009). A good many INGOs ascribe globally to an ethos of working primarily through local partner organizations, but because of limited local capacity they find themselves needing to still implement most of their programs directly through paid staff in Myanmar. Indeed this limitation in capacity is the major constraint restricting most INGOs wanting to partner with local civil society, and this is particularly significant for bigger INGOs with large or more specialized programs. For example, while the global practice of Care International is to minimize the number of its own staff and work primarily through local partners, in Myanmar it has a large staff that directly implements 95 percent of its programs (Agland, *Care* 2009). This is something Care International is now addressing, but developing the sort of shared culture, ideals, and beliefs it looks for in a genuine partner, as well as the capacity of partners, takes time.

Care International is not alone. Médecins du Monde (MDM) likewise discussed the fact that it works in direct implementation of projects in Myanmar to an extent it is not happy with, and it would not usually accept in other countries, directly running its own HIV/AIDS clinics and other programs without having the time and resources it would prefer to devote to capacity building local NGOs.

> *We absolutely want to build local capacity of local NGOs, CBOs, informal groups, whatever. . . . And we would like to do hospital cooperation. . . . [But for now] we are operating as if we are in an emergency situation, and we are not in an emergency.* (Lancelot, *MDM* 2009)

There are several reasons MDM attributes to this. One is limited budgets for projects in Myanmar, constraining it to almost have to choose between its programs or capacity development of potential partners. Another is its inability to find suitable partner organizations. In 2006 MDM conducted a survey to identify suitable partner organizations.

> *We found some NGOs claiming to be involved in HIV/AIDS, but . . . [it] turned out to be a total disaster. We could not find a single bona fide NGO [with active HIV/AIDS programs]. Maybe we did not know where to look, that is possible. . . . We think things have now changed. . . . We were so busy doing real care and prevention directly, we somehow missed that there was in the last—I would date it maybe five years—I think there has been the development of a very active civil society.* (Lancelot, *MDM* 2009)

MDM's desire and commitment to partner are not in dispute, but limited local capacity has been a major constraining factor until now. Like MDM, many INGOs in Myanmar would prefer to focus on technical cooperation and capacity building of local NGOs and civil society, even of government departments, as they do in other countries, rather than direct program implementation. The limiting factors are most commonly scale, governance, and management and evaluation skills of potential partners. Many of the emerging civil society groups wanting to partner with can't even write reports in English, so unless INGO leaders have sufficient Burmese language ability themselves, partnership opportunities are greatly restricted (Griffiths, *TLMI* 2009; LRC and Oxfam 2010). A lack of these capacities makes genuine partnership difficult.

Developing potential partner organizations has, therefore, become a conscious high priority for many INGOs over the past couple of years. Several organizations, including Oxfam, ActionAid, SWISSAID, and the Burnet Institute, for example, have all made conscious decisions to implement almost all programs through local partnerships and build local capacity rather than directly implement programs themselves, despite this limited local capacity (Dorning, *Burnet* 2009; O'Leary, *ActionAid* 2009; Salai, *SWISSAID* 2009; Wells, *Paung Ku* 2009).

For example, SWISSAID likes to consider the local partner as the more important side of the relationship, and one of its principles is to attempt to commence a partnership not based on the project as much as on who the partner is and how the process and partnership is constructed (Salai, *SWISSAID* 2009). Several centers have been set up to directly further civil society partnerships and capacity development, including Paung Ku (Wells, *Paung Ku* 2009), the Local Resource Centre (Herzbruch, *LRC* 2009), and the Capacity Building Initiative (Ngwe Thein, *CBI* 2009). The greatest challenges INGOs face are identifying suitable candidates and then building their organizational capacity and taking them from being small and unregistered organizations into ones with sufficient size and management skill to partner, often also involving assistance with the process of attempted registration. Capacity development of technical skill is far less of a difficulty.

One of the key issues discussed in the literature regarding partnership by large international agencies with much smaller civil society and LNGOs anywhere is that, rather than being a mutual trust relationship based on shared goals, principles, understandings of poverty, and so on, such partnerships often slide toward patron–client patterns because of the knowledge and resource disparity (Fowler 1998, 140). Partnerships rarely genuinely empower local organizations or help them gain credibility and develop their autonomy and effectiveness. "A precondition for authentic partnership is dealing with asymmetric power relations, particularly for donors to delegate 'bounded authority' to the people on the ground which are context-specific" (Yonekura 2000, 44).

Partnerships based on long-term commitment, shared responsibility, reciprocal obligation, shared credit for results, mutuality, and balance of power are not common in any area of life and quite uncommon on the field with development (Fowler 2000a, 3). It is therefore perhaps unsurprising that a common criticism made by LNGOs in Myanmar is that where large INGOs do partner with them, the INGOs "see the local partners as their implementers, not in any sense of true partnership" (Dorning, *Burnet* 2009). Most LNGOs working in partnership with INGOs feel a power imbalance in the relationship, due to INGO control of knowledge, skills, and funding, although the INGOs do not perceive the power imbalance as often (LRC and Oxfam 2010).

LNGOs perceive their strength to be the provision of local knowledge, but in many cases they complain about decision making mostly lying with the international partners. While this is not an uncommon criticism globally, it persists in Myanmar even where the INGO is aware of the issue and significant attention is given to minimizing its impact. The size of the INGO–LNGO power disparity is such that many LNGOs have a fear of large international agencies coming in and rolling over really good local initiatives (Dorning, *Burnet* 2009).

Dealing with such asymmetric power relations when local civil society is so limited in capacity and vulnerable is a particularly thorny problem, and one that most agencies are still grappling with. Oxfam, for example, deals with this by not expecting all partners to be equal, identifying a range of "project partners" who interact around implementation of programs, while concurrently focusing on significantly developing the capacity of a few "strategy partners" who have demonstrated both strategic innovation and that they adequately share the culture, ideals, and beliefs of Oxfam (Win, *Oxfam* 2009).

Likewise, SWISSAID distinguishes between three types of partnerships based on the capacity of the partner organization, from newly formed community-based organizations to mature local organizations with clear vision and mission who are able to effectively manage complex projects, negotiate with other donors themselves, and apply for registration (LRC and Oxfam 2010). SWISSAID then retains long-term, largely nonfinancial partnerships with strategic partners who share a common interest and ethos.

The fact that most local organizations are not registered is an additional obstacle to partnerships for many INGOs. Many local organizations consider the greater risk of being scrutinized and controlled disincentives, such that they do not wish to pursue registration (e.g., Source 11 2009; Source 12 2009; Source 30 2009; Source 32 2009; Source 37 2009; Source 38 2009; Source 39 2009), and registration has been nigh impossible for some other local organizations. However, many international institutional donors don't want to take the risk of investing money into groups that are not registered, so a not uncommon practice has developed whereby INGOs partner with smaller unregistered organizations to facilitate international funding for local unregistered organizations. It can be tricky: "You find funding, but you have to carry it for them since institutional donors will not take the risk of investing money in a group that is not registered, that is not controllable" (Lancelot, *MDM* 2009). Duffield (2008, 36) provocatively referred to this practice in Myanmar as "aid laundering," citing an example of funds flowing from an international donor through a UN agency to an INGO, who administered the funding on behalf of an unregistered local NGO who would not otherwise be funded. He suggests this is directly "due to the restrictive international climate." Hopefully the domestic political reform and thawing in international relations will soon remove the necessity for these sorts of practices.

Agencies like MDM find not only that they need to find funding for small, unregistered, local organizations and carry it on their own books but also that their lack of size and management capacity means that the best things MDM can do is find small amounts of money to access capacity-building programs for LNGOs from other NGOs or the United Nations. They then seek to "*push these people to organize*," then scale up what they are doing if the LNGOs can reach a scale to register (Lancelot, *MDM* 2009). However, having to operate as an LNGO under such an umbrella of an INGO exacerbates power and control issues (Source 20 2009).

One other issue resulting from the relatively small number of LNGOs who do have experience and reasonable organizational capacity is that multiple INGOs and donors often cluster around them competitively, something that can undermine their autonomy and ability to operate (Source 33 2009; Source 37 2009; also LRC and Oxfam 2010).

Two recent reports raise several other concerns regarding potential issues stemming from partnerships in Myanmar with LNGOs of limited organizational capacity. Caution is expressed over the fact that most LNGOs are led by leaders from minority groups, meaning partnership can itself potentially favor minorities, exacerbating ethnic tension capacity (Desaine 2011). Paung Ku, a local consortium focusing on capacity building of local NGOs and CBOs, agrees, expressing concern at the number of examples of partnership with INGOs increasing interpersonal, intercommunity, and interethnic tension. Likewise, most LNGOs are led by a single charismatic leader in whose hands most of the power lies, who operates with a team of staff, mirroring the authoritarian structures of the state and the military. Indeed, some appear to be attracted to the NGO sector for the advancement in status it can afford: "The NGO sector offers a rare opportunity for the pursuit of power by leaders, besides military, armed groups and recent political parties" (Desaine 2011, 106). In such a context, partnerships can carry a dangerous potential to concentrate power to a few individuals, undermining the community support and democratic representation civil society should bring (Wells 2009).

Desaine (2011) notes that to register LNGOs need to act in ways that respect and help the state save face, limiting their capacity to confront or attempt to change the system (Desaine 2011, 106). This idea that civil society should "confront" the state and "change the system" is a very limited view of the role of civil society in authoritarian states, where respect for "face" and connections with authorities are elements of context-sensitivity that can enhance voice and where change is often more evolutionary than a radical transfer of power. It does mean, however, that publicly most registered civil society in Myanmar concentrates primarily on meeting practical needs within the society.

In conclusion, then, despite the complications of developing and maintaining INGO–LNGO partnerships, the Burmese nationals and LNGOs interviewed definitely want to see more of these capacity-building relationships, particularly with unregistered civil society groups and as partnerships that deliberately design capacity-building elements into the implementation of shared projects.

Faith-Based and Religious Organizations

Approaching this research, the focus was on the complex sociopolitical issues and not on religion or culture. Interview respondents were therefore not directly asked questions relating to religion or culture. Nonetheless, several INGO respondents chose to raise religion and the faith-base of many civil society and LNGO actors as an issue in regard to INGO stakeholder relations.

Religion is a defining force within culture across much of the world, and the importance of sensitivity to culture in development was discussed extensively in chapter 2. Nonetheless, religion and faith-based institutions have largely been marginalized and ignored in the development discourse and treated as either irrelevant or an impediment (Marshall 2001; Ver Beek 2002; Selinger 2004; Clarke 2011). As the UNFPA (2010) points out, "Too often the strengths (efficacy, commitment, knowledge, networks and influence) and experience of FBOs are overlooked by development planners," as well as in forming development partnerships. Not uncommonly local religious leaders and institutions are either ignored or seen as empowered elite whose excessive influence needs to be countered through more equitable, participatory approaches. Concerns focus around the potential for abuse of the traditional power religious leaders possess and around probable proselytization. As a result, many faith institutions have chosen to position themselves outside the development sector when working to improve lives in the local community, often viewing the work and approaches of development institutions with equal cynicism (Marshall 2001; Clarke 2008).

Most religious adherents do not separate their religious belief from the economic and political spheres of their lives. For development to be effective and sustainable, it thus must seriously account for the role of religion as a powerful aspect of public culture, and faith-based organizations (FBOs) as significant actors in development (Tyndale 2000; Selinger 2004; WFDD 2001). Faith and religious organizations are often a powerful source of social capital in communities (Candland 2000). Avoidance of the topic of spirituality or of religious institutions and organizations results in less effective development (Ver Beek 2002), and transparency about the beliefs (including secular beliefs) of outsiders is especially sensitive in this regard.

Myanmar is a deeply religious society, making these issues particularly pertinent:

> *This is a very religious society here in Burma, and we set up quite an artificial barrier between religion and community development when we have to always keep it separate. . . . That is not to say that we should be tolerant of groups that may want to use development work to proselytize or convert others to their religion. . . . But I think that international agencies . . . [for] fear of that . . . want to separate it so much that it becomes artificial for local community.* (Tegenfeldt, *Hope* 2009)

Prior to the recent boom of new actors in the civil society space, local religious institutions and what might be loosely termed FBOs were the most prevalent civil society in Myanmar (Steinberg 1997). Even today most civil society in the country has a religious base or motivation. The higher status position the culture affords religious leaders, and the perception by officials that religious groups will remain largely apolitical, gave these organizations an advantage under SLORC/SPDC military rule, allowing them to operate more freely than most nonreligious civil society groups. As one Burman Buddhist former manager with a UN agency remarked,

> *Where natural CBOs have perished, church or religious organizations have not. . . . There is a very great religious toleration in Myanmar . . . [and] there is a big role being played by faith-based organizations, who have taken up a very big and challenging role, especially after 1988. . . . The church leaders and religious organizations provide a very important link between the "rulers" and the "ruled."* (Source 41 2009)

As a result, a very large percentage of civil society groups today either are FBOs or have religious connections. Most others, because of their religious roots or the sincere religious beliefs of their members, are what the LRC describes as strongly "values driven," meaning workers are highly motivated by spiritual beliefs such as the earning of merit (LRC and Oxfam 2010, 32–33).

It is natural for INGOs that are faith-based to partner with local FBOs. What is more unusual is that a number of respondents from secular INGOs noted that when they partner with local organizations, they too were more likely to partner with FBOs than secular NGOs. Several secular INGOs even suggested that working with local religiously affiliated partners is often beneficial in Myanmar (Source 19 2009; Agland, *Care* 2009). The country director of one secular INGO remarked, *"Most of our local partners have a religious affiliation. It helps a lot"* (Source 20 2009).

However, working with local religiously connected civil society can have complications. The lack of resources of these local FBOs means that they often operate out of a religious premises, a complication for many secular INGOs and bilateral donors (Source 20 2009), raising fears of INGO programming becoming linked to proselytization efforts by local religious institutions. Indeed, a recent report suggested that most local NGOs and civil society have a religious (or sometimes an ethnic or political connection) and therefore often have additional agendas they seek to pursue alongside or through their social activities (Desaine 2011).

On the positive side, local faith-connected agencies are more likely to operate under some form of registration. Likewise, because they have been around longer and have a natural connection to their faith organizations internationally, agencies with a religious connection are more likely to have organization, scale, and governance more in keeping with Western requirements (Source 20 2009). Those groups from Christian backgrounds, in particular, have often been able to maintain connections with the global Christian community and thus often better understand the requirements of Western agencies and have better English skills to support this.

The Buddhist *sangha* generally have better connections with local authorities than do Christian FBOs and provide significant social cohesion in Buddhist communities, being, as Goodwin-Dorning (2007, 16) expresses it, "cultural guardians of knowledge" in a range of significant areas. However, one director of a secular (not faith-based) INGO cautioned,

> It is much harder to work with the sangha. We have tried it. If the concept of participatory development is weak within the church, then within the sangha it is a lot more alien. . . . [When] people donate to

the head monk, and the head monk decides how the money is spent. (Source 20 2009)

The *sangha* traditionally had the primary role in education and still play a substantial role in this area (Goodwin-Dorning 2007). They also redistribute food and provide emergency housing and so on to the extremely poor in their communities. However, beyond meeting such immediate needs in a more ad hoc fashion, as a Buddhist informant expressed it,

> *Buddhist monks historically have not been good at social work, but they do take a charitable role providing food for the poor and opening monastic schools that provide both food and education to children.* (Source 41 2009)

Nonetheless, partnering with FBOs has largely proven effective, particularly when they include *"representatives from both the Buddhist and Christian communities. . . . But that is difficult"* (Source 20 2009).

The feedback from local LNGOs is that INGOs far too readily bypass local religious and FBOs, rather than approach them as part of the community and part of civil society (Source 37 2009; Source 41 2009; Saboi Jum, *Shalom* 2009; Salai, *SWISSAID* 2009). Myanmar culture includes respect for religious leaders and volunteering with religious organizations, both of which are advantages INGOs should build on rather than resist because of some foreign secular organizational ideology (Source 41 2009).

Smaller, Newer INGOs

Most newer and smaller organizations in Myanmar work through partnerships (at least initially), either working under the MOU of another INGO or implementing small projects without official approval in urban-fringe areas that do not have access restrictions, operating *"under the radar"* and partnering with a local registered company, an unregistered local organization, or a faith-based group (Source 8 2009; Source 11 2009; Source 12 2009; Source 14 2009; Source 25 2009). This latter model, in particular, is widely used by INGOs based outside the country who do not yet have permanent local or expatriate staff inside Myanmar and do not have an MOU with the government for their projects. Under this arrangement, the local organization becomes the project implementer, and the INGO primarily provides funding and possibly training, project design, and evaluation through periodic visits. One commented,

"We don't have a generic work of our own. We've primarily worked with people that are already doing it and build our model from theirs" (Source 14 2009).

As a consequence of the restrictions they face, their projects often remain few and much smaller than those of registered organizations. Working through local partners, these INGOs often do not need to maintain much direct interaction with local township officials or military personnel (Source 14 2009). However, as they grow, the pressure for some sort of official status increases, and with no MOU they do face a range of additional restrictions. For example, they are unable to apply for travel permission and are thus often restricted in terms of the regions they can visit. One regional manager explained the consequences for project monitoring and evaluation:

> *We recently completed our first project evaluation, with a foreigner traveling in. However, the foreigner could not access the villages. I, too, have not been able to go to many of our places, so it is hard to get accurate evaluations.* (Source 11 2009)

In some cases the intent is to maintain this arrangement indefinitely, to avoid the need for excessive interaction with officials. This is particularly true of smaller INGOs, who do not feel they have the resources to commit to the implications of registration. However, others suggested it was part of a strategy to personally build rapport with local authorities through delivering several successful development projects, with a view toward potentially ultimately negotiating their own MOU and placing personnel inside the country in the longer term. When that happens, however, the change in roles and in the nature of the relationship between the INGO and the LNGO can be quite problematic and often results in the INGO finding new local partners (Source 28). Naturally, each of these organizations sought anonymity in this research.

During interviews in 2009–10 several organizations working from outside the country in this manner indicated they would love to bring in staff and open an office immediately, but the complexity of negotiating an MOU was keeping them out. More than one such organization described how they had limited their projects and funding into Myanmar because of complications in their relationship with their partner, stemming largely from not having personnel on the ground often enough or because their unregistered partner organization feared that if the program grew too much or became too effective, it would attract unwanted attention. The rate of new agencies opening offices in Myanmar as a result of the political reform is therefore hardly surprising, although it does pose real concern about the additional demands so many new agencies all wanting partnerships place on the limited local capacity.

Partnerships and Capacity-Building Government Officials

> If a white elephant is defined as something expensive to maintain and useless, then international Burma policy has many white elephants! But if there is one I would recommend we change quickly, it is capacity building . . . technical capacity. (Thant Myint-U 2011)

> *We should not think of the government authorities [as] our enemies. We should receive their assistance for the benefit of the people.* (Salai, *SWISSAID* 2009)

Building the capacity of government agencies and departments, and strengthening state institutions and civil service, are widely seen as essential for sustained economic development (e.g., ESCAP/ADB/UNDP 2007). A few UN agencies, such as the FAO, have a sufficient mandate and good relationship to work in close partnership with and capacity build Myanmar government departments (Imai, *FAO* 2009). The FAO has been working in Myanmar since 1978 and operates out of government facilities in Yangon, advising the government on agricultural policy, running a range of capacity-building programs, and running joint emergency and rehabilitation programs alongside the ministry of agriculture. Such UN agency leaders are highly pragmatic about their role: "*Our work is apolitical, it is technical . . . working with the host government in the country will allow us to best help the people we want to help*" (Ghermazien, *FAO* 2009). "*Every country has politics . . . we have to work together [with the government]. . . . If you come here as a guest to contribute to this country, you have less problems*" (Imai, *FAO* 2009). Still, despite the freedom in their mandate and long-term close working relationships with the government, even the FAO acknowledge that "*many restrictions happen*" (Imai, *FAO* 2009).

Most other agencies, whether multilateral or INGO, lack such a mandate or the funding to work closely with government departments. For most INGOs, partnership with government officials and departments is very complex and fraught with tension. On one side, restrictions applied by donors, boards, and the international community to prevent funds flowing to those connected to the regime often include officials down to the township (local government) level (Source 1 2009). On the other side, many officials are deeply suspicious of the motives of INGOs and their donors (Source 16 2009; Source 31 2009; Source 50 2009).

> *They don't want input. They are not interested in it. At a very high level, MOH [Ministry of Health] very much does not particularly wish to participate. International staff do not have access to hospitals, officially. I am not allowed to walk into a hospital. Most hospital directors would not allow me to walk in to their wards. . . . The first, big reason we don't have a lot of care cooperation with MOH is because they don't want it.* (Source 18 2009)

This tension is easing, but as this book goes to press, Western bilateral donors have not yet eased restrictions on use of development assistance in partnership projects aimed at capacity development of government ministries and agencies or included Myanmar within the funding criteria of programs specifically aimed at building the capacity of government agencies.

Many government officials are NLD supporters, as demonstrated by the fact the NLD won all four seats in the administrative capitol contested in the April 2012 by-elections. However, the openly democratic aspirations of many INGOs and the electoral success of Aung San Suu Kyi and the NLD are a cause for concern to those in the government who disagree with NLD policy. "*The [former] regime believe INGOs are not just there to do a specific task but to organize politically against the regime*" (Source 50 2009). Likewise, many officials in higher positions in the departments don't want partnership "*because they don't want the strings which they feel are attached to aid; they don't feel they can control aid*" (Lancelot, *MDM* 2009).

This fierce independence and second-guessing of motives by officials on both sides is nothing new. It not only stems from the strained relationships between Burmese military governments and the international community over recent decades but also reverberates with the Burman–British struggles of the colonial era and the democratic postindependence state—as well as echoes centuries of tension and posturing between Burmese monarchs and European expansionism dating back to the sixteenth century.

What is actually surprising is the extent to which government officials at all levels are putting this aside and showing a willingness to work with their own civil society and the international community. Most INGOs find that most local authorities do want help and do want partnership, so long as it is genuine and nonpolitical.

They are very much concerned that they need, and would very much love to receive, some help, as long as they can manage the contradiction—as long as their technical people can receive the aid without it becoming a political thing. (Lancelot, *MDM* 2009)

Many agencies have deliberately invited township-level officials to their training events for some time. One bilateral donor spoke of the positive experience they had providing specific technical assistance and training to township-level officials during the fight against avian flu in the mid-2000s: they *"found ministries to be very professional and motivated . . . [with] no leakage of money"* (Source 1 2009). However, building partnership relationships with government officials requires *"spending a little more time and effort building relationships [with officials] here than in other countries . . . because relationships are often clearer in other countries"* (Tumbian, *WV* 2009). And because of the international tension, political forces on both sides have long worked against partnership. One INGO manager complained about the inequalities that their funding guidelines forced them to perpetrate on officials, not allowing them to pay the travel expenses of low-paid civil servants attending their training when they do pay these expenses for all other participants, something *"very frustrating for us and for them"* (Agland, *Care* 2009).

Several years ago one INGO implemented a three-way partnership in a community-level livelihood program, between themselves, a local implementing partner, and a government agency (Source 25 2009). The INGO provided funding, strategy, and training, while the local partner handled all direct implementation in the community. No funding went to the government agency, and despite the strained nature of the relationship, they found that including officials in the partnership promoted healthy dialogue and coordination. However, another agency attempting similar involvement expressed frustration that in such approaches, local officials are almost certain to be included in INGO projects, rather than any genuine partnership being generated (Agland, *Care* 2009).

Myanmar is perceived to be highly corrupt, and this is certainly true in business practice (TI 2011). However, Western concerns about corruption of officials in development partnerships appear to be overstated to this point:

I have had less problems with corruption in Burma than in Laos or Thailand. . . . The problem is mostly with business . . . there is definitely less corruption when it comes to aid (except exchange rate, big issues) because most locals are concerned about the poverty of the people. (Source 31 2009)

This correlates with Pedersen's research, which found that

neither manipulation of aid for political purposes nor corruption is a huge problem for those organizations that remain vigilant, or at least, not greater than in a number of other fragile states. (Pedersen 2010, 123)

This may change with a large influx of additional funding and organizations, but it is an encouraging fact to this point.

Likewise, not all officials at all levels are tainted with the same regime brush, as is commonly intimated by some in the wider international community. Reflecting on her own experience, the Western adviser to one unregistered LNGO noted,

I learned to differentiate government from civil servants, and many of them are committed to their own people and their own people getting educated. There are some really, really good people in the civil service. (Source 37 2009)

Thus despite the obstacles, many INGOs expressly indicate that if they were given more freedom, this would be something they would do more frequently. One key Burmese worker with a UN agency, who, because he is Burmese, had a great deal of experience working in communities without the presence of the government liaison officers that accompany foreign staff, argued that INGOs need to find ways to overcome the clear tensions and competition and that cooperation or partnership with officials is an essential component of facilitating the political change the outside world is seeking in Myanmar:

Once the INGO leaves, the local authority comes and claims the credit. That does not mean anything. We should allow that. We should see that as a positive thing—let them take ownership, support it! . . . A key role for INGOs is to gain trust from the government. The government knows it needs to change but feels threatened. We need to allow them to own the changes at the village level. Only the INGOs can offer that—the local people can't. The INGO must learn to work with (but not through) the government. (Source 41 2009)

When communities take the lead on an integrated development project, they sometimes take the initiative to instigate inclusion of township officials on their own, when they have good relationships with local authorities already and believe partnership with them is the most efficient way to achieve their development goals (Source 30 2009).

Partnering with government officials still requires access to funds with little in the way of restrictions. Respondents who have done so describe the positive outcomes that come from partnering with officials. For example, when Cyclone Nargis struck, The Leprosy Mission International (Griffiths, *TLMI* 2009) realized both that this was going to be a big issue for people with disabilities and that the Social Welfare Department was going to be overloaded with proposals—so it rang the department and asked what additional equipment it would need to be able to process the coming administrative mountain, and provided it. Prior to that it had been working with local partners but finding things hard going, and while it did this with a motive to ensure people with disabilities were cared for after the cyclone, it found the strengthened relationship most empowering for its work.

> *When their seniors come, they get top marks for having done a good job. . . . Them getting top marks because we helped them gives them flexibility to grant more operational freedom to us. We did this not with the aim of greasing the relationship, but . . . [later] they just said, "Do whatever you want to do, we know you, we trust you, just go and do it. We'll sign the papers later"—[even in areas we] haven't really had operating permission before.* (Griffiths, *TLMI* 2009)

TLMI was subsequently commissioned to write a disability protection plan and disability access guidelines for public buildings in Naypyidaw under the SPDC and now since the elections to help draft disability legislation to be introduced into the new parliament. To TLMI, this clearly demonstrates the extent to which constructive engagement around mutual priorities can bring enhanced influence for change and is a requisite for lasting development outcomes in the country (Griffiths, *TLMI* 2011).

> *Relationship building often comes through being willing to recognize and work with the agendas of other people. . . . No matter who's in charge of the country in the future, the same group of civil servants are going to provide these services, so up-skilling and resourcing them is not necessarily putting money into the hands of restricted people. And by strengthening their hand, it strengthens their ability to do a lot of good things that they want to be doing.* (Griffiths, *TLMI* 2009)

Many respondents agreed that

if we are going to see any kind of long-term development going the way we want it to go in Myanmar, we are going to have to start now to build up the level of the people who work in the administration. Because, whether there is reform or outright change, we are going to have to work with the same people . . . [but] we can't currently do that. (Source 20 2009)

Thus, at one level this translates into building the capacity of officials within townships, departments, and ministries, often in some very basic ways:

If they don't know how to use a typewriter, let alone a computer, where are you leaving the next persons who are going to take over the country, who have better intentions than the ones we have today? You are really giving them an impossible starting point. (Source 20 2009)

At a deeper level, it can mean actively involving officials in projects:

I came to this situation seeing my government counterparts as an intrusion into the work that we were trying to do in communities and therefore trying to keep them away from meddling. . . . What I learned right away was that if we used an approach of trying to make friends of our counterparts and using very transparent ways of working, we could in fact either work together, or they would be too busy to spend time trying to monitor what we were doing. . . . If we treated them as obstacles or as ones who wanted to interfere, that would almost be a self-fulfilling prophecy. . . . [But if] in some ways we treat them as a partner . . . solicit their input . . . government counterparts, or even special branch police or military intelligence, can sometimes be a better ambassador for me than I could ever be for myself. (Tegenfeldt, Hope 2009)

Duffield (2008) argued that the main role of INGOs in Myanmar is to "push back, contain or modulate the effects of unchecked, arbitrary personal power" by all connected to the regime. Clearly many UN and INGO leaders have not agreed for some time. For example, several years ago the country liaison for the ILO argued that a key obstacle to effective long-term development in Myanmar is the absence of a cohesive civil service that can implement the high-level policy initiatives agencies are currently negotiating with senior officials (Marshall, *ILO* 2009). Given the current rate of reform and the easing or suspension of many international sanctions, capacity building of government agencies and the civil service is increasingly essential. Funding and mandate restrictions that limit partnership with officials are a point of great frustration, and given the emphasis on poverty alleviation in President Thein Sein's inauguration speech (NLM 2011b) and subsequent reform, INGOs are increasingly arguing that this is the right time to explore capacity-building partnerships (Herzbruch, *LRC* 2011).

The danger, of course, in building a good relationship with government officials is that *"you may be perceived from the outside as being too close; you have to tread a fine line"* (Source 15 2009). Many of the UN and INGO leaders making these comments, particularly those who self-assess their work in Myanmar as more effective, felt the need to defend themselves against being labeled regime apologists. For example,

> *The reason I am here and working inside the country is not because I see the systems as any better than my colleagues on the other side of the border see them. The reason I am here is because I think these systems are really evil, they are really bad for the people. And the people will benefit, including those in the military will benefit, from change in these very destructive systems that are in place now. Lest people think, and some people do think, or would like to describe me, as too close to the regime and that is why I am here. Absolutely not! The reason I am here is because there is a lot of suffering, it is due to the bad systems that are in place, and those systems need to change.* (Source 16 2009)

Rights-Based Approach

Definitions of a rights-based approach (RBA) to development diverge greatly. One definition suggests that RBA simply means ensuring every program, policy, or process of development remains conducive to, and furthers the realization of and overall respect for, universally recognized human rights (Gouwenberg 2009). However, an RBA usually conceptualizes poverty "as the direct result of disempowerment and exclusion" (ACFID 2009, 5). Since exclusion constitutes a denial of human rights, an RBA seeks to address poverty by empowering rights-holders. A central aim of an RBA is thus "a positive transformation of power relations" for those in poverty (Nyamu-Musembi and Cornwall 2004, iii). The grounding of such an approach in human rights legislation makes it distinctively different to other approaches to development, repoliticizing development work. To many, an RBA wants to be a normative framework for development that "puts politics at the very heart of development practice" (Nyamu-Musembi and Cornwall 2004, 2).

Rights-holders are usually seen to be citizens. Domestic governments are usually seen to be the prime duty bearer (ACFID 2009), as the authority vested with the responsibility under human rights law to ensure the rights of citizens are not violated by either themselves or other actors. In theory, there is a diversity of duty bearers. Governments themselves are not monolithic, with a diverse range of levels of government, public service departments, and government-sponsored organizations, as well as the army and more independent government agencies. Other duty bearers include businesses, civil organizations, community members, and even the international community, all of whom may have obligations as duty bearers under international human rights law.

An RBA seeks to hold duty bearers to account under international human rights legislation, empowering the poor "to claim their rights and to change the social structures that keep them poor" (ACFID 2009, 6). In particular, the RBA seeks to assist marginalized poor people to assert their rights to a fair share of existing resources and power, including provision of basic services and an equitable application of the law, "making the process explicitly political" (Nyamu-Musembi and Cornwall 2004, 3).

In practice, the primary duty bearer is widely taken to be the national government—particularly in a state with a reputation of state violation of human rights—and an RBA is often seen as a "vehicle for increasing the accountability of government organisations to their citizens" (Ferguson 1999, 23).

RBA is a contentious topic among INGOs in Myanmar and seen by practitioners to almost always refer to holding government officials or agencies accountable, including the army and USDP. Several organizations interviewed have adopted the RBA globally as their approach to development yet, in order to "do no harm" and not put people at risk, until 2011–12 worked in Myanmar in a more reserved way, advocating basic services in recognition that poverty itself is a violation of human rights (Source 24 2009). The ILO, with its mandate to work against forced labor, already spends most of its time advising citizens of its rights under existing Myanmar law. It suggests that existing national laws provide a reasonable framework in many areas and that awareness raising of rights under these laws is a critical part of development. However, it finds that even when people understand their legal rights, very few are brave enough to exercise them (Marshall, *ILO* 2009).

In 2009, many interviewees felt an RBA was not appropriate in Myanmar since *"the law is in the mouth of the generals; there is nothing down on paper, no real rule of law because what is written can always be manipulated"* (Source 16 2009). Some see the RBA as built on concepts not *"relevant in Myanmar given neither the people nor military leaders believe there are rights"*:

> *This country does not believe there are rights. They believe there are needs, but not that there are rights. That is not just the military leaders; that is the rank-and-file person. The concept of rights is not . . . very common.* (Tegenfeldt, *Hope* 2009)

Others suggest that many government ministers and key officials actually

> *are aware of human rights principles, are concerned, and are trying to improve on them . . . but they have very little budget in which to operate. . . . [Therefore,] criticism is not helpful when officials genuinely are concerned.* (Source 31 2009)

Inescapably, part of the issue of talking about rights in Myanmar is the fact that international governments and agencies have long couched their most stinging rebukes in human rights language, to the extent the SPDC government repeatedly responded by arguing that human rights allegations were being exploited to destabilize the state and were being raised by certain countries for political advantage more than out of genuine humanitarian concern (e.g., see NLM 2009). One of the greatest obstacles to progress on human rights globally is said to be a "lack of understanding of the psychological legacy of imperialism and colonial rule" (Yasuaki 1999, 104), and most nations who are the targets of the most serious criticism for human rights violations were, like Myanmar, previously victims of military intervention and economic exploitation via colonialism under slogans like "humanity" and "civilization." Over the years human rights has appeared to many former colonial states "like nothing more than another beautiful slogan by which great powers rationalize their interventionist policies" (Yasuaki 1999, 104). Opponents argue the concept of rights has been co-opted as "another weapon in the arsenal of Western countries in their efforts to bring recalcitrant Third World nations to heel in their 'New World Order' . . . to judge third world governments" (Aziz 1999, 39).

SLORC and SPDC reactions to human rights allegations reflected these feelings, reverberating with the Burmans' fierce desire to maintain independence and rebuff the history of dominance by European powers discussed in chapter 3. The SPDC regularly countered human rights allegations by arguing the hypocrisy of the West in pursuing such claims and that the upshot of the work of human rights activists is that the people of Myanmar are further denied their human rights by actually restricting the right of the people to economic growth and development (Ware 2010; see, e.g., U Soe Tha 2006).

Things are changing fast in Myanmar, with, for example, the formation of the Myanmar National Human Rights Commission in 2011. One common argument about universal rights, however, is that to overcome the concerns of some that human rights are used to mask cultural imperialism in former colonial states, alternate language must often be employed, and local variation in the implementation of rights may be required (An-Na'im and Hammond 2002). Several INGOs in Myanmar argue that human rights gains are being made, particularly in areas such as forced labor, human trafficking, disability, and child protection, but largely not using the language of human rights or the RBA.

Interestingly, several interviewees expressed the view that poverty itself had one of the greatest impacts in denying the rights of the people (Source 24 2009; Source 28 2009). Pedersen agrees, suggesting, "Poverty has emerged as the most acutely felt constraint on human rights for the majority of people across the country" (Pedersen 2009, 2). This is a widely accepted view: Mary Robinson, former UN high commissioner for human rights, long argued that extreme poverty is "the most serious form of human rights violation in the world today" (UNDP 2003b, iv). Certainly, the Vienna Declaration of the World Conference on Human Rights observed, "The existence of widespread extreme poverty inhibits the full and effective enjoyment of human rights" (UN 1993, Article I.14).

This perspective on human rights and poverty does imply greater sharing of responsibility between the Burmese government and the international community than an RBA sometimes engenders (Ware 2010). Those agencies interviewed who self-assessed their work as most effective in these areas (e.g., Source 6 2009; Source 16 2009; Source 31 2009; Griffiths, *TLMI* 2009; Tegenfeldt, *Hope* 2009; Win, *Oxfam* 2009) believe the RBA agenda is better pursued by building relationships with authorities and appealing for assistance nonconfrontationally rather than using the language of responsibilities and rights with an adversarial approach.

Having said this, just as the space for active citizenship appears to be expanding in the shifting political landscape of Myanmar, so too does the space for human rights and an RBA to development. Discussion with one LNGO leader in Yangon in December 2011 was particularly illustrative. During a discussion of their current work, he explained that when he had encountered an uncooperative local official recently, he reminded the official of his rights and told the official what he needed to do to comply with Burmese law (Source 51 2011). This informant appeared nervous, even guilty, to be telling me this incident. This had not been a premeditated response, and he clearly expressed disbelief both at what he had done and at the positive outcome it provoked. Still, the fact that he adopted rights language in an unplanned exchange, and that it produced the desired outcome, shows an emboldening of LNGOs and an expanded civil space in which a rights discourse may now emerge.

Advocacy

Many question whether advocacy works in Myanmar or has produced any significant outcomes. INGOs point to a wide range of policy change and development to show that advocacy can work, such as in areas of human trafficking, drug control, disability strategy, sustainable forestry, and HIV-malaria-TB prevention (Allan 2009). TLMI points to recent invitations for INGOs to assist in drafting legislation surrounding disability, the elderly, and the protection of women and children (Griffiths, *TLMI* 2011). The story of the Network Advocacy Group's empowerment of fisher-folk associations to advocate on their own behalf is another clear example. One of the limitations for work in Myanmar, though, is that these advances generally take place quietly and receive little press or credit in the international arena. President Thein Sein's enthusiasm for the alleviation of extreme rural poverty could also be taken as an advocacy win.

However, progress in advocacy seems as related to the issue as it does to the methodology and approach, with items related to the military or national security or involving budgetary reallocations making less progress, and change related to technical matters or local needs is more likely to succeed than calls for political policy change. For example, despite a great deal of advocacy, increases to the government health and education budget have been minimal (Source 19 2009).

Respondents widely agreed that sustainable change is not possible through village-by-village interventions alone but will require major policy change to address, for example, education, health care, and infrastructure deficiencies, and secure things like property rights and access to finance. "*[Advocacy] is really the main thing we need to do*" (Lancelot, *MDM* 2009). Yet most INGOs are "*particularly hesitant to pursue fully rational advocacy strategies that would do a better job of leading to more complete overall development in any sense*"

(Source 30 2009). The reforms of 2011–12 have led officials to be far more attentive to community opinion and needs, and those citing the greatest success argue there is enormous space for advocacy. One UN informant argued, "*Most organizations . . . don't engage and negotiate boldly enough behind closed doors. When we push back nonconfrontationally, but boldly, they generally move closer to a consensus or compromise solution*" (Source 42 2009). Yet these same organizations implied vulnerability for such work by seeking assurances of anonymity for these answers to this fieldwork!

Given that power in Myanmar has traditionally been seen as personal, most successful advocacy in Myanmar is personal and nonconfrontational. This is still true and is typical in authoritarian contexts where participatory public advocacy is often inimical to change because of the nature of the political culture. Advocacy NGOs working in authoritarian contexts can easily adopt means that impact negatively on policies and on the needs of the poor (Tadros 2009), violating the "do no harm" principle. One respondent suggested effective advocacy in Myanmar was "*silent advocacy*" (Source 20 2009), by which she meant away from any public spotlight. The Myanmar Red Cross speaks of "*informal advocacy*" or "*situation sensitive advocacy*" (Tha Hla Shwe, *MRC* 2011). "*We can't work in an advocacy-based way*" (Source 20 2009). Oxfam prefers to speak of advocacy as "*building relationships*" and notes that success is very dependent on the individuals involved (Win, *Oxfam* 2009).

Indeed, "*the word 'advocacy' itself, in some cases, makes people afraid*" (Tumbian, *WV* 2009):

> "*Advocacy*" *is not so nearly as helpful a term as "dialogue." I would much rather talk about dialogue and engagement than about advocacy. A Western form, a marketing approach, a civil-rights-based approach to advocacy is simply inappropriate here, but that does not mean you can't have an advocacy strategy that uses a whole range of tools and techniques to progress exactly the same messages in a very different way, using very different media.* (Allan, *Spectrum* 2009)

The most effective approach appears to be through exploring needs and issues together with officials, with no confrontation and no blame, just looking for ways to meet needs together. "*It is more like seeking support or seeking to supplement what the community has already done to help themselves*" (Source 24 2009). World Vision explained this advocacy as "*report[ing] needs to the government, so they know and so they can even support us by sending their technical people*" (Tumbian, *WV* 2009).

Øyen (2002) argues that such a pedagogical element to advocacy in order to change the minds of authorities is often required anywhere in the world:

> Much of the resistance to poverty-reducing practices is due not only to the antagonists' self-interest and the potential loss they may have from redistributive measures; much of their hostility stems from a lack of concrete knowledge about poor people and the causes and consequences of poverty. (Øyen 2002, 25)

This approach is most contextual, too, in that under traditional political ideology derived from the ideas of *kamma* and the *dhammaraja* (discussed in chapter 3), Burmese rulers are very aware of their responsibilities toward the poor and the need for development. Producing development and overseeing a prosperous nation are seen as both the righteous act of a good ruler and a means to demonstrate their legitimacy to rule. However, these are secondary priorities after the immediate need for state security and control of power have been established, so advocacy approaches that threaten security or challenge the position of authorities can quickly become counterproductive. Avoiding confrontation therefore opens the opportunity to appeal to inherent motives of Burmese political rulers to assist the needy as a form of legitimizing their power.

Effectively, such an approach involves adopting methods described in the literature for involving elites in poverty alleviation, despite their vested interests lying elsewhere. Hossain and Moore argue that elites in poverty alleviation do not depend on the elites being altruistic. They argue for

> involv[ing] national elites in constructive dialogue about the nature, causes of and solutions to poverty, in ways that will maximize their empathy and engagement with the issue, and minimize the danger that they will feel railroaded into responding. (Hossain and Moore 2002, 5)

Hossain and Moore (2002, 10) propose constructing "persuasive narrative around notions of joint gains" rather than by attempting to blame or shame elites into change. This is precisely the approach INGO leaders in Myanmar have found most effective, where advocacy has worked.

> *Our approach is to make them understand what the reality is . . . we give them real information, bring them to reality, bring them to the*

field, so they can understand what the reality of the situation is. Why would you make other people ashamed? . . . If you want to win, don't make other people feel like they have lost. (Source 6 2009)

MDM, as a specific example, was engaged in 2009 in an advocacy campaign seeking to gain acceptance for needle and syringe exchange, as part of an HIV/AIDS strategy. Possession of syringes is widely taken as proof of drug addiction and can constitute enough evidence to put people in jail (Lancelot, *MDM* 2009). MDM has had success in terms of the needle and syringe exchange program idea being accepted by the Ministry of Health, but the obstacle it has found is (1) to have official policy change endorsed at the highest level and (2) to have the police and the army take ownership of such a change. One of the greatest issues, MDM has found, is a lack of understanding on its side of government decision-making processes and therefore on how to go about targeting an advocacy campaign of that nature to work through the remaining obstacles.

Such influence must be exercised person to person. Using the media, political pressure, or writing has not been effective in Myanmar, at least not until this current juncture. One respondent emphasized that many officials at the township level are genuinely concerned about many of the same issues as development agencies but are hamstrung by policies and budgets (Source 31 2009).

Accountability

Eyben (2008) argues that mutual accountability in international development is not so much about the parties holding each other to account for performance against preestablished objectives as about the messy complexity of relationship and process, with notions of mutual responsibility: "Much of what proves with hindsight to be effective aid may well be an outcome of relational approaches, although such approaches are rarely valued or reported" (Ebyen 2008, 3). This conception of accountability appears particularly apt in Myanmar, where agencies need to overcome the strained relationship between the West and the Myanmar government in order to operate freely and cooperatively.

Accountability and transparency were not initially within the question framework for this research, but once several interview participants raised the issue, questions about accountability were incorporated in the later interview cycle.

INGOs with the greatest ease of access to sensitive parts of the country have strong relationships with authorities, built largely through highly transparent dealings with officials. Many invest significant time and personnel into government relations (e.g., Agland, *Care* 2009; Griffiths, *TLMI* 2009; Purnell, *WVI* 2011; Tegenfeldt, *Hope* 2009). Transparency is key. Many are

> *even more transparent [than usual]. . . . The entire thing that is at stake . . . is to build trust. . . . So we are absolutely transparent in everything we do . . . we are trying really to build trust with them, that they see the value of us working with them [and] spread that message that international aid—that it can really bring development and improvement, and that it is not just political spying.* (Lancelot, *MDM* 2009)

World Vision explained,

> *We go and talk with the local authority—they know us and question us about what we're planning to do. And we are very transparent with them: This is our planning, this is long-term development, this is the type of development where people should participate and do [things] for themselves, people should develop their own decisions about where they would like to go for the future. So everything should be transparent with the local authority. And then through the local authority, they say, "OK you can go. That village is very poor. Why don't you start from that village?"* (Tumbian, *WV* 2009)

The Myanmar government is, of course, not all that transparent in return. However, that is perhaps sometimes more a matter of bureaucratic capacity as intent. *"I don't think they want to be nontransparent, but they don't want to be required to give more than they can provide"* (Lancelot, *MDM* 2009).

Interestingly, however, given the level of transparency in direct relationships with officials, reports being delivered to higher levels of authority are not always as transparent. One INGO country director explained,

> *We tell [our contacts in the department] exactly what we are doing and ask for their advice on what to put into our written reports—people in the department advise back what to write up and what not to write up. It creates more trouble for them if we report everything. One colleague insisted on proper reporting of what they actually did, which caused problems.* (Source 20 2009)

Another went so far as to suggest,

There is a manipulation of figures culture which is a disaster for any aid program, because you can't get any figures for a baseline or any figures on impact. And if you publish any figure on impact you are putting yourself in danger because you are not supposed to publish any research of any sort. So that is a major obstacle to any sort of cooperation. I really think that is a culture that has permeated the UN as well. The UN . . . they literally said to me, use your research data where you want and when you want, but please, could you report it like this and like this. (Source 18 2009)

At least one INGO leader voiced concern that "*INGOs here seem to be less open to information sharing [with other INGOs] than we found them in [other country named], as if they mimic the government and become less transparent themselves*" (Source 18 2009).

The unprecedented relief cooperation in the wake of Cyclone Nargis seems to have significantly improved the level of cooperation and information sharing between international agencies with, for example, eighteen agencies cooperating very openly in an impact study after the March 2011 earthquake and an interagency discussion of salary scales for local staff being held in 2011 (Herink, *WV* 2011). Still, it is interesting these comments about a lack of INGO transparency were made a full year after the cyclone. Journalists working longer term in the country have likewise noted reluctance by INGOs to talk about their work. One suggested he had noted much greater reluctance for INGOs to go on record and talk about their activities after the purge in the military leadership in 2004, and that since then that they preferred their work to remain more "*under the radar*" of the media (Goddard, *MT* 2009). Another commented,

NGOs will say, "Everything is fine, the government is cooperative," but at the bar they often suggest a different story. . . . NGOs think that if they complain the government might kick them out, so when we ask them about their work and relationship with the government, as a reporter, they say to us that all is OK. (Long, *MT* 2009)

In terms of accountability to donors, many respondents readily agreed that they maintain a very low publicity profile of their work, both in Myanmar and overseas (in donor countries). "*Caution is wise*" when it comes to publicizing projects outside the country, and some country directors are particularly sensitive to advise visitors from other parts of their organization about being careful that they don't put anything in their promotional materials that would upset either the Myanmar government or the people outside of the country (Source 6 2009). In part this is recognition of the government's sensitivity that opponents exploit portrayals of poverty. But it does highlight the complexity of accountability toward donors. Likewise, allowing donors to visit and see with their own eyes is often not possible, many times external project evaluations are limited or not possible, and flexibility in the application of project funding to changing situations is often required. Accountability and disclosure are generally good with large institutional donors but often minimal with small donors and the general public.

Conclusions on Context-Sensitive Development With Stakeholders

This research has drawn out many of the key adaptations made by INGOs to facilitate greater effectiveness in stakeholder relations as they implement community development programs within Myanmar. Such contextualization that they describe in their development approach can be linked directly to restrictions stemming from both the Myanmar government's domestic politics and the international community's response to this.

INGOs approach working with civil society, local NGOs, and officials quite differently in Myanmar than they would in most other countries, finding the need to limit or seriously adapt most of these activities because of the macro-political context. Contextualization in these interactions has been explored in this chapter through the development approaches of partnership, capacity building, advocacy, RBA, and accountability. It was shown that after long being suppressed, "informal" civil society has become quite strong in Myanmar over recent years. The need to partner with and build the capacity of this sector is widely recognized within the INGO community; however, efforts are complicated as much of this civil society is unregistered (and difficult to register) and lacks both the scale and the organizational capacity required for effective partnership with most INGOs. Partnership and capacity development usually also emphasize work with government departments, which is heavily restricted by both domestic and international politics and so rarely undertaken in any significant manner. Most speak of the need for such civil service capacity development, and where cooperative work has been attempted, those involved speak highly of the outcome.

LNGO leaders and many INGO leaders feel development must take religion particularly seriously. While religion can often be a cause of division and conflict, because of their strong connections with the community and the role of faith in Myanmar, faith-based organizations (FBOs) and religious leaders or institutions seeking to work with the community in development-like projects should be actively engaged as a means of both bonding and bridging social capital. Many, therefore, advocate deliberate inclusion of local FBOs, religious leaders, and religious institutions into partnerships and to participate in programs.

A rights-based approach, being defined as holding the government to account for human rights publicly and by a public educated in their rights, is inherently political. The government's long domination of the political space has therefore meant such an approach has not been effective in this format. However, many INGO informants insist that a nonconfrontational strategy of advocacy toward the same goals is becoming very fruitful. By nonconfrontational advocacy, these leaders speak more of a dialogue away from media spotlight and mass mobilization, referring to a process reminiscent of strategies designed to involve the elite in development through an exploration of needs together in a no-blame fashion. To avoid exposing civil society to undue risk, this sort of advocacy is primarily undertaken by INGOs directly with government officials, although some local civil society is now independently taking some interesting initiatives as well. Permission to operate, the possibility of partnership, and effectiveness in advocacy are built on the quality of relationships, so in a context where political will and international funding for partnership or civil service capacity development is low, INGOs instead seek to build personal contact and trust with officials primarily through activities involved in being absolutely transparent. As such, the more effective INGO initiatives in Myanmar seek to be transparent with officials to an extent well beyond levels of accountability that they would usually undertake in other countries.

7

Dancing With the Devil but Not Holding Hands: Negotiating the Restricted Humanitarian Space

It is vital that Burma be opened up to greater NGO presence, both local and international, so that pressing development issues can be addressed. In adopting an engagement agenda of this kind, it will be important to accept that initially it will entail considerable hard work for no more than limited benefit. It will not deliver the instant democracy sought by many political activists and some external powers. . . . Engagement with the generals who have done so much to damage Burma will be, paradoxically, the best way to deliver tangible benefits to its citizens. . . . The world needs to find ways to move on and engage with its domineering military rulers . . . focusing on underpinning economic and social change [to] open up options for incremental political reform. (Holliday 2008b, 52)

Looking across the empty coffee mugs and small café table, John (not his real name) kept quizzing me about working in Myanmar. John was the director of a philanthropic foundation, it was 2011, and he was exploring the possibility of funding a proposed INGO development project in Myanmar. But John struggled to see past the stereotypical media images and the newsletters he received from various advocacy groups describing the oppression of Karen and Kachin Christians.

Preferring to call the country Burma, John inquired about government restrictions, surveillance and interference in projects by the authorities, and all the obstacles to working in Myanmar. Not an interview participant, John had visited Myanmar just once, some time ago.

"How do you get money in? How freely can INGOs work? Aren't they heavily scrutinized? So what sorts of projects can NGOs actually do in Burma, and how effective are they, really?"

He had many questions, but the implication was clear. Political restrictions by the regime surely limited any real effectiveness, suggesting it was perhaps not yet time to fund projects in Burma. He listened politely, but my responses clearly conflicted with the mental image he had of the context. I could see skepticism reflected on his face.

The conversation was almost a direct correlation with the interview with Ann Lancelot, country representative in Myanmar with the French INGO Médecins du Monde in 2009. She articulated a viewpoint many of the interview participants shared:

> For me, I have a huge advocacy responsibility inside MDM, to explain to them that this country has a different operation mode. We don't get enough money. We need to get more money in the country. Political oppression or not, political oppression is not the issue: there is a huge humanitarian need that is not covered. The sanctions are a disaster.
>
> I am building that internal advocacy, and I have a few people on the board who are very much online and willing to listen to that. We must also build a more structured advocacy toward donors and donor countries, especially toward France. We have a good cooperation toward the French ambassador, to try to convince French corporations to put more money into this country. I have received US$4,000 this year from French corporations covering two trainings of local staff—because I went and begged at the French embassy. They are ashamed of that, rightly, the French ambassador, that he has so little money to spend on aid. And yes, the French are one of the first contributors to the EU. . . .
>
> So there is a huge responsibility NGOs have to build advocacy toward donors and donor countries, and that is one of the things we need to do.

INGOs working in Burma operate in a difficult environment. On the one hand, INGOs face international criticism . . . [often] paint[ing a] simple black-and-white picture of the situation [that] is counterproductive. On the other hand, INGOs do find it difficult to work within the constraints of the situation in Burma. (Tegenfeldt 2001, 115)

The pace of reform in Myanmar has taken most commentators by surprise, and the international community is responding in kind with increases to international assistance, suspension of sanctions, and broadening of aid mandates. In February 2012, in response to "unprecedented" democratic reforms, the European Union pledged a substantial additional 150 million euros in aid over 2012–13 (Wilson 2012). While this is still to be channeled through the INGOs and UN agencies, this is a big increase in EU funding that (on its own figures) has averaged only 11 million euros a year since 1996. Then, after the largely free and fair by-elections that saw Aung San Suu Kyi and forty-three other NLD representatives elected in April 2012, British prime minister David Cameron visited Myanmar. The result of his visit was the surprise suspension of almost all EU sanctions.

Australia, the second largest bilateral donor to Myanmar (at present), has quickly followed suit—and gone a step further. Australia announced a 30 percent increase in development assistance to Myanmar following the April by-elections. Then, as I was making final edits to this book in June 2012, Australia's foreign minister, Senator Carr, traveled to Myanmar and announced groundbreaking policy changes and new aid commitments. After discussions with President Thein Sein and Aung San Suu Kyi, Senator Carr announced the suspension of Australia's remaining sanctions against Myanmar, declaring,

> The point has been reached where lifting sanctions is the best way to promote further progress. . . . We have moved beyond coercion, and coercive measures no longer contribute to the reform process. . . . Engagement, through exposure to international standards and best practice, will also help improve accountability and transparency. (Carr 2012b)

At the same time, Senator Carr announced further increases in development aid that will take Australian assistance for Myanmar to more than A$100 million a year by 2015 (Carr 2012a). What is perhaps most significant, however, and something going well beyond the European Union decisions, is the Australian announcement that aid mandates will be expanded to allow funding of capacity development projects for government agencies and departments. Senator Carr announced that Australia will "work with the Myanmar Government to identify aid priorities and build its capacity to deliver essential services. As democratic reforms continue, we hope to establish a formal relationship on development cooperation" (Carr 2012a). As an example of such a capacity-building partnership project, Senator Carr announced a project in which academics from two Australian universities will be funded to undertake capacity building of the Myanmar National Human Rights Commission and to work with them to identify human rights priorities in parliamentary practices, the rule of law, and the judicial system (Carr 2012d).

These are very substantial changes by both the EU and Australia, and they will be very welcome boosts to poverty alleviation and development programs in Myanmar. The magnitude of their impact is yet to be felt, although both Australia and the European Union warn that sanctions have only been suspended, not lifted, and that they are watching closely; if there is a reversion to hard-line policies or a backing away from reform, they warn that previous restrictions will be quickly reinstated. Nonetheless, such changes in funding, sanctions, and mandate restrictions are not yet universally supported. While the Obama administration has announced it will reestablish an in-country mission for USAID and has doubled aid to Myanmar, total assistance from the United States still amounts to just US$37 million (USAID 2011). The United States has not, at this point, lifted or suspended most of its sanctions against Myanmar or substantially increased foreign aid mandates, and it still uses its influence to limit the mandates of UN agencies such as the World Bank and UNDP in Myanmar.

The majority of Myanmar is poor, and despite severe limitations in the capacity of government departments, the Myanmar government is still the best-placed agent to address the greatest number of needs. As Wilson (2012) notes,

> The key areas where ordinary people in Myanmar are deprived of opportunity and assistance include education, health, employment and improved livelihoods in the agricultural sector. In almost all situations, existing government networks have substantially greater potential to deliver outcomes sooner and on the scale needed given Myanmar's population of 60 million. (Wilson 2012)

Yet despite this, and despite the level of reform over the past year, bilateral assistance by Western donor countries apart from Australia is still restricted to be provided only by multilateral agencies, INGOs, and LNGOs, and most donors retain strict preconditions limiting partnership with government agencies and the opportunity to capacity build officials or civil service agencies.

This may change in the near future and would have significant implications. However, whether or not more donors move to implement development cooperation with the Myanmar government, and capacity-building projects with government agencies, this chapter explores INGO perceptions of the major constraints they have felt on their poverty alleviation and development programs in the country over the past few years. Hopefully this chapter will serve simply as a historical analysis of the impact of previous sanctions policy, restricted development assistance, and narrow aid mandates against Myanmar, and as such it will offer a critique of these policies from the viewpoint of INGO in-country managers. Such lessons are of value for understanding of historical context and as lessons for development assistance in other internationally isolated states. However, in the meantime this analysis remains highly relevant to the future direction of US policy toward Myanmar.

In interviews commencing in 2009, the greatest area of concern INGO managers expressed about their work in Myanmar was the impact Myanmar's strained international relations had on program effectiveness. Foremost among their concerns were their ability to access the people and communities most in need, and their level of funding to implement projects to address these needs. This chapter therefore presents the perspective of INGO managers in regard to this restricted humanitarian space and then analyzes these restrictions from several theoretical perspectives in order to evaluate the intent, efficacy, and future applicability of Western development policy as it has been applied toward Myanmar. In the light of the findings from this field research, as well as the reform undertaken by the regime and the demands of humanitarianism and global justice, this chapter concludes that the current repositioning by Australia, the European Union, and the international community more generally is long overdue.

Gaining Access

While it seems almost so obvious as to be trivial, two preconditions for effective INGO development interventions are the ability to gain access and funding. In the context of Myanmar, because of the political tensions both inside and outside the country, neither has been able to be taken for granted. Several INGO country directors spoke in 2009 of being confronted by the extra level of complexity in obtaining access and funding when they arrived in Myanmar from postings in other developing countries, including from conflict zones and failed state contexts (e.g., Source 18 2009; Source 24 2009; Source 30 2009). Context-sensitivity thus begins in dealings with international stakeholders and the Myanmar government, to expand the space in which they can operate within the country.

At least until a year ago, INGOs working inside Myanmar argued that the greatest immediate constraints on their poverty alleviation, health, education, and livelihood programs stemmed not from the Myanmar government but from the limited funding and restrictive mandates applied by the international community. This is a significant challenge, claiming as they were that international restrictions limited their ability to address poverty far more seriously than the very real but less impacting restrictions applied by the Myanmar government.

Access to Myanmar communities has been complicated by the competing strategic concerns held by the international community and the government. On the one side, the government has been slow to negotiate MOUs, has been equally slow to issue visas, and then has often restricted the places and sectors INGOs may work in and their travel to visit project sites. Only a few years ago the European Commission (CEC 2007) suggested these serious access restrictions threatened the whole humanitarian space in Myanmar. On the other side, Western governments, international donors, organizational boards, and the international community as a whole have long used direct and indirect restrictions on the humanitarian space in Myanmar as an attempt to put political pressure on the regime—as the United States continues to do. One in-country representative of a major bilateral donor pointed out that the greatest consideration for Western governments, which has tempered humanitarian assistance to the people of Myanmar, is that aid must *"not keep the regime in power one day longer than would otherwise be the case"* (Source 1 2009). Prioritization of this concern restricts the work of INGOs.

Creating Space With the International Community

When contrasting these two pressures, even in 2009 before the recent domestic political reform, INGO respondents almost uniformly suggested that the greatest constraints on their humanitarian and development efforts come not so much from the Myanmar government as the international community. For example,

> *Many external people will say that it is the government that constrains so much of what we do. I guess I feel that much more it is the international environment in which the country is forced to operate because of sanctions and policy that is having a much bigger impact. When I say, "having a much bigger impact," I mean on what work it is possible to do at this point in time, as opposed to the fundamental humanitar-*

ian situation in the country, which is of course the direct result of the country's historical, cultural, political context over a very long period of time. (Allan, *Spectrum* 2009)

While many agree that the fundamental issues of poverty in Myanmar are closely connected with domestic politics and political history, when questioned about restrictions from the Myanmar government, most respondents countered with examples of solutions or examples of what they actually can do in the country. What has long frustrated INGO managers at least as much as domestic restrictions have been the restrictions on aid funding and the ongoing restrictions on mandates by the international community, particularly because they believe they are largely based on false, stereotypical perceptions. Examples of their responses include the following:

The reality on the ground is not what is portrayed by the Diaspora or those that work in the camps on the Thai-Burma border. . . . Cyclone Nargis demonstrated that you can deliver effective humanitarian aid. (Agland, *Care* 2009)

The regime, they do things I find completely abhorrent. They are difficult to deal with. But they are not always as bad as the picture that is painted. I find it equally abhorrent that the people outside the country feel the need to "garnish the lily," lie through their teeth, exaggerate. . . . I find that equally obnoxious [and] extremely unhelpful. (Marshall, *ILO* 2009)

A lot of Western media coverage of Myanmar is not fair. (Tumbian, *WV* 2009)

Relative to some other countries, there are restraints here, but there are restraints in other countries as well. If we take the longer term context as well as put it in the context of other third world or more difficult countries, Myanmar is not nearly as much of an anomaly as Western media and policies would lead us to believe. (Tegenfeldt, *Hope* 2009)

Pedersen made a similar argument when he suggested,

There is no doubt that the military leaders are hostile to economic and administrative reforms that would directly weaken their hold on power, and less than enthusiastic about community development and other programs that contravene national notions of development, which lag several decades behind current international thinking. There is no doubt either that both the state and society lack the capacity to absorb and effectively apply large amounts of assistance, or that this capacity will have to be built up gradually ahead of any major new financial commitments. The international aid community, however, is hardly unfamiliar with such obstacles, but has a range of strategies and tools available that are used in other countries with arguably less government commitment to development and less potential for long-term success. (Pedersen 2008, 269–70)

Limited mandates are also a considerable restriction for some organizations. Most organizations face restrictions on partnering with government departments and officials, as previously discussed. Some are also restricted in terms of sectors they are permitted to work within. This is particularly true for multilateral agencies like the UNDP and ILO, whose mandate restrictions mean they work in Myanmar more like INGOs than they would in most other contexts, with programs largely independent of the government.

As a result of these Western restrictions on the humanitarian space, many INGOs that work in Myanmar have found the need for continual advocacy toward their own boards, donors, country offices, and governments, to present their perceptions of the in-country context, as described by the vignette at the start of this chapter. This is becoming somewhat easier, as diplomats, bilateral donors, and organizational boards are becoming increasingly sympathetic toward change in Myanmar. However, the attitude of INGO country managers can be summed up with the statement, "*As long as you can get assistance to the people and do so with integrity, you should do it . . . humanitarian aid must flow*" (Walker, *WVM* 2009). Any politically motivated restrictions on aid to people in need are an anathema to humanitarian ideals.

One respondent suggested that the single greatest challenge in Myanmar has been "*to make this local context understood by the international community*" (Tumbian, *WV* 2009). He explained his strategy of bringing organizational marketing managers and country-desk managers from home offices to Myanmar, so they can go home and communicate the context more effectively within their national offices and with private donors. There is also an antipathy by foreign donors toward funding unregistered LNGOs. Many complain that they are not able to promote what they know and can do "*with glossy brochures like those on the border do, so then donors say they can't support NGOs in-country based on the advocacy from the border"* (Source 20 2009). This further limits both their programs and those of their INGO partners.

Creating Space With Myanmar Domestic Politics

Having said all this, INGOs working in Myanmar certainly have long found working with the Myanmar government restrictive. It is not possible for INGOs to operate in Myanmar without in some way connecting with or gaining approval from the government. Things are improving, but one participant colorfully described it as being like *"dancing with the devil but not holding hands"* (Source 15 2009).

A typical comment was, *"We in NGOs and the UN could do a lot more if we got better access"* (Source 20 2009). The European Commission (CEC 2007) reports that travel restrictions and lack of access to project sites directly led to two of its INGO projects being suspended in 2005. The core of the issue, as one journalist observed, is,

> *The regime believes INGOs are not just there to do a specific task but to organize politically against the regime. That general suspicion, to the point of paranoia, is the key obstacle.* (Source 50 2009)

Myanmar is *"a complex operating environment"* (Massella, *OCHA* 2009) for aid agencies. *"To operate effectively in Myanmar you must be astute politically. You spend a lot of time trying to intuit what the authorities are thinking."* Things are improving but are still not always smooth. However, even under the SPDC operating conditions in Myanmar were not unique, being similar to many other difficult environments: "attempts to register and control NGOs are reminiscent, for example, of Sudan" (Duffield 2008, 35).

INGOs with MOUs devise creative ways around some of the restrictions in their MOUs; Duffield cites an example of an INGO *stretching* its MOU (as he expresses it) by conducting a livelihood project under an MOU for preventative health, arguing it allows people to be able to pay for medical care. Those without MOUs circumvent restrictions through partnerships with LNGOs or joint projects with other INGOs.

Over the past two decades there has been a dramatic increase in access given to INGOs, with both

> *geographical access having increased, as well as the types of sectors and issues being worked on having been expanded . . . that often times is*

not appreciated, particularly by those who have only been around for the last three to five years. (Tegenfeldt, *Hope* 2009)

Access did become a little more restrictive after the removal of Prime Minister Khin Nyunt in 2004; he *"provided space for INGOs to operate in a way that the regulations did not limit operations too significantly"* (Source 31 2009). Until Cyclone Nargis, the process of negotiating an MOU with the government became "more laborious and uncertain" after his removal, but space to operate again expanded after Cyclone Nargis. INGOs noted a tightening and increasing delays between early 2009 until well after the November 2010 elections. Several attributed this to uncertainty and election security more than a deliberate longer-term restriction of the humanitarian space, although it may also have been a backlash from hard-liners who felt that too much had been given away in the access provided after Cyclone Nargis, given the lack of other restrictions surrounding the elections. Access has steadily improved since the inauguration of Thein Sein and the new government.

Almost universally INGOs suggest the most essential factor facilitating access is relationships and trust built with individual officials, at both township and ministry levels. Decision making in government departments is based on personal politics. It all depends on the right relationships with the right officials.

The response you get from one person can be completely different from the response you get from another person. Some are really positive; others are the complete opposite. They are not a coherent group. (Massella, *OCHA* 2009)

Once trust is built with senior officials within a department, INGO staff find they have good access to various people under them (Agland, *Care* 2009). Until then, access can be difficult. These relationships open the door to more formal agreements later.

It's all about relationships. . . . If you have an MOU but don't have the relationship, you can't do anything. If you have the relationship but no MOU, you can do anything. (Griffiths, *TLMI* 2009)

There is no doubt that the government restrictions and all the travel restrictions and everything else have a real impact on the ability people have to operate. . . . But on the ground it really boils down to how good your networks are and your relationships with local authorities. . . . Most effective organizations really invest a lot in getting those local relationships really solid. (Dorning, *Burnet* 2009)

As one INGO manager expressed,

I am not sure that we'd actually do anything very much different to what we are currently doing because, while there are restrictions and so on, it is hard to tell what we might change. . . . I think that the model that we've got is working well. (Source 14 2009)

INGO respondents with the longest association with Myanmar have observed that "*it takes several years to be accepted by officials*" (Walker, *WVM* 2009). Burmese nationals and long-term INGO leaders agree that "*a big drawback in the INGO world is that directors and staff come and stay for two to three years . . . by the time they know enough about the culture and the context, they leave*" (Source 41 2009). Instead they argue INGOs should aim to retain good leaders in-country as long as possible, "*so they build shared experiences and lives with national leaders*" (Walker, *WVM* 2009). It is the strength of the trust within these relationships that has allowed many INGOs the space they have with the Myanmar government to operate.

One other significant observation from the interviews is that larger organizations with higher profile international reputations or significant funding bases appear to be able to negotiate MOUs more quickly and gain wider access. Larger and better-resourced organizations have greater expertise and can more easily demonstrate their humanitarian rather than political motives. While this might be an issue of resources and expertise, it might also be an indicator of status, where organizations that might be termed "higher-status organizations" are granted better access, while smaller organizations with lower status do seem to struggle to negotiate official access to operate in Myanmar (Source 11 2009; Source 14 2009; Source 20 2009; Source 30 2009; Source 21 2009).

Obtaining Funding

Recent announcements of major funding increases have already been noted. However, until very recently heavy restrictions in funding have been one of the major restraints on development effectiveness. Until now international governments and major donors have maintained that "*the necessary preconditions for long-term development are not currently in place in Myanmar,*" as Moore (2009), deputy director general (Asia) for Australia's AusAID program, expressed it. They imply that without political reform, poverty reduction and development efforts are very limited in their impact, at best. That reform, of course, appears to now be underway, and funding is increasing rapidly from most donors apart from the United States. It is, however, coming off a very low base; even after recent increases Myanmar receives only US$8 of international assistance per person annually, compared with US$68 for Laos, US$49 for Cambodia, and US$39 for Vietnam (Carr 2012a). Major foreign donors are still particularly concerned at the government's expenditure on the military and harbor suspicions senior officials divert funds into personal bank accounts. They ask, "*Why should we put more in when they don't?*" (Source 1 2009).

It is therefore not surprising that INGOs, which believe that much poverty reduction *can* be achieved in Myanmar despite the politics, have found funding one of the greatest challenges to working in Myanmar—and found the political conditionality attached to Myanmar's aid funding most frustrating. Many see an injustice inherent in a token high moral ground position being taken with a poor country that is already isolated, where it poses virtually no economic cost to the West (see also Camroux and Egreteau 2009). One Western in-country bilateral donor representative spoke candidly, lamenting the low funding levels offered by both their own government and the wider international community, arguing,

> *Looking through a human rights lens, these guys are not much worse than Laos, Vietnam, Cambodia, even Thailand. The thing that gets under people's skin about Burma when you have been here for a while is, yes, they are bastards—but are they really any worse than any of these other countries we are happily playing with? Some of these are making no attempt at democracy, others just using it for corruption.* (Source 1 2009)

The issue of conditionality on aid, particularly in fragile states, has already been discussed. Many have argued that attempts to impose reform through conditionality are ineffective (e.g., Anderson 2005; Clayton 1994; Santiso 2001) and have argued the need for both increased funding and less conditionality on humanitarian aid to Myanmar (ICG 2008, 2011a; Pedersen 2009; Steinberg 2009; Thant Myint-U 2009b). Nonetheless, significant restrictions on the amount and use of aid in Myanmar are a reality.

Cyclone Nargis brought additional funding, but it also brought many new agencies; both funding and the number of agencies in Myanmar more than doubled during 2008–9. However, that increased funding was for emergency humanitarian needs and fell off quickly while most agencies have remained. On the positive side, one agency reported, *"A lot of donors are now interested in funding work inside the country who have been traditionally only funding the border-related prodemocracy work"* (Dorning, *Burnet* 2009). However, *"INGOs who came in without a solid base of other funding are [in 2009] finding it hard; some are leaving or reducing their office and staff"* (Source 1 2009). Hopefully recent funding increases will alleviate the pressure, but with the increased number of new organizations entering the country and the still very low levels of official development assistance, competition over funding and the funding squeeze are likely to continue for the foreseeable future.

This shortage of funds directly impacts programs. *"You have to cut corners at times . . . you struggle to gain an efficiency that you might gain in other programs with a different level of scale"* (Allan, *Spectrum* 2009).

> *We have never had the long-term stability in our programs to [build participatory and integrated programs] . . . you tend to have scattered projects all over the country, wherever you can get funding . . . you implement a three-year project in one year.* (Agland, *Care* 2009)

Restricted Humanitarian Assistance: Sanctions and Aid

Restricted Humanitarian Assistance

This claim by INGOs, that the greatest restriction on the humanitarian space for interventions alleviating extreme poverty over the past few years has come from Western sanctions and restrictions on aid, is possibly the most contentious of the findings of this research. It is thus worthy of further analysis. This next section will examine this international dimension of the sociopolitical context from the perspectives of international relations theory, development theory, and contemporary political philosophy.

Behind the comments of these INGO leaders is the fact that, despite the Asian constructive engagement, Myanmar's connectedness to the international community and, particularly, international aid flows has remained particularly restricted. Most major donors have remained concerned about excessive military expenditure, macroeconomic policy, poor governance, human rights abuses, and the suppression of democracy.

According to the International Crisis Group (ICG), in 2008, shortly before Cyclone Nargis, Myanmar received the least ODA of any of the United Nations' least developed countries, at just 5 percent of the average assistance given on a per capita basis. This restriction in development assistance appears highly disproportional, especially when contrasted with assistance given to other least developed countries with "similarly repressive governments" that received substantially more aid: Laos twenty-two times more, Sudan nineteen times more, and Zimbabwe seven times more on a per capita basis (ICG 2008, 15). Table 7.1 contrasts ODA levels with GDP for Myanmar with a number of regional and LDC reference countries prior to Cyclone Nargis and the global financial crisis and then again for 2010.

ODA to Myanmar more than doubled in response to Cyclone Nargis, reaching US$10.80 per capita in 2008 (UNDP 2010) and creating an improved environment of development cooperation in Myanmar (Sadandar 2010), as this research has demonstrated. However, this was a temporary,

Table 7.1

Gross Domestic Product and Official Development Assistance Indicators
for Myanmar and Reference Least Developed Countries

	GDP per Capita (PPP US$)		ODA per Capita (US$)		
	2005	2007	2005	2007	2010
Singapore	29,663	40,907	Donor	Donor	Donor
Thailand	8,677	8,135	Donor	Donor	Donor
Indonesia	3,843	3,712	11	27	7
Vietnam	3,071	2,600	23	29	34
Cambodia	2,727	1,802	38	46	52
Laos	2,039	2,165	50	68	67
Myanmar	**1,027**	**904**	**2.9**	**4**	**7**
Sudan	2,083	2,086	51	55	47
Zimbabwe	2,038	—	28	35	59
Congo, Rep	1,262	3,511	362	34	325
Ethiopia	1,055	779	27	29	43

Source. UNDP (2007, 2009); data.worldbank.org.
Note. The 2010 and 2011 UNDP *Human Development Reports* have not been used, as GDI figures have replaced GDP figures, preventing meaningful direct comparison to periods prior to the global financial crisis and Cyclone Nargis.

emergency-response increase. The return to previous levels has been partially offset by smaller, ongoing increases from a number of donor governments, but ODA to Myanmar still remains particularly low in comparison to other least developed countries, rising modestly to US$7 per capita in 2010. The unintended adverse humanitarian impact of such highly restricted aid has been widely observed (see, e.g., Badgley 2004b; Hadar 1998; Holliday 2005, 2008a, 2008b, 2009, 2011b; Horsey 2009; ICG 2002, 2004, 2006, 2008, 2009, 2010b, 2011a; James 2004; Pedersen 2008, 2009, 2010; Seekins 2005; Taylor 2004; Thant Myint-U 2009b).

Restricted aid has been one dimension of the international coercive pressure designed to compel the regime into adopting democratic and human rights reform, as it remains for the United States. It also reflects donor concerns that increasing humanitarian aid may have sent the wrong signals, inadvertently prolonging authoritarian rule and stymieing political change (Source 1 2009). The absence of the rule of law, a lack of administrative capacity, and a number of specific policy shortcomings (such as a lack of property rights) have also been of concern, undermining the macroeconomy to the extent that the preconditions for growth have not been considered to yet be in place (Moore 2009). Thus donors have implicitly questioned Myanmar's absorptive capacity for development assistance and the probability of fungibility.

The argument in favor of sanctions, from a humanitarian perspective, relies on the idea that the formal and informal economy are largely independent of each other, that the poor primarily derive their incomes from the informal sector, and that the informal sector is not dependent on foreign investment or markets (Burma Campaign 2004; Asia Society 2010a). It therefore argues that sanctions targeted at the formal economy have minimal impact on the vast majority of Myanmar's people. Oehlers (2004) argues that these structural and institutional characteristics of the Burmese economy make sanctions an effective device against the military regime, without causing harm to the poor:

> It may reasonably be presumed the negative consequences arising from sanctions will have greatest impact on the military and its closest associates. Far from the blunt and indiscriminate tool it is often accused of being, in the case of Burma at least, sanctions appear to be surprisingly well targeted and capable of exerting considerable pressure on the military regime. (Oehlers 2004, 43)

It is significant to note that Oehlers recognizes this is a presumption. Certainly, the majority of the poor are primarily connected to the informal economy, and it is domestic policy not economic sanctions that are the greatest immediate cause of the economic difficulty faced by most of the poor. However, the level of poverty and the depth of multidimensional deprivation mean that even a marginal impact on the poor will have a significant effect on their well-being, and this assessment ignores the fact that many poor do also connect with the formal economy. In a command economy, what hurts the leadership hurts the people.

World Vision, for example, found that the May 2003 imposition of further US sanctions had the largest impact on factory workers in the textile industry (James 2004). US and European sanctions have "significantly hampered growth in export sectors such as agriculture, fishery, and garments, as well as tourism, which are a crucial source of jobs and income for millions of impoverished families" (Pedersen 2010, 116). Taylor (2004) argues that sanctions have created an economic malaise that has deepened the poverty of most people in the country, while weakening the prospects of sustainable democratization and making resolution of the fundamental issues more difficult through postponement and polarization.

As Moore (2011) suggests, the crucial questions are "How do we make the welfare of the people our main priority? And would an increase in international assistance lend too much legitimacy to the regime?" Australia and the European Union are repositioning aid levels quite differently, but the United States continues to be concerned about the need for coercive pressure, and the signals significant change in policy could send.

International Relations Analysis: Sanctions as Norm Socialization

Risse and Sikkink (1999) offer a theory of the role of sanctions in socializing norm-violating states to international norms, illustrating their model with a discussion of socialization to human rights norms. This theory fits closely with the Western response to Myanmar and offers useful analysis of sanctions policy.

According to their model, socialization pressure is triggered when a particularly flagrant violation of an international norm activates a transnational advocacy network that succeeds in putting the norm-violating state on the international agenda. Such a transnational advocacy network, they suggest, will typically attempt to shame the norm-violating state by labeling it as a "pariah" state that does not belong to the community of civilized nations, then begin documenting and publicizing human rights violations.

Such a transnational advocacy network began to coalesce against Myanmar after the brutal crackdown on demonstrations in 1988, particularly when Suu Kyi was arrested in 1989. It was solidified when the NLD won the 1990 elections but was subject to mass arrest rather than a transfer of power. Advocates quickly labeled Myanmar an uncivilized "pariah" state, highlighting human rights abuses and calling for sanctions.

According to the Risse and Sikkink model, the initial reaction of most norm-violating states to such overt confrontation is to refuse to accept the applicability of international human rights norms to their case and to challenge international jurisdiction. SLORC did exactly this. In response, transnational advocacy networks almost always advocate material pressure, from targeting the key interests of regime officials to making aid conditional on human rights performance. Regimes vary greatly in their vulnerability to this sort of pressure, based largely on the strength of their desire to maintain good standing with the states applying the pressure.

Several Western governments responded to Suu Kyi's arrest by severing or downgrading diplomatic links and slashing aid, particularly budgetary support assistance (Pedersen 2008). The US Congress passed the Customs and Trade Act, enabling the president to impose sanctions, although then-president Bush declined to do so. Suu Kyi was awarded the Sakharov Prize and the Nobel Peace Prize in 1991, to enhance the legitimacy of the opposition. The United Nations appointed a special rapporteur for human rights in Burma in 1992, and the UN General Assembly and Human Rights Council began passing resolutions against Burma/Myanmar. The response from the regime was to explain its need to ensure order and security in the face of foreign and ethnic threats to national security, to claim that international pressure was in violation of the UN principle of state sovereignty, and to talk about Western hypocrisy and the right to development (Ware 2010). Such a response fits closely with Risse and Sikkink's model, although several authorities see an irony in using sanctions to attempt to isolate the regime:

> It is ironic that as the regime seeks once more to disengage from the rest of the world that the world considers disengagement in the form of sanctions as a weapon for change in Burma. (Perry 2007, 175)

> The irony is that western threats feed into the founding ideology of the military regime, which needs external enemies to justify its harsh rule and divert attention from its economic and other failures. (Pedersen 2010, 116)

Increased pressure from the transnational advocacy network is aimed at enlarging the space for domestic groups, amplifying their demands in the international arena. This can result in a backlash and further repression against activists; however, further repression is costly to the government in terms of both domestic and international legitimacy. Where further repression occurs, Risse and Sikkink suggest, transnational advocacy will increasingly call for donor countries to make foreign aid contingent on human rights.

Again this fits the Myanmar saga closely. Suu Kyi was released from house arrest in 1995, but she was issued a travel ban, which she repeatedly defied, provoking confrontations. Concerted advocacy stepped up pressure in response. Aid budgets were further slashed, and the US Congress debated the Free Burma Act, which called for the imposition of stiff economic and trade sanctions against both Burma and any countries that traded with or provided aid to Burma (a clause later dropped). When the act passed with amendments in 1997, President Clinton quickly imposed an arms embargo, a ban on new investment, the suspension of bilateral aid, withdrawal of trade privileges, visa restrictions on senior leaders, and a veto of any loan or financial support by international financial institutions (Oehlers 2004). The European Union (EU) followed the same year with an arms embargo, withdrawal of trade privileges, a visa ban on senior leaders, and the suspension of aid.

The impact of the initial 1998 crackdown and the abortive election of 1990 on aid flows to Myanmar and then the further impact of the 1997 bans by the United States and European Union were immediate and dramatic, as shown clearly in Figure 7.1. Sanctions were further tightened in 2003, in the wake of what American diplomats and the NLD claim to have been a deliberate ambush on Suu Kyi and her supporters by the regime, and after which she was taken into "protective custody" (Seekins 2005). The United States banned all imports "mined, made, grown or assembled" in Myanmar, together with halting all US dollar transactions in and out of the country (Oehlers 2004). The European Union, Japan, Canada, and Australia also reassessed their positions. However, humanitarian assistance had already been minimalized to such an extent that the additional sanctions caused little further effect on the already low ODA. The spike in ODA for 2008–9 relates to emergency assistance after Cyclone Nargis rather than an ongoing increase in ODA, and levels are currently back to around US$7.50 per person annually.

Returning to Risse and Sikkink's model, their most important contribution is the observation that as international pressures continue to escalate, the first steps toward institutionalizing international norms into domestic practice are often initially intended only as cosmetic tactical concessions to pacify criticism rather than steps to institute real reform. However, by changing their discursive practice, they unintentionally open greater space for opposition and

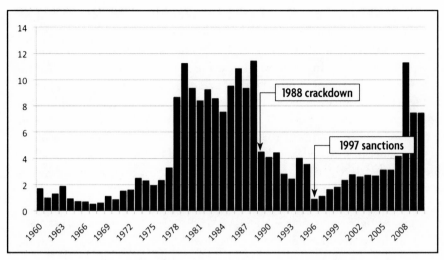

Figure 7.1   Official development assistance (ODA) to Myanmar 1960–2010 in US$ per capita. *Source.* World Bank, data.worldbank.org.

reform. The first aim of transnational socialization pressure should therefore be to force the target regime to offer concessions that may initially be only tactical rather than sincere reforms.

Many argue that sanctions against Myanmar have lacked coercive force, not being universally adopted (e.g., Holliday 2005; Pedersen 2008; Steinberg 2010a; Taylor 2004; Thant Myint-U 2009b; Thant Myint-U in McDermid 2009). The significant contribution of Risse and Sikkink is recognition that the role of sanctions should not be about coercion at all but be about socialization and that the indicators of success should initially be tactical concessions and incremental change, not radical reform.

Klotz (1996) elaborates this distinction between coercion and socialization, arguing that coercion relies on threatening state survival. Since sanctions anywhere are generally incapable of inflicting that high a cost on the target state, he finds that sanctions are almost always an ineffective instrument of coercion. Socialization, on the other hand, seeks to promote the desire for acceptance within the international community. Sanctions, he argues, can sometimes do this well. Klotz concludes that what is essential is not that pressure be applied comprehensively by all international actors, as is often argued, but that pressure is both targeted against key regime interests and that it quickly adjusts in response to concessions and other decision making or actions within the target state.

It is hard to see how funding interventions that bypass government officials to deliver assistance directly to the extremely poor via UN and INGO agencies constitutes a key interest of the regime and therefore why such aid should ever have been included within the socialization pressure against Myanmar. This aside, decades of international pressure have now resulted in significant reform, culminating in the 2010 elections, the new president and quasi-civilian government, and now the election of Aung San Suu Kyi and members of the NLD in by-elections in April 2012. Whether these are the result of Western sanctions, Asian engagement, or internal drivers of change is debatable. Nonetheless, these clearly do constitute significant concessions to the domestic opposition, if not the international community.

Other significant concessions have been also achieved, including cooperation in regional forums addressing HIV/AIDS and human trafficking (Moore 2011), declaration of forced labor as illegal with some effort made to enforce this (Pedersen 2010), and policy changes in areas such as drug control, disability, and sustainable forestry (Allan 2010).

Risse and Sikkink's model, and Klotz's argument, therefore insist that socialization pressure must readjust quickly in response to these concessions and the ongoing reforms in the country, something the INGOs in this fieldwork strongly advocate. The socialization model requires markers of improved international social acceptability be exchanged for reform.

Development Theory: Competing Political and Apolitical Approaches

The same debate emerges if we analyze the issue through a development theory rather than an international lens. Underlying this analysis is an altercation between contrasting political and apolitical approaches to international development, accentuated in the case of Myanmar by the highly strained and politicized context. A paper by Nelson (2007) characterizes these as an approach motivated by Millennium Development Goals (MDGs) and a rights-based approach (RBA). Nelson sees these two approaches as fundamentally conceptually different.

> The MDGs mobilize the classic development sector tools. . . . The MDGs are a careful restatement of poverty-related development challenges, in language that avoids reference to rights. . . . The RBA rests . . . on internationally recognized human rights standards and principles, to which governments and donors are obliged to adhere. . . . Rights-based approaches . . . tie development to the rhe-

torical and legal power of internationally recognized human rights. (Nelson 2007, 2041)

It is this clash of understandings of the nature and resolution of poverty that lies at the heart of the disagreement between international development approaches to Myanmar.

The RBA has been termed "empowerment through external pressure" (Nyamu-Musembi and Cornwall 2004). It seeks "to analyse inequalities which lie at the heart of development problems and redress discriminatory practices and unjust distributions of power that impede development progress" (OHCHR 2006, 15). When applied, it enables people to recognize their rights as enshrined in the *Universal Declaration of Human Rights*, works to build their capacity to claim these rights, and works with the state, as the primary duty-bearer, to strengthen state capacity to respond and be accountable in fulfilling these human rights (Nyamu-Musembi and Cornwall 2004). The RBA uses recourse to international law to guarantee "a protected space where the elite cannot monopolize development processes, policies and programs" (OHCHR 2006) and as such is explicitly political, putting politics at the heart of development (Nyamu-Musembi and Cornwall 2004). Of some concern, however, is the question of who exactly is empowered for which rights, by what "external pressure," applied by whom.

By contrast, the MDG approach insists on political neutrality for development assistance with a focus on poverty alleviation, allocated on a needs basis, targeting assistance to the most poor and vulnerable. Nelson observes that the Millennium Declaration and the MDGs were deliberately constituted in apolitical terms. An expectation that humanitarian poverty alleviation be apolitical is likewise brought out by many others. For example, the Brazilian ambassador to the United Nations noted to the General Assembly in 1991,

> Humanitarian activities . . . must by definition be disassociated from all shades of political consideration. They are, by definition, neutral and impartial. . . . The secret of effectiveness in the humanitarian field is that even when nations disagree on everything else, even when they clash, they can still agree that . . . suffering must be relieved. (cited in Minear and Weiss 1993, 24)

Baulch (2006) argues donors should allocate aid based on the level of poverty and the ability to make an impact "in accordance with the priorities set out by the MDGs" rather than on political considerations. Alesina and

Dollar (2000, 33) express similar concern that too often aid is not given in response "to the variables that make aid effective in reducing poverty . . . [but] is dictated as much by political and strategic considerations as by the economic needs and policy performance of the recipients."

While some argue the two approaches are entirely consistent (ACFID 2009; OHCHR 2006; UNDP 2003a, 29), others recognize only a "limited convergence between the two agendas" (Alston 2005, 761). To Nelson (2007), the inherent conflict is between the key agents mobilized and policy recommendations espoused by the two approaches. The MDGs were couched in strictly humanitarian terms that seek to make developing country governments, donors, UN agencies, and NGOs all mutually accountable, with a focus on international cooperation to address the issues created by poverty, and without any inherent reference to cause or blame. The RBA, by contrast, focuses on national governments as primary duty-bearers, seeks to empower populations to make substantive claims against these governments, and is couched in international legal terms. The MDGs want the best-equipped actor to address specific poverty needs, drawing on best practice international development to meet the most severe needs as a priority. The RBA seeks to reform systemic causes of poverty by demanding change of political power structures.

As already noted, Duffield (2008) argues that aid agencies create space to operate in Myanmar through strict adherence to these humanitarian principles and constant reassurances to all sides that they are adhering strictly to the principle of apolitical humanitarian assistance. This finding is strongly borne out by these fieldwork responses, where deviation from apolitical neutrality could threaten the operating space granted by the Myanmar government. With neutrality, however, aid agencies are confident they could substantially deliver more aid to effectively alleviate more of the suffering they see, even if continuing to bypass the government. They thus argue the greatest restriction on the humanitarian space is caused by the international community and therefore that humanitarian funding (and mandates) should be significantly increased.

Political Philosophy: The Demands of Global Justice
Holliday (2011a) observes what may be considered a flaw in this logic, namely, that a new idea of humanitarianism has emerged since the end of the cold war that denies the old principles of impartiality, apoliticality, and neutrality and is instead ambitious to engage politically to redress the root causes of injustice.

> In a post-Cold-War era of humanitarian engagement driven by generic notions of global justice, [Myanmar] has for years looked to

be a prime candidate for political reform, and the main task facing the rest of the world has long seemed crystal clear: helping to make it happen. (Holliday 2011a, 2)

Holliday therefore explores theories of contemporary political philosophy and global justice in relation to Myanmar, concluding that "a *prima facie* case for external engagement with Myanmar is readily made" based on the obligations of our shared humanity (Holliday 2011a, 145), but finds it far less clear exactly how such engagement should be undertaken and what issues specifically it needs to address.

To analyze any such foreign intervention, Holliday (2011a) proposes a typology of possible interventions by various actors, suggesting they may involve expressive or aggressive pressure, and consensual or belligerent engagement, by either state or civil actors. These possibilities are summarized in Table 7.2.

Since 1988, Western state and civil actors have primarily responded to the Myanmar regime with a range of both expressive and aggressive pressure (diplomacy, advocacy, sanctions, and boycotts), with restricted consensual engagement through limited bilateral assistance and INGO engagement. However, the old regime was primarily concerned with foreign investment, trade, and financial sanctions, not humanitarian aid, so this form of consensual engagement had little bargaining power. Asian regional neighbors, on the other hand, have primarily acted through consensual corporate engagement and (in some cases) bilateral assistance and limited expressive diplomatic pressure. This has thus had marginally more impact.

Holliday argues that in determining an appropriate response to the global justice demands of contemporary political philosophy, insiders must play a leading role, and the dismissal of the views of regional neighbors such as China, India, and ASEAN is "worrying"; their voice should be "an essential

Table 7.2

Holliday's (2011a) Proposed Typology of Engagement Options for External Actors

	State Actors	**Civil Actors**
Expressive pressure	Diplomacy	Advocacy
Aggressive pressure	Sanctions	Boycotts
Consensual engagement	Bilateral assistance	INGO/corporate engagement
Belligerent engagement	Military intervention	Cross-border terrorism

moral and practical precondition for external engagement with Myanmar"
(Holliday 2011a, 142).

The conclusion of his extensive analysis of the demands of contemporary
political philosophy and global justice is to call for increased expressive pressure (diplomacy and advocacy), a readjustment and evaluation of the extensive
repertoire of aggressive pressures applied by Western powers against Myanmar, and an increase in consensual engagement by the West—particularly an
increase in INGO engagement. He expresses great concern at the imbalance
in which so little Western consensual engagement has been attempted. While
ascribing this imbalance mainly to "the difficulties put in the way of internal
action by the Myanmar authorities" (Holliday 2011a, 164), he advocates a
major increase in effort be given to such intervention, "led from the grassroots
through civic action, undertaken . . . by UN agencies and INGOs . . . a recast-
ing of major power engagement" (Holliday 2011a, 172). This field research
concurs that despite serious restrictions applied by the Myanmar government,
there is considerable scope for increased INGO consensual engagement with
the regime to be effective.

Challenging Western Responses

A wealth of scholarly research has thus arisen to suggest that humanitarian aid
to Myanmar should be significantly expanded, in line with the calls made by
INGOs. From a sanctions perspective, the range of tactical concessions made
by the regime requires a repositioned response, and humanitarian assistance
offers the best option to do that in a manner that supports reform without otherwise strengthening the regime. From a humanitarian perspective, whether
one ascribes to an apolitical or actively political humanitarian approach, development theory and contemporary political philosophy both call for increased
intervention in the form of development assistance and cooperation.

Steinberg, for example, argues,

> The international community has been more concerned about the
> impact of political repression on human rights than on any human
> rights issues arising from endemic extreme poverty, yet the latter is
> equally important and is something the international community
> may both have had a hand in contributing to, and the power to
> help address, at least to some extent. (Steinberg 2010b, 3)

The opportunity now exists to acknowledge domestic political reform by
increasing assistance to the poor and vulnerable, in a way that reduces conflict

in the international political relationships. Australia and the European Union are leading the way, and so long as reform continues the United States should quickly follow. As Pedersen (2010, 117) expresses it, we now have the opportunity to redress the fact that "the Burmese people for the past 20 years have been denied the international assistance normally provided to the world's most vulnerable." "It would be a massive wasted opportunity if the West failed to engage with this new government, to assess their willingness to take the country in a different direction, and to convince them that improved relations are possible if they do so" (TNI 2010, 10).

It has been argued for some time that Western policy toward Myanmar, particularly the US sanctions policy, has been "too crude, blunt, and one dimensional" (Holliday 2005) and needs to develop a more nuanced approach. The Asia Society's (2010a, 36) recommendation paper to the Obama administration argues that "there are now many more opportunities to engage effectively in humanitarian and community development programs than there were in the past" and that aid agencies now have productive relationships with mid- and lower-level civil servants. While opposing budgetary support for the regime, the Asia Society recommends significantly increased humanitarian funding, as well as capacity building of the technical skills of civil servants, particularly in ministries involved in economic management, and the governance skills of elected politicians. If adopted these would constitute significant new directions in US policy, bringing it far closer to the Australian position.

Aung San Suu Kyi and the NLD initially took a hard line on sanctions and a cautious stand on aid:

> It makes little political or economic sense to give aid without trying to address the circumstances that render aid ineffectual. No amount of material goods and technical know-how will compensate for human irresponsibility and viciousness. (Suu Kyi 1995a, 245)

Nonetheless, the NLD position on aid has always been nuanced enough to reject aid for the government while supporting strictly humanitarian aid (ICG 2002), and the NLD claims it has never opposed purely humanitarian aid (Suu Kyi 2010). The recent change of policy by Australia and the European Union come with Suu Kyi's full endorsement. "Poverty has emerged as the most acutely felt constraint on human rights for the majority of people across the country" (Pedersen 2009, 2), while "aid has, arguably, emerged as our best tool for promoting better governance and human rights in Burma" (Pedersen 2009, 1).

Further significant expansion of the humanitarian space through increased funding and mandates, as the INGOs in this field research call for, expresses sensitivity to both the domestic and the international sociopolitical context. Such a move offers the opportunity to alleviate extreme poverty, test the sincerity of the new government's reform, and strengthen the ability of local authorities to provide basic needs, while socializing officials to the benefits of cooperation with international actors and capacity building civil society, starting a process of bottom-up democratization.

8

Conclusions and Recommendations

[The international community should] educate itself to the complexities that are Burma/Myanmar and some possible avenues for alleviating its problems. So when the time comes, and it surely will, outside communities will be able to appreciate the nuanced issues and step forward with the sensitivity necessary to help intelligently, in contrast to many less effective responses in the past. We on the periphery should minimally follow the physicians' code: do no harm. (Steinberg 2010b, xxxi)

Steinberg was right. The time has come. This is a critical juncture, and sensitivity to the context is now more important than ever. As reform gains momentum and the door of opportunity opens, what Myanmar needs are people from the outside who are willing to help and who "appreciate the nuanced issues" sufficiently to "step forward with the sensitivity necessary to help intelligently."

This book has examined key issues involved in context-sensitive development through a case study exploring the manner in which INGOs operate in Myanmar. Myanmar offers an interesting and illustrative example for this study, being a difficult political context for development due not to collapse of state institutions but to international isolation and internal conflict. The Myanmar context involves significant postcolonial sensitivities and multiple political actors, each with their own competing strategic concerns. Myanmar presents a confluence of significant need with restricted access and resourcing, limited mandates, a suspicious authoritarian government, and deep reservations by international donors and governments based in part on shallow understandings and misconceptions. It therefore offers a very useful case study by which to begin filling the gap in the existing literature on the roles INGOs and international agencies need to play in adapting global principles, approaches, and strategies to specific and often complex sociopolitical contexts.

This research has examined how INGOs contextualize their operations and projects out of sensitivity to the sociopolitical context they face in this so-called "pariah state" in order to maximize development effectiveness in Myanmar and to help further define the role INGOs and international agencies need to play as actors in participatory context-sensitive development more generally.

Sociopolitical Context-Sensitive Development

INGO Roles in Context-Sensitive Development: Extension of Participatory Development Approach

The results of the field research, presented in Part 3, clearly demonstrate the significant impact the sociopolitical context of Myanmar has had on the implementation of international best practice and global development approaches in order to maximize development effectiveness within a context. This book has documented the contextualization INGOs have made to interventions in local communities, in relationships with other stakeholders, and in expanding the humanitarian space.

Not all INGOs are as equally sensitive to sociopolitical context. The research outcomes presented in Part 3 represent those approaches that the broader INGO community has assessed as being most effective within this context, based on several separate stages in assessing effectiveness. First, interview participants were asked to self-assess the effectiveness of the approaches they talked about during the interview. While there are serious limitations to self-assessment, it is significant that there were several instances of INGOs providing an honest assessment that this is what they are doing, but it is not being very effective or does not appear to be working well.

To address personal bias, self-assessments of effectiveness were correlated with snowball sampling referrals. At the end of each interview, participants were asked to refer other organizations or individual development professionals they perceived to be good examples of effective context-sensitive development programs in Myanmar. The frequency of referral to particular organizations and individual leaders was taken as a proxy measure of effective context-sensitive approaches. Findings based on these self-assessments and referrals were then confirmed using the Delphi method, in which preliminary findings were presented to a forum of INGO country representatives, with feedback and discussion following. Selected follow-up interviews were also undertaken. In this way, less effective approaches were discarded, and approaches perceived by the INGO community in Myanmar to be the most effective and context-sensitive are the ones that have been documented.

An extension of current models of the roles that different development actors play in sociopolitical context-sensitive development was proposed at the end of chapter 2, based on a combination of the participatory development model and social change theory. Figure 2.1 diagrams the conclusion that each actor needs empowerment to innovate within the level of context at which he or she is embedded but should primarily act as facilitators to empower those embedded at more local levels of context. Actors should step in to assist with contextualized decision making at a lower level only when other sociopolitical factors prohibit the empowerment of these actors. Thus local communities should act as primary decision makers at the micro-level of development, local NGO or civil society partners at meso-levels, and INGOs at more macro-levels.

The most complex factors requiring sensitivity in many contexts are cultural. "Culture-sensitive development" has therefore been discussed at length over the past several decades, with the participatory development model providing the conceptual basis for empowering communities and LNGO or civil society actors embedded within the local knowledge systems to direct highly context-sensitive decision making. Another factor commonly creating great complexity for development is conflict, whether continuing violence or immediate postconflict situations. In the most extreme cases, these "fragile" states manifest as "failed" states. The issues are highly political, and the literature demands great context-sensitivity to this sociopolitical context by the international agency, not just by relying on the local knowledge and participation of local partners. However, apart from manifestly conflict or failed-state contexts, little has been documented about the role and type of sensitivity required of the international agency in sensitivity to complex sociopolitical factors at this more meso-macro level. Sensitivity to context by international agencies is not well documented.

The significant innovation of the extended participatory model presented in this book has been to conceptualize INGOs as composed of two discrete actors: in-country INGO staff who have a field orientation, and INGO head office staff with a policy, branding, and global practice orientation. Tension between these two sets of actors in most INGOs is clearly drawn in the literature but usually examined from an organizational management perspective. This book has taken this distinction and applied it to the issue of empowerment for participatory development, concluding that much of this tension is derived from the neglect of discussion of INGO roles in contextualization in the development literature.

This extended model therefore suggests that context-sensitive development requires significant empowerment of INGO in-country staff by INGO head offices to facilitate their innovation, based on local knowledge of in-country sociopolitical factors in the same manner as empowerment of local communities and partners is emphasized by the participatory-empowerment model. In effect, this extension conceptualizes postcolonial sensitivities and national–international power dynamics as forms of conflict, significant toward development effectiveness even if remaining nonviolent. INGO in-country staff are the actors embedded in such a national–international context who need empowerment to act and make decisions within their spheres of insider participation.

Context-sensitive development therefore requires the empowerment of senior in-country INGO staff to gain in-depth understanding of the political, cultural, and historical context and the decision-making ability to deviate from organizational norms and approaches as required to make the most contextual responses. It requires their empowerment both to innovate context-sensitive solutions to complex stakeholder relations and to innovate context-sensitive ways to facilitate the innovation of communities and local partners. This empowerment of INGO in-country staff must be sufficient to overcome the normalizing forces within large organizations, often manifesting within INGOs through things like monitoring, evaluation, and reporting procedures, as well as the rotation of staff on short-term contracts.

The variation in effectiveness and context-sensitivity reported by different INGOs during this fieldwork research suggests different levels of such empowerment by the different organizations. It is notable that the personnel most commonly recommended during the snowball sampling were commonly those who had been in the country longest and had the deepest historical, political, and cultural understanding. Many, however, had been forced to change organizations in order to stay within the country after contract periods had expired. This suggests that facilitating deeper understanding of the context and culture by senior national and foreign in-country staff is an important key to empowering all INGO in-country staff to innovate and facilitate more context-sensitively and suggests expatriate INGO managers should remain in-country longer.

However, one of the reasons the participatory development model advocates the devolution of responsibility for contextualization to local communities and partners is the propensity for the power relations inherent in the

INGO–LNGO and INGO–community relationship to undermine their empowerment and decision making. Further empowerment of INGO in-country staff poses the risk of INGOs reasserting control over local development, at the expense of the empowerment of local partners and communities. There remains, therefore, a need for greater theorization and discussion around the limits on the role of INGOs in innovation, along the lines called for by Radcliffe (2006b), to ensure maximal empowerment of both local partners and communities *and* INGO in-country staff.

Extension of Conflict-Sensitive Development: Importance of Historically Informed Understandings

This book has also explored the relevance of conflict-sensitive development ideas to Myanmar, finding in particular that firmly grounding development in a historically informed in-depth understanding of the sociopolitical context, as emphasized in the literature, is extremely relevant to Myanmar. The Conflict Sensitivity consortium (2004) defines conflict as "two or more parties [who] believe that their interests are incompatible, express hostile attitudes or take action that damages other parties' ability to pursue their interests." Most conflict is thus not currently violent.

Conflict-sensitive development recognizes that development has the capacity to contribute proactively to conflict prevention and peace building if the root causes of conflict are understood and explicitly addressed, while careless development can exacerbate conflict by fueling long-held fears and provoking unintended negative reactions. The relationships between the Myanmar government and both the democratic opposition and the ethnic minorities are both clearly marred by substantial conflict. However, tension in the relationship between the international community and actors within Myanmar also require a conflict-sensitive approach, with hostility between the international community and the Myanmar regime often expressed by efforts toward regime change and stubborn isolation, respectively. In that sense, this research has extended the application of conflict-sensitive development ideas to an internationally isolated state, a so-called "pariah state," by enlarging the context to embrace the conflict with the international community. The international community, particularly the West, should be seen not as an impartial mediator but as a political actor within a significant, ongoing conflict.

Sensitivity to context requires understanding historical and contemporary sociopolitical factors in depth, as well as the interaction between them and development interventions. It requires acting on this understanding in ways that either align with these factors or always keep them clearly in mind, respecting the views and processes embodied by them, including these national and international political tensions. It must therefore commence with a detailed analysis of the context, its causes, all actors, and their dynamic interaction. Interventions must be based on an in-depth understanding of the political, economic, sociocultural, and historical context and the structural and proximate causes of conflict, including the triggers provoking fears and reactionary responses.

A thorough examination of the historical origins of the conflicted politics in and surrounding Myanmar identified three major historical narratives contributing significantly to the values and strategic concerns of the major contemporary actors. These narratives relate to major historical timeframes and continue as residues, as it were, resonating within and helping to shape all sides of the contemporary sociopolitical context. These narratives are (1) traditional ideology and values about power, rulership, and political legitimacy derived from the patterns of the precolonial, monarchical period; (2) postcolonial sensitivities and security fears aggravated by the colonial experience and history of interaction with the West; and (3) the enduring impact of the political and economic crises of the nationalist struggle for independence, WWII, and the subsequent civil war.

Regimes of the past two decades (and beyond) have acted out of a polity derived in large part from traditional Burman ideology about power, rulership, and political legitimacy, ideas that were the central organizing patterns of monarchical rule prior to colonialism. These values were described in this research in terms of seven perceptions about power and political legitimacy that still resonate in polity today. While most readily observable today in the actions of traditional elements within the military elite, they are also often evident throughout the contemporary social structure. These perceptions include zero-sum ideas about personalized, centralized power; the importance of controlling or eliminating rivals; and the legitimacy derived from demonstrating order and control, as well as nondependence on external powers. These perceptions suggest development approaches that are more likely to be resisted and others that may gain ready acceptance. They highlight, for example, that advocacy and the capacity building of state institutions with independent powers are likely to be resisted by some until there has been time for a significant shift in mind-set. They also suggest, however, that political leadership has a moral responsibility for reformation and provision and therefore that most regime officials almost certainly have intrinsic political and personal motivations favoring provision of welfare, poverty alleviation, and development under the right circumstances. A well-thought-through constructive engagement strategy is therefore likely to have considerable success, as indeed we are increasingly seeing, even with those for whom traditional zero-sum perceptions of power continue to dominate.

The colonial experience and history of interaction with the West has been a thorny issue, fueling distrust of the West by many military elite today. The form of colonial administration, as well as the approach to ethnic politics and economic development that offered little benefit to the Burmese people, underscored the fierce Burmese priority on independence from foreign domination and fanned ethnic differences into almost intractable issues. The economic crisis and violent ethnic-civil conflict at independence only exacerbated these and cemented the leading role of an authoritarian military apparatus. Foreign support for communist and ethnic rebellions inflamed Burman fears of foreign intervention and created a siege mentality that still widely persists within the strategic concerns of the military hierarchy.

Conflict-sensitive development seeks to ensure "human security," defined as freedom from both fear and want, and thus seeks to reduce the reasons for fear. Conflict-sensitive development requires consolidation of relationships between actors, and strengthening of institutions capable of containing and transforming conflict. The literature shows that agencies working in conflict areas need to focus on building and sustaining constructive relationships between actors and focus on addressing political and socioeconomic inequalities and also shows that capture of development by one actor undermines effectiveness.

These narratives suggest that some development approaches, such as a strongly rights-based approach led by Western agencies, are likely to provoke postcolonial reactions and are unlikely to be fruitful without significant improvement in the relationship between the regime and the international community. They also suggest that in such a contested context in which the international community is also partially implicated, blaming the current political, economic, or humanitarian situation solely on governance failures by the regime is highly provocative. A more sympathetic examination of the complexity of the political and economic trauma within the country should evoke a less self-righteous approach, which this research into the approach of INGOs in Myanmar has demonstrated to be far more conducive to evoking change.

This research has shown that a deep understanding of historical factors such as these that have shaped the fears, sensitivities, and notions of the state held by the different political actors offers significant explanatory power about approaches that provoke negative reactions and effective alternative development approaches.

Igboemeka (2005) found in her study of the perceptions of development agencies about aid effectiveness in Myanmar that external actors do not recognize or reflect in-country understandings of the context sufficiently well and that a more thorough understanding of the challenging sociopolitical context is required by all actors. This research has verified that insufficient analysis of the sociopolitical dynamics and conflicting ideology significantly undermines development effectiveness.

How INGOs Operate Context-Sensitively in Myanmar

This research has drawn out many of the key adaptations INGOs make to this sociopolitical context, particularly by those responding conflict- and context-sensitively to the sorts of dynamics and factors outlined. It thus documents INGO context-sensitive development implemented to improve effectiveness within Myanmar. The contextualization described by INGO participants relates directly to restrictions stemming from this conflicted domestic and international politics, particularly to Myanmar government polity and problems within the international community's approach toward the country.

Context-Sensitive INGO Development in Communities

INGOs contextualize their development activities within local communities in Myanmar primarily by tweaking and intensifying effort toward a number of key outcomes, rather than by limiting community empowerment. This is a significant finding given the authoritarian and highly restrictive governance that has been widely considered by those outside the country to be a severely limiting factor. Broadly speaking, context-sensitive INGO development places additional emphasis on highly participatory development, creating a process to overcome not-insignificant obstacles of fear and skepticism and allowing a greater timeline to elicit genuine involvement. It seeks approval and involvement of local officials and the elite, while safeguarding against capture by such powerful groups through very deliberate emphasis on equity issues. It therefore directly addresses power imbalances based on a diverse range of marginalizing factors, including gender, ethnicity, religion, political affiliation, and age, and seeks transformation in the way in which people see each other, building social cohesion and developing community consensus decision-making processes. Sensitivity to the local context thus involves efforts at peace building, at building social capital, and in conflict-sensitive development.

Highly participatory development in this format is seen as very relevant and effective in Myanmar, perhaps even more so than in many other contexts.

The end goal of many INGOs in community participatory development is long-term local sustainability by capacity building the emergence of village-level community-based organizations. However, to "do no harm" most INGOs have felt the need to help these emerging local civil groups to remain in co-operative relationship with officials, depoliticizing community-level development. Most INGOs therefore have taken on most advocacy with regional- and national-level officials themselves. In this sense, INGOs have only recently begun to develop active citizenship, in terms of empowering communities to advocate with authorities on their own, concluding that it was not possible or desirable before now.

INGO leaders also felt development must take the people's religion particularly seriously, so while often related to division and conflict, opportunities to employ it as an avenue of strengthening both bonding and bridging social capital should be utilized. They therefore advocate deliberate inclusion of local FBOs, religious leaders, and religious institutions in community development and in capacity-building work.

INGO leaders who have been in the country longer also highlight the importance a personal fluency in the Burmese language provides and thus advocate much longer terms for senior appointments by INGOs to the country, with a budget to become fluent in the language and to learn the history and culture before taking on their role.

Context-Sensitivity in Stakeholder Relations

INGOs likewise approach working with other development stakeholders, including civil society, local NGOs, officials, and other INGOs, quite differently in Myanmar than they would in most other countries, having found the need to limit or seriously adapt many of these activities because of the conflicted macro-level sociopolitical context.

Contextualization in these interactions has been explored in this book through the development approaches of partnership, capacity building, advocacy, a rights-based approach, and accountability. It was shown that after long being suppressed, "informal" civil society has become quite strong in Myanmar over recent years. The need to partner with and build the capacity of this sector is widely recognized within the INGO community; however, efforts are complicated, as much of this civil society is unregistered (and has been difficult to register until now) and lacks both the scale and the organizational capacity required for effective partnership.

Globally, partnership and capacity development usually also emphasize work with government departments and harmonization with government objectives. However, partnership with officials has been heavily restricted by both domestic and international politics, and so capacity development even of local officials is rarely undertaken in any significant manner. New opportunities are just emerging as Australia has led the way with new announcements of a desire to support capacity building of government agencies and a willingness to engage in much greater development coordination. Most INGOs speak of the need for such civil service capacity development, and where cooperative work has been attempted, those involved speak highly of the outcome.

A rights-based approach to development, defined as publicly holding the government to account for human rights by a public educated in their rights, is inherently political. The government's domination of the political space in Myanmar has therefore meant such an approach has not been effective in this format and has not been considered the most effective approach by many INGOs in Myanmar. It remains a contentious question among INGOs however, a growing number of INGOs are beginning to pursue development in Myanmar in these terms. At the same time, many INGO informants insist that a nonconfrontational strategy of advocacy toward the same rights and goals is more fruitful. By "nonconfrontational" these leaders speak of dialogue away from media and mass mobilization, referring to a process more reminiscent of strategies for mobilizing elite involvement through an exploration of needs together in a no-blame fashion. To avoid exposing civil society to undue risk, this sort of advocacy has primarily been undertaken by INGOs directly with government officials, although some local civil society groups are independently commencing interesting and very effective advocacy initiatives as well.

Context-Sensitivity and Negotiating the Restricted Humanitarian Space

INGOs seek to build strong personal trust with officials, given access to the humanitarian space to operate and effectiveness in advocacy are built on the quality of such relationships. In a context where domestic and international political will is particularly low, they largely do this by attempting to be absolutely transparent with government officials and donors, to an extent often well beyond levels of accountability that they would usually undertake in other countries. To attempt to expand the humanitarian space sufficiently to fulfill their mandates regarding poverty alleviation, INGOs therefore also direct significant advocacy toward their own donors, governments, and boards.

The insights documented in this research offer something of a blueprint for organizations working in Myanmar and the prospect of incremental change and effectiveness in alleviating poverty in Myanmar. More broadly, this research highlights the clear need for development practitioners to understand the local context and be ready to adapt global development approaches to specific contexts, for every unique context. Myanmar simply highlights this need because of an acutely difficult context. This research thus highlights the lack of substantive research into the sociopolitical contextualization of development, and the tendency of the international and academic community to espouse a global ideal without sufficient emphasis on contextual alternatives and adaptations in implementation.

Sociopolitical Context as the Basis of INGO Adaptations to Context

These adaptations to the development approaches adopted by INGOs are clear responses to the complex sociopolitical context and have contributed to the current national reform agenda. The first INGOs reentered the country in the early 1990s, with steady growth in numbers and the scale of projects until the rapid expansion in response to Cyclone Nargis.

Highly participatory development as a response to the marginalization and fear many poorer people felt under military rule, particularly those from ethnic minorities, has helped alleviate some of that fear and empower the voice of the poor. It has also been a means of building a broad-based foundation for social change that reassesses traditional beliefs about power, authority, and legitimacy. Grassroots democratization and widespread participation in development processes has required reconciliation, and INGOs have emphasized equity. While not a driver of national sociopolitical reform, these are a necessary complement to it. By addressing grievances and inequalities at the community level and being engaged in larger-scale peace initiatives, INGOs have sought to support and model the national reconciliation that is hopefully now being embarked upon. And by often approaching development through more humanitarian rather than rights-based principles, INGOs have not only gained additional access to poor communities but also helped build trust between the Myanmar government and the international community. Nonconfrontational INGO advocacy on behalf of communities and issues not only has achieved positive outcomes on particular issues but also has challenged the preconceptions of Myanmar officials who had inherited the suspicions and fears of the past and expanded the space for civil society.

Context-sensitive development has therefore met both the immediate needs of the people whose poverty is being addressed by INGO programs, while also smoothing the way for larger social change through this sensitivity.

Further Research

At the conclusion of this study, there remain several areas requiring further research. These include the need for further theorization around the roles of various actors in context-sensitive development, particularly the role of INGOs in innovation or in advocating or facilitating innovation in a manner that does not devalue local knowledge or disempower local communities or partners, compromising the strengths and gains made by the participatory model.

Another key area of further research is to examine the areas of similarity and divergence in context-sensitive development between various difficult contexts, including failed, securitized, and internationally isolated (so-called "pariah") states. For example, a comparative study of how context-sensitive development works under the same ideas of participation, equity, sustainability, active citizenry, sensitivity to culture, partnership, capacity building, rights, advocacy, and accountability across a number of difficult states, such as perhaps Zimbabwe, Sudan, Afghanistan, Iraq, and even North Korea, would make a very interesting and illuminating study. Theorization and much greater clarification of policy by international agencies toward internationally isolated (so-called "pariah") states, in particular, are needed. This gets to the heart of competing apolitical and overtly political humanitarian conceptions and has great implications for poverty alleviation and development among millions of impoverished people in a range of difficult countries on the international scene.

Another interesting research area is to examine the extent to which context-sensitive development offers an antidote to the common critique that most INGO development is still steeped in imperialistic and neocolonial ideas. A study documenting the extent to which the best context-sensitive development is or is not perceived to align with broader societal aspirations and is or is not perceived by recipients to be imperialistic or neocolonial would be a significant study, with the potential of improving access and effectiveness within difficult contexts.

Afterword

After many decades of isolation and stagnation, Myanmar is now in the midst of rapid and significant change. Parliamentary elections in 2010 and the release of Aung San Suu Kyi have now resulted in members of the National League for Democracy being elected as members of parliament (MPs); historic visits by US secretary of state Hillary Clinton, UK prime minister David Cameron, and Australian foreign minister Bob Carr, among others; and the suspension or easing of sanctions by most countries. The United States and Canada have upgraded diplomatic relations, and Myanmar has been offered chairmanship of the Association of South East Asian Nations (ASEAN) for 2014. Trade unions have been legalized, media censorship has been relaxed, Suu Kyi has visited abroad and been allowed to return, and civil society and community associations are using new freedoms to negotiate for freedoms and rights in ways previously unheard of.

I began the research for this book in mid-2009, and a lot has occurred since then. I am struck by several thoughts as I contemplate the magnitude of these changes in the light of this book going to press. First, the reform is very real, and it is occurring much faster than almost anyone expected. Second, along with the people of Myanmar, I fervently desire this change to continue, deepen, and broaden, bringing greater well-being and security to millions and resulting in lasting social change. And third, change is always difficult and usually resisted, meaning the more things change, the greater the need for context-sensitivity.

Traditional political ideologies and attitudes toward power, together with the significant postcolonial sensitivities and powerful interests that have long impacted Myanmar politics, continue not far below the surface. The current reform hinges largely on three individuals: President Thein Sein, Speaker of the Lower House Thura Shwe Mann, and Aung San Suu Kyi. As Suu Kyi noted to reporters during her recent visit to Thailand, Thein Sein is in his late sixties and does not have an obvious successor. The nomination of former general Myint Swe last month as the country's next vice president highlights this fragility: Myint Swe is believed to be fiercely loyal to former senior general Than Shwe and to be ready to protect the vested interests of the military. While the methods adopted by the reformers are far more honorable and offer real freedoms, they still appear to build on the same traditional forms of political legitimacy and values about the nature of power. Meanwhile, real problems still exist: human rights abuses continue to be documented in conflict areas, and cronyism and corruption remain major national problems. Elected MPs from the National League for Democracy complain about discriminatory access to funding for infrastructure and service development in their electorates. And ethnic tensions over the "Myanmarification" of ethnic minorities recently erupted into street violence in Rakhine State and into organized armed conflict in Kachin State.

One of the biggest challenges facing President Thein Sein's government is lifting the country's poorest people out of abject poverty. This will be a monumental challenge requiring changed Western attitudes to facilitate international development partnerships. To this point, while the European Union and Australia have suspended almost all sanctions, such development cooperation remains some way off. The United States still retains many sanctions, demanding far greater levels of reform before offering further concessions. International financial institutions have been granted only a limited mandate to conduct assessment missions in Myanmar, with the United States continuing to restrict their ability to implement programs in partnership with the government. Indeed, with the significant exception of Australia, major Western bilateral aid donors still heavily restrict or prohibit capacity-building development partnerships with government agencies.

Thus, despite the significant gains made by the current reform, both domestically and internationally, the same set of serious issues and sensitivities remains. To be effective, poverty alleviation and development in Myanmar will need to be aware of context-sensitive issues, now as ever.

Anthony Ware
July 24, 2012

Glossary of Myanmar Terms

bodhisatta a being already enlightened, remaining voluntarily to teach the path to others; an emergent Buddha; occasionally claimed by or about Burmese kings

cakkavatti a universal monarch (world conqueror) in Theravada Buddhist thought

dhamma Pali form of *dharma*; the natural and moral teaching or law; the uncreated ethical, rational, and eternal law of the universe; a blend of nature and justice

dhammaraja literally, "lord of the law," an ideal ruler who restores political, moral, and religious order, creating an environment in which people have peace and prosper, thus being able to spend time gaining merit

dukka the first Buddhist noble truth; suffering; unsatisfactoriness

hpoun amount of innate merit or glory a person possesses, effectively a measure of the level of their *kamma*, a concept not dissimilar to *mana* in Polynesia

hsaya teacher, whether religious or secular

kamma Pali form of *karma*; the law of cause and effect; personal destiny or fate as determined by the result of volitional personal acts

nibbana soteriological goal of Buddhism

samsara the Buddhist cycle of rebirth

sangha the order of Buddhist monks; collective term for the monkhood

tanha the second Buddhist noble truth; the cause of *dukka*: desire, grasping, or attachment

tatmadaw the Myanmar armed forces

Thakin master; a term equivalent to *sahib* by which the British were addressed, taken as the name of the nationalist party founded by Aung San and U Nu, and a title claimed by members of the party

List of Interview Participants

Interview Participants Who Consented to Be Identified

Agland, Brian. Country Director, *Care International*. July 2009, Yangon.

Ahamad, Shihab Uddin. Country Director, *ActionAid Myanmar*. April 2012, Yangon.

Allan, David. Director, *Spectrum*, and Former Country Coordinator, *World Concern*. July 2009, Yangon.

————. June 2011, Yangon.

Aye, Matthew. Director, *Karen Development Network*. June 2011, Yangon.

Berenguer, Bryan. Bogale Office, *Welthungerhilfe*. July 2009, Yangon.

Bobby Mg. CEO, *Network Activities Group*. April 2012, Yangon

Dorning, Karl. Country Representative, *Burnet Institute*. July 2009, Yangon.

East, James. Asia Pacific Regional Director—Communications, *World Vision International*. July 2009, Bangkok.

Feindt, Regina. Country Director, *Welthungerhilfe*. July 2009, Yangon.

Gang, Sun. Country Coordinator, *UNAIDS*. July 2009, Yangon.

Ghermazien, Tesfai. Senior Emergency and Rehabilitation Coordinator in Myanmar, *Food and Agricultural Organisation*. July 2009, Yangon.

Goddard, Geoff. Former English Editor, *Myanmar Times*. July 2009, Yangon.

Griffiths, Mike. Country Director, *The Leprosy Mission International*. July 2009, Yangon.

————. June 2011, Yangon.

Havens, Douglas. Country Director, *Adventist Development and Relief Agency*. July 2009, Yangon.

Herink, Chris. Country Representative, *World Vision Myanmar*. June 2011, Yangon.

Herzbruch, Birke. NGO Liaison Officer, *Local Resource Centre.* July 2009, Yangon.

———. June 2011, Yangon.

Imai, Shin. Representative in Myanmar, *Food and Agricultural Organisation.* July 2009, Yangon.

Lancelot, Anne. Country Representative, *Médecins du Monde.* July 2009, Yangon.

Long, Douglas. English Editor, *Myanmar Times.* July 2009, Yangon.

Marshall, Steve. Liaison Officer, *International Labour Organisation.* June 2009, Yangon.

Massella, Antonio. *UN Office for the Coordination of Humanitarian Affairs,* Field Coordinator and Deputy Head of Office. July 2009, Yangon.

Ngwe Thein. Project Manager, *Capacity Building Initiative.* July 2009, Yangon.

O'Leary, Moira. Policy and Project Advisor, *ActionAid Myanmar.* July 2009, Yangon.

Purnell, David. East Asia Region Senior Director Operations, *World Vision International.* July 2009, Bangkok.

———. July 2011, Bangkok.

Romano, Gaetano. Country Representative, *Terre des Hommes—Italy.* July 2009, Yangon.

Saboi Jum. Director, *Shalom Foundation.* July 2009, Yangon.

Salai, Khin Maung Aye. Country Coordinator, *SWISSAID Myanmar.* July 2009, Yangon.

Simmons, Peter. Chairman, *GraceWorks Myanmar.* September 2009, Melbourne.

———. July 2011, Melbourne.

Taylor, James. Country Director, *International Development Enterprises.* July 2009, Yangon.

Tegenfeldt, David. Senior Advisor, *Hope International Development Agency.* June 2009, Yangon.

———. June 2011, Yangon.

Tha Hla Shwe. President, *Myanmar Red Cross.* June 2011, Yangon.

Thein, Ngwe. Project Manager, *Capacity Building Initiative.* July 2009, Yangon.

Tumbian, James. Country Representative, *World Vision Myanmar.* July 2009, Yangon.

Walker, Roger. Former Country Representative, *World Vision Myanmar.* March 2009, Melbourne.

Wells, Tamas. Project Manager, *Paung Ku Project (Save the Children).* July 2009, Yangon.

———. June 2011, Yangon.

Win, Chaw Su. Coordinator Strategic Programme and Organisation Development, *Oxfam GB*. July 2009, Yangon.

Zaw, Aung. Editor in Chief, *The Irrawaddy*. July 2009, Chiang Mai.

List of Anonymous Interview Sources

Source 1. Country Coordinator for a bilateral donor. July 2009, Yangon.

Source 2. Country Coordinator for a bilateral donor. July 2009, Yangon.

Source 3. Country Coordinator for a major international donor. July 2009, Yangon.

Source 4. Country Representative for an INGO. July 2009, Yangon.

Source 5. Country Representative for an INGO. July 2009, Yangon.

———. June 2011, Yangon.

Source 6. Former Country Representative for an INGO. July 2009, Yangon.

Source 7. Country Representative for an INGO. June 2011, Yangon.

Source 8. Regional Director of an international FBO working into Myanmar through partnership with a local company. July 2009, Bangkok.

Source 9. Regional Director for an INGO. July 2009, Bangkok.

———. July 2011, Bangkok.

Source 10. Regional Manager for an INGO. July 2009, Bangkok.

Source 11. Regional Director of an international development FBO working into Myanmar through partnerships. August 2009, Chiang Mai.

Source 12. Regional Director of an international development FBO working into Myanmar through partnerships. July 2009, Chiang Mai.

Source 13. Regional Director of an international development FBO working into Myanmar through partnerships. July 2009, Chiang Mai.

Source 14. Director of an international development FBO working into Myanmar through partnerships. August 2009, Melbourne.

Source 15. Country Director of an INGO. July 2009, Yangon.

Source 16. Senior Advisor to an INGO. June 2009, Yangon.

———. June 2011, Yangon.

Source 17. Country Representative for an INGO. June 2011, Yangon.

Source 18. Country Representative for an INGO. July 2009, Yangon.

Source 19. Country Representative for an INGO. July 2009, Yangon.

Source 20. Country Program Manager for an INGO. June 2009, Bangkok.

Source 21. Country Representative for an INGO. July 2009, Yangon.

Source 22. Country Director for an INGO. July 2009, Yangon.

Source 23. Country Representative for an INGO. July 2009, Yangon.

Source 24. Policy and Project Advisor for an INGO. July 2009, Yangon.

Source 25. Strategic Coordinator for an INGO. July 2009, Yangon.

Source 26. Country Director for an INGO. July 2009, Yangon.

Source 27. Liaison with an INGO. July 2009, Yangon.

Source 28. Project Manager with an INGO. July 2009, Yangon.
————. June 2011, Yangon.

Source 29. Project Manager with an INGO. July 2009, Yangon.

Source 30. Director of an LNGO/former country coordinator for an INGO. July 2009, Yangon.
————. June 2011, Yangon.

Source 31. Former Country Representative for an INGO. March 2009, Melbourne.

Source 32. Director of a local development FBO working under a company registration. July 2009, Yangon.

Source 33. Director of a registered LNGO. July 2009, Yangon.

Source 34. Director of a registered LNGO. July 2009, Yangon.

Source 35. Project Manager with a registered LNGO. July 2009, Yangon.

Source 36. Director of a registered LNGO. June 2011, Yangon.

Source 37. International adviser to an unregistered LNGO. July 2009, Yangon.

Source 38. Director of a local unregistered orphanage. July 2009, Yangon.

Source 39. Director of an unregistered LNGO. July 2009, Yangon.

Source 40. Director of an unregistered LNGO. July 2009, Yangon.

Source 41. Former Senior Manager with a UN agency. July 2009, Yangon.

Source 42. Deputy Head of a UN agency. July 2009, Yangon.

Source 43. Country Coordinator of a UN agency. July 2009, Yangon.

Source 44. Country Representative of a UN agency. July 2009, Yangon.

Source 45. Project Manager with a UN agency. July 2009, Yangon.

Source 46. Liaison with an INGO. June 2009, Yangon.

Source 47. Journalist. July 2009, Yangon.

Source 48. Journalist. July 2009, Yangon.

Source 49. Journalist. July 2009, Chiang Mai.

Source 50. Journalist. March 2009, Melbourne.

Source 51. Director of a registered LNGO. December 2011, Yangon.

References

Every effort has been made to ensure that the URLs in this book are accurate and up to date. However, with the rapid changes that occur in the World Wide Web, it is inevitable that some pages or other resources will have been discontinued or moved, and some content modified or reorganized. The publisher recommends that readers who cannot find the sources or information they seek with the URLs in this book use one of the numerous search engines available on the Internet.

ACFID. 2009. *Millennium Development Rights: How Human Rights-Based Approaches Are Achieving the MDGs. Case Studies from the Australian Aid and Development Sector*. Canberra: ACFID.

ActionAid. 2010. *The Fellowships Programme in Myanmar: Critical Stories of Change*. ActionAid: Yangon.

Addison, Tony, ed. 2005. "WIDER Special Issue: Conflict and Peace-building: Interactions between Politics and Economics." *The Round Table* 94 (381).

Africa Peace Forum, Center for Conflict Resolution, Consortium of Humanitarian Agencies, Forum of Early Warning and Response, International Alert and Saferworld. 2004. *Conflict-Sensitive Approaches to Development, Humanitarian Assistance and Peacebuilding: A Resource Pack*. London: Africa Peace Forum, Center for Conflict Resolution, Consortium of Humanitarian Agencies, Forum of Early Warning and Response, International Alert and Saferworld. conflictsensitivity.org.

Alamgir, Jalal. 1997. "Against the Current: The Survival of Authoritarianism in Burma. *Pacific Affairs* 70 (3): 333–50.

Alesina, Alberto, and David Dollar. 2000. "Who Gives Foreign Aid to Whom and Why?" *Journal of Economic Growth* 5:33–63.

Alexander, Lindsay, Canan Gündüz, and D. B. Subedi. 2009. *What Role for Business in "Post-Conflict" Economic Recovery? Perspectives from Nepal*. Economic Dimensions of Peacebuilding Case Study Series. London: International Alert.

Allan, David. 2009. "Same Place, Some Changes: Positive Engagement Examples in Myanmar and Thoughts for the Future." Paper presented at the ANU Myanmar/Burma Update Conference, Australian National University, August 17–18.

———. 2010. "Positive Engagement in Myanmar: Some Current Examples and Thoughts for the Future." In *Ruling Myanmar: From Cyclone Nargis to National Elections*, edited by Nick Cheesman et al., 236–66. Singapore: ISEAS.

Alston, Philip. 1995. "The Rights Framework and Development Assistance." *Development Bulletin* 34:9–12.

———. 2005. "Ships Passing in the Night: The Current State of the Human Rights and Development Debate Seen through the Lens of the Millennium Development Goals." *Human Rights Quarterly* 27 (3): 755–828.

Amarasuriya, Harini, Canan Gündüz, and Markus Mayer. 2009. *Rethinking the Nexus between Youth, Unemployment and Conflict: Perspectives from Sri Lanka*. Economic Dimensions of Peacebuilding Case Study Series. London: International Alert.

Anand, Sudhir, and Amartya Sen. 1996. *Sustainable Human Development: Concepts and Priorities*. Discussion Paper Series, Office of Development Studies. United Nations Development Programme.

———. 2000. "Human Development and Economic Sustainability." *World Development* 28 (12): 2029–49.

Anderson, Ian. 2005. *Fragile States: What Is International Experience Telling Us?* Canberra: AusAID.

An-Na'im, Abdullahi A., and Jeffrey Hammond. 2002. "Cultural Transformation and Human Rights in African Societies." In *Cultural Transformation and Human Rights in Africa*, edited by Abdullahi A An-Na'im. London: ZED Books.

Arensberg, Conrad M., and Arthur H. Niehoff. 1964. *Introducing Social Change: A Manual for Americans Overseas*. New York: Aldine.

———. 1971. *Introducing Social Change: A Manual for Community Development*. New York: Aldine.

Asia Society. 2010a. *Current Realities and Future Possibilities in Burma/Myanmar: Options for U.S. Policy*. Asia Society Task Force Report. asiasociety.org.

———. 2010b. *Current Realities and Future Possibilities in Burma/Myanmar: Perspectives from Asia*. Asia Society Task Force Report. asiasociety.org.

Aung-Thwin, Michael. 1979. "The Role of Sasana Reform in Burmese History: Economic Dimensions of a Religious Purification." *Journal of Asian Studies* 38 (4): 671–88.

———. 1983. "Divinity, Spirit, and Human: Conceptions of Classical Burmese Kingship." In *Centres, Symbols, and Hierarchies: Essays on the Classical State of Southeast Asia*, edited by Lorraine Gesick, 45–86. Southeast Asian Studies Series No. 26. New Haven, CT: Yale University Press.

———. 1985. *Pagan: The Origins of Modern Burma*. Honolulu: University of Hawai'i Press.

AusAID. 2005. *Australian Aid: Approaches to Peace, Conflict and Development*. Canberra: AusAID.

———. 2010. *Fragile States and Australia's Aid Program*. AusAID. ausaid.gov.au.

Aziz, Nikhil. 1999. "The Human Rights Debate in an Era of Globalization: Hegemony of Discourse." In *Debating Human Rights: Critical Essays from the United States and Asia*, edited by Peter Van Ness. New York: Routledge.

Ba Kaung. 2011. "Burmese President Halts Myitsone Dam Project." *The Irrawaddy*, September 30. irrawaddy.org.

Badgley, John H. 2004a. *Reconciling Burma/Myanmar: Essays on U.S. Relations with Burma*. Vol. 15, no. 1. Seattle, WA: NBR Analysis, The National Bureau of Asian Research.

———, ed. 2004b. "Strategic Interests in Myanmar." In *Reconciling Burma/Myanmar: Essays on U.S. Relations with Burma*, edited by John H. Badgley, vol. 15, no. 1, 13–27. Seattle, WA: NBR Analysis, The National Bureau of Asian Research.

Badgley, John H., Robert H. Taylor, David I. Steinberg, Helen James, Seng Raw, Kyaw Yin Hlaing, and Morten B. Pedersen. 2004. "Executive Summary." In *Reconciling Burma/Myanmar: Essays on U.S. Relations with Burma*, edited by John H. Badgley, vol. 15, no. 1, 73–85. Seattle, WA: NBR Analysis, The National Bureau of Asian Research.

Baird, Mark. 2009. *Service Delivery for the Poor: Lessons from Recent Evaluations of Australian Aid*. Canberra: Office of Development Effectiveness, Australian Agency for International Development. ode.ausaid.gov.au.

Baliamoune-Lutz, Mina, and Mark McGillivray. 2008. *State Fragility: Concept and Measurement*. Helsinki, Finland: United Nations University World Institute for Development Economics Research.

Banfield, Jessica, and Jana Naujoks. 2009. *Enabling Peace Economies through Early Recovery: Perspectives from Uganda*. Economic Dimensions of Peacebuilding Case Study Series. London: International Alert.

Banuri, Tariq, Goran Hyden, Calestous Juma, and Marcia Rivera. 1994. *Sustainable Human Development, from Concept to Operation: A Guide for the Practitioner*. New York: United Nations Development Programme.

Barnett, Homer G. 1942. "Invention and Culture Change." *American Anthropologist* 44 (1): 14–30.

———. 1953. *Innovation: The Basis of Social Change*. New York, Toronto, and London: McGraw-Hill.

Bastin, Rohan. 2010. "Global Governance and the Corporate State." Paper presented at the Reconceptualising Development Workshop: Centre for Citizenship, Development, and Human Rights, Deakin University, Melbourne, October 29.

Baucus, Max. 2011. "Baucus Hails Senate Renewal of Sanctions against Burma." Statement by the senate committee chairman, released by the US Department of State, September 15, 2011.

Baulch, Bob. 2006. "Aid Distribution and the MDGs." *World Development* 34 (6): 933–50.

Bernstein, Henry. 2000. "Colonialism, Capitalism, Development." In *Poverty and Development into the 21st Century*, edited by Tim Allen and Alan Thomas. Oxford, UK: Oxford University Press.

Bleiker, Roland. 2003. "A Rogue Is a Rogue Is a Rogue: US Foreign Policy and the Korean Nuclear Crisis." *International Affairs* 79 (4): 719–37.

Bolton, John R. 2005. "Remarks to the Press on the Situation in Burma." December 16, 2005. web.archive.org.

Braden, Su, and Margorie Mayo. 1999. "Culture, Community Development and Representation." *Community Development Journal* 34 (3): 191–204.

Bradford, Wylie. 2004. "Purchasing Power Parity (PPP) Estimates for Burma." *Burma Economic Watch* 1 (1): 4–18.

Bray, Daniel. 2009. "Social Accountability for Development Effectiveness: A Literature Review." In *Promoting Voice and Choice: Exploring Innovations in Australian NGO Accountability for Development Effectiveness*. Deakin, Australia: ACFID.

Brehm, Vicky. 2000. "Culture, Context and NGOs." *OnTrac*, no. 16, September 2000. intrac.org.

Browne, Stephen. 2007. *Aid to Fragile States: Do Donors Help or Hinder?* Discussion Paper No. 2007/01. Helsinki, Finland: United Nations University World Institute for Development Economics Research.

Brunner, Ronald D. 2004. "Context-Sensitive Monitoring and Evaluation for the World Bank." *Policy Sciences* 37 (2): 103–36.

Buncombe, Andrew. 2011. "Burma Benefits as UK Targets Aid Money on Fight for Democracy." *The Independent*, February 14, 2011.

Burma Campaign. 2004. *The European Union and Burma: The Case for Targeted Sanctions.* London: Burma Campaign UK. ibiblio.org.

Callahan, Mary P. 2000. "Cracks in the Edifice? Changes in Military-Society Relations in Burma since 1988." In *Burma-Myanmar: Strong Regime, Weak State*, edited by Morten B. Pedersen et al., 22–51. Adelaide: Crawford House.

———. 2004. *Making Enemies: War and State Building in Burma.* Singapore: Singapore University Press, National University of Singapore.

———. 2010. "The Endurance of Military Rule in Burma: Not Why, but Why Not?" In *Finding Dollars, Sense and Legitimacy in Burma*, edited by Susan L. Levenstein, 54–76. Washington: Woodrow Wilson International Center for Scholars.

Campbell, Kurt. 2011. " 'Winds of Change' in Burma, but Extent Not Known: Campbell." *The Irrawaddy*, September 22. irrawaddy.org.

Camroux, David, and Renaud Egreteau. 2009. "Normative Europe Meets the Burmese Garrison State: Policies, Processes, Blockages . . . and Future Possibilities." Paper presented to the ANU Myanmar/Burma Update Conference, Australian National University, August 17–18.

Candland, Christopher. 2000. "Faith as Social Capital: Religion and Community Development in Southeast Asia." *Policy Sciences* 22:355–74.

Carment, David, and Albrecht Schnabel. 2001. *Building Conflict Prevention Capacity: Methods, Experiences, Needs.* UNU Workshop Seminar Series Report. Ottawa and Tokyo: International Development Research Centre and United Nations University. idrc.ca.

Carr, Bob. 2012a. *Australia to Double Aid to Myanmar by 2015.* Thoughtlines with Bob Carr. June 8. bobcarrblog.wordpress.com.

———. 2012b. *Australia to Lift Sanctions against Myanmar.* Thoughtlines with Bob Carr. June 8. bobcarrblog.wordpress.com.

———. 2012c. "Kangaroo in Corner of Emerging Neighbour." *The Daily Telegraph*, June 11, 2012. dailytelegraph.com.au.

———. 2012d. *Support for Rights of the Child and Human Rights in Myanmar.* Thoughtlines with Bob Carr. June 8. bobcarrblog.wordpress.com.

Cary, DLA Piper Rudnick Gray. 2005. *Threat to the Peace: A Call for the UN Security Council to Act in Burma.* DLA Piper Rudnick Gray Cary: Report commissioned by The Hon Vacláv Havel and Archbishop Desmond M. Tutu. unscburma.org.

CEC. 2007. *Towards a European Consensus on Humanitarian Aid: Report on Responses to Crises—DRC, Pakistan, Lebanon and Burma/Myanmar.* Accompanying the Communication from the Commission to the European Parliament and the Council, COM(2007) 317 final–SEC(2007) 782. Brussels: Commission of the European Communities, Commission Staff Working Document. ec.europa.eu.

Chambers, Robert. 1983. *Rural Development: Putting the Last First.* London: Longman.

———. 1994. "Participatory Rural Appraisal (PRA) Analysis of Experience." *World Development* 22 (9): 1253–68.

———. 2005. *Ideas for Development*. London: Earthscan.

Charney, Michael W. 2009. *A History of Modern Burma*. Cambridge: Cambridge University Press.

Chin, Robert, and Kenneth D. Benne. 1976. "General Strategies for Effective Changes in Human Systems." In *The Planning of Change*, edited by Warren G. Bennis et al., 3rd ed., 22–45. New York: Holt, Rinehart and Winston.

Clark, Allen L. 1999. "Myanmar's Present Development and Future Options." *Asian Survey* 39 (5): 772–91.

Clarke, Gerard. 2008. "Faith Based Organisations and International Development." In *Development, Civil Society and Faith-Based Organisations: Bridging the Sacred and the Secular*, edited by Gerard Clarke and Michael Jennings. London: Palgrave Macmillan.

Clarke, Matthew. 2006. "Aid and Development in Conflict." In *Aid in Conflict*, edited by Matthew Clarke, 1–8. New York: Nova Science.

———. 2009. "Over the Border and under the Radar: Can Illegal Migrants Be Active Citizens?" *Development in Practice* 19 (8): 1064–77.

———. 2011. *Development and Religion: Theology and Practice*. Cheltenham: Edward Elgar.

Clayton, Andrew. 1994. *Governance, Democracy, and Conditionality: What Role for NGOs?* Oxford, UK: INTRAC.

Cleaver, Frances. 2001. "Institutions, Agency and the Limitations of Participatory Approaches to Development." In *Participation: The New Tyranny?*, edited by Bill Cooke and Uma Kothari, 36–55. London and New York: ZED Books.

Clements, Kevin. 2006. "Conflict and Security Sensitivity: A Pre-requisite for Effective Development Assistance." In *Aid in Conflict*, edited by Matthew Clarke, 11–19. New York: Nova Science.

Collignon, Stefan. 2001. "Human Rights and the Economy in Burma." In *Burma: Political Economy under Military Rule*, edited by Robert H. Taylor, 70–108. New York: Palgrave.

Commonwealth Foundation. 2008a. *Culture: What Is Development Missing?* London: Commonwealth Foundation.

———. 2008b. *Putting Culture First: Commonwealth Perspectives on Culture and Development*. London: Commonwealth Foundation.

Conflict Sensitivity. 2004. *Conflict-Sensitive Approaches to Development, Humanitarian Assistance and Peacebuilding: Tools for Peace and Conflict Impact Assessment*. Conflict Sensitivity Consortium. conflictsensitivity.org.

———. 2009. "Homepage." conflictsensitivity.org.

———. 2011. "The Consortium." conflictsensitivity.org.

Conn, Harvey. 1984. *Eternal Word and Changing Worlds: Theology, Anthropology, and Mission in Trialogue*. Grand Rapids: Zondervan.

Cooke, Bill, and Uma Kothari. 2001. "The Case for Participation as Tyranny." In *Participation: The New Tyranny?*, edited by Bill Cooke and Uma Kothari, 1–15. London and New York: ZED Books.

Cornwall, Andrea. 2002. *Making Spaces, Changing Places: Situating Participation in Development*. IDS Working Paper 170. Brighton, UK: Institute of Development Studies, University of Sussex.

Coward, Noel. 1931. *Mad Dogs and Englishmen* (song lyrics). traditionalmusic.co.uk.

CPCS. 2008. *Listening to Voices from Inside: Myanmar Civil Society's Response to Cyclone Nargis*. Phnom Penh, Cambodia: Centre for Peace and Conflict Studies. centrepeaceconflict-studies.org.

Craig, David, and Doug Porter. 1997. "Framing Participation." *Development in Practice* 7 (3): 229–36.

CSO. 2011. *Central Statistical Organisation*. Myanmar Ministry of National Planning and Development. Available from the csostat.gov.mm website.

Culbert, Samuel A. 1976. "Consciousness-Raising: A Five Stage Model for Social Change." In *The Planning of Change*, edited by Warren G. Bennis et al., 3rd ed., 231–44. New York: Holt, Rinehart and Winston.

Dale, Reidar. 2004. *Development Planning: Concepts and Tools for Planners, Managers and Facilitators*. London: ZED Books.

Dapice, David. 2003. *Current Economic Conditions in Myanmar and Options for Sustainable Growth*. Medford, MA: Global Development and Environment Institute, Tufts University.

Dapice, David, Tom Vallely, and Ben Wilkinson. 2009. *Assessment of the Myanmar Agricultural Economy*. Cambridge, MA: Harvard Kennedy School. ash.harvard.edu.

Davidson, John. 2010. "Lessons for a More Effective Aid Program." Paper presented at the conference Development and Aid Effectiveness: Interrogating Pedagogies in International Development Studies, University of Canberra, Office of Development Effectiveness Assistant Director General, November 18–19.

Deleuze, Gilles, and Felix Guattari. 1991. *What Is Philosophy?* Translated by Hugh Tomlinson and Graham Burchell. New York: Columbia University Press.

Denzin, Norman K., and Yvonna S. Lincoln, eds. 2000. *Handbook of Qualitative Research*. Los Angeles: Sage.

Desaine, Lois. 2011. *The Politics of Silence: Myanmar NGOs' Ethnic, Religious and Political Agenda*. Bangkok: IRASEC, Research Institute on Contemporary Southeast Asia. irasec .com.

DFID. 2010. *UKAid in Burma Factsheet*. Rangoon: UK Department for International Development. dfid.gov.uk.

Diokno, Jose. 1978. "The Real Reasons for Authoritarianism." Speech delivered at the Sean McBride lecture, Dublin.

Donnison, F. S. V. 1970. *Burma*. London: Ernest Benn Limited.

Doyal, Len, and Ian Gough. 1991. *A Theory of Human Need*. London: Macmillan.

Duffield, Mark. 2008. "On the Edge of 'No Man's Land': Chronic Emergency in Myanmar." Working Paper, Department of Politics, University of Bristol. bris.ac.uk/politics.

EarthRights. 2009. *Total Impact: The Human Rights, Environmental, and Financial Impacts of Total and Chevron's Yadana Gas Project in Military-Ruled Burma (Myanmar)*. EarthRights International. earthrights.org.

EC. 2007. *The EC–Burma/Myanmar Strategy Paper 2007–2013*. Brussels: European Commission. ec.europa.eu.

ECOSOC. 1950. *Review of Consultative Arrangements with Non-government Organizations*. Resolution 288 (X). New York: United Nations Economic and Social Council. un.org.

Edwards, Michael. 1989. "The Irrelevance of Development Studies." *Third World Quarterly* 11 (1): 116–35.

EEAS. 2011. *Myanmar (Burma)*. European External Action Service of the High Representative of the Union for Foreign Affairs and Security Policy. eeas.europa.eu.

Egreteau, Renaud. 2008. "India's Ambitions in Burma: More Frustration Than Success?" *Asian Survey* 48 (6): 936–57.

EIU. 2008. *Country Profile: Myanmar*. London: Economist Intelligence Unit.

ESCAP. 2007. *Ten as One: Challenges and Opportunities for ASEAN Integration*. Bangkok: United Nations Economic and Social Commission for Asia and the Pacific. unescap.org.

———. 2008. *Statistical Yearbook 2008*. Bangkok: United Nations Economic and Social Commission for Asia and the Pacific. unescap.org.

———. 2010. *Paths to 2015: MDG Priorities in Asia and the Pacific—Asia-Pacific MDG Report 2010/11*. Bangkok: United Nations Economic and Social Commission for Asia and the Pacific. undep.org.

ESCAP/ADB/UNDP. 2007. *Access to Basic Services for the Poor: The Importance of Good Governance*. Asia-Pacific MDG Study Series. Report No. ST/ESCAP/2438. Bangkok: United Nations Economic and Social Commission for Asia and the Pacific, United Nations Development Programme, and the Asian Development Bank.

Eyben, Rosalind. 2008. *Power, Mutual Accountability and Responsibility in the Practice of International Aid: A Relational Approach*. Working Paper 305. Brighton, UK: Institute of Development Studies, University of Sussex. ids.ac.uk.

Eyben, Rosalind, Naila Kabeer, and Andrea Cornwall. 2008. *Conceptualising Empowerment and the Implications for Pro Poor Growth: A Paper for the DAC Poverty Network*. Brighton, UK: Institute of Development Studies, University of Sussex. ids.ac.uk.

Eyben, Rosalind, Thalia Kidder, Jo Rowlands, and Audrey Bronstein. 2008. "Thinking about Change for Development Practice: A Case Study from Oxfam GB." *Development in Practice* 18 (2): 201–12.

Farrelly, Nicholas. 2010. "Beyond Burma's Stalemates." *Inside Story*, December 31, 2010. inside.org.

FCO. 2011. *Travel Advice by Country: Burma*. (British) Foreign and Commonwealth Office. Retrieved March 8, 2011, from fco.gov.uk.

Fechter, Anne-Meike, and Heather Hindman. 2011. *Inside the Everyday Lives of Development Workers: The Challenges and Futures of Aidland*. Sterling, VA: Kumarian Press.

Feeny, Simon, and Matthew Clarke. 2009. *The Millennium Development Goals and Beyond: International Assistance to the Asia-Pacific*. London: Palgrave Macmillian.

Ferguson, C. 1999. *Global Social Policy Principles: Human Rights and Social Justice*. London: UK Department for International Development.

Ferretti, Silva. 2010. *Fellows and Civil Society*. Yangon: ActionAid Myanmar.

Fink, Christina. 2000. "Burma: Human Rights, Forgotten Wars, and Survival." *Cultural Survival*, 24 (3).

———. 2001. *Living Silence: Burma under Military Rule*. London: ZED Books.

Foreign Policy. 2010. "The Failed States Index 2010." *Foreign Policy*, July/August 2010. foreignpolicy.com.

Foster, George M. 1962. *Traditional Cultures and the Impact of Technological Change*. New York: Harper and Row.

———. 1969. *Applied Anthropology*. Boston: Little, Brown.

Fowler, Alan. 1998. "Authentic NGDO Partnerships in the New Policy Agenda for International Aid: Dead End or Light Ahead?" *Development and Change* 29 (1): 137–59.

———. 2000a. "Introduction: Beyond Partnership—Getting Real about NGO Relationships and the Aid System." *IDS Bulletin* 31 (3): 1–13.

———. 2000b. *The Virtuous Spiral: A Guide to Sustainability for NGOs in International Development*. London: Earthscan.

Frantz, Telmo Rudi. 1987. "The Role of NGOs in the Strengthening of Civil Society." Supplement. *World Development* 15:S121–27.

Freire, Paulo. 1972. *Pedagogy of the Oppressed*. Harmondsworth: Penguin.

Fritzen, Scott A. 2007. "Can the Design of Community-Driven Development Reduce the Risk of Elite Capture? Evidence from Indonesia." *World Development* 35 (8): 1359–75.

Furnivall, J. S. 1941. *Progress and Welfare in Southeast Asia: A Comparison of Colonial Policy and Practice*. International Research Series. New York: Secretariat, Institute of Pacific Relations.

———. 1991. "The Fashioning of Leviathan: The Beginnings of British Rule in Burma." In *Reprint from the Journal of the Burma Research Society*, vol. 29 no. 1 April 1939, pp. 3–137. Canberra: Australian National University, Department of Anthropology. First published 1939.

Geary, Grattan. 1886. *Burma after the Conquest: Viewed in Its Political, Social and Commercial Aspects from Mandalay*. London: Sampson Low, Marston, Searle and Rivington.

Godnick, William, and Diana Klein. 2009. *The Challenges of Supporting "Alternative" Economic Opportunities for Peacebuilding: Perspectives from Colombia*. Economic Dimensions of Peacebuilding Case Study Series. London: International Alert.

Goodenough, Ward. 1963. *Cooperation in Change: An Anthropological Approach to Community Development*. New York: Russell Sage Foundation.

Goodwin-Dorning, Karl. 2007. "Children as Beneficiaries and Participants in Development Programs: A Case Study in Burma (Myanmar)." PhD diss., Victoria University.

Gouwenberg, Anna E. 2009. *The Legal Implementation of the Right to Development*. A study of the Grotius Centre for International Legal Studies. The Hague: Leiden University. grotiuscentre.org.

Gray, David E. 2009. *Doing Research in the Real World*. Los Angeles: Sage.

Guijt, Irene. 2007. "Assessing and Learning for Social Change: A Discussion Paper." Institute of Development Studies, University of Sussex.

Guijt, Irene, and Meera Kaul Shah, eds. 1998. *The Myth of Community: Gender Issues in Participatory Development*. London: Intermediate Technology.

Guo Xiaolin. 2009. *Democracy in Myanmar and the Paradox of International Politics*. Stockholm: Institute for Security and Development Policy. isdp.eu.

Haacke, Jürgen. 2006. *Myanmar's Foreign Policy: Domestic Influences and International Implications*. London: Routledge, for the International Institute for Strategic Studies.

Hadar, Leon. 1998. *U.S. Sanctions against Burma: A Failure on All Fronts*. Trade Policy Analysis No. 1. Washington, DC: Centre for Trade Policy Studies, Cato Institute. cato.org.

Hagen, Everett E. 1957. "The Process of Economic Development." *Economic Development and Cultural Change* 5 (3): 193–215.

Hall, D. G. E. 1956. *Burma*. 2nd ed. London: Hutchinson's University Library.

Hall, Jo, and Jude Howell. 2010. *Good Practice Donor Engagement with Civil Society*. Canberra: Office of Development Effectiveness, Australian Agency for International Development and London School of Economics. ode.ausaid.gov.au.

Harkavy, Robert E. 1981. "Pariah States and Nuclear Proliferation." *International Organization* 35 (1): 135–63.

Harvey, Geoffrey E. 1925. *History of Burma from the Earliest Times to 10 March 1824, the Beginning of the English Conquest*. London: Longmans, Green.

Herskovits, Melville J. 1937. "The Significance of the Study of Acculturation for Anthropology." *American Anthropologist* 39 (2): 259–64.

Hettne, Bjorn. 1995. *Development Theory and the Three Worlds: Towards an International Political Economy of Development*. Essex: Longman.

Hildebrand. 1848. *Economics of the Present and the Future*. Frankfurt: Literarische Anstalt.

Hilhorst, Dorothea, and Nadja Schmiemann. 2002. "Humanitarian Principles and Organisational Culture: Everyday Practice in Médecins Sans Frontières–Holland." *Development in Practice* 12 (3–4): 490–500.

Hirschman, Albert. 1958. *The Strategy of Economic Development*. New Haven, CT: Yale University Press.

Hla Min. 2000. *The Political Situation of Myanmar and Its Role in the Region*. Yangon: Office of Strategic Studies, Ministry of Defense.

Holliday, Ian. 2005. "Rethinking the United States' Myanmar Policy." *Asian Survey* 45 (4): 603–21.

———. 2007. "National Unity Struggles in Myanmar: A Degenerate Case of Governance for Harmony in Asia." *Asian Survey* 47 (3): 374–92.

———. 2008a. "Beyond Burma versus the World." *Far Eastern Economic Review* 171 (5): 48–51.

———. 2008b. "Breaking Out of Burma's Time Warp." *Far Eastern Economic Review* 171 (2): 49–52.

———. 2009. "Raising the Stakes in Burma." *Far Eastern Economic Review* 172 (5): 25–29.

———. 2010a. "Beijing and the Myanmar Problem." *Pacific Review* 22:479–500.

———. 2010b. "Ethnicity and Democratization in Myanmar." *Asian Journal of Political Science* 18 (2): 111–28.

———. 2011a. *Burma Redux: Global Justice and the Quest for Political Reform in Myanmar*. Hong Kong: Hong Kong University Press.

———. 2011b. "Extending a Hand in Myanmar." *Dissent* 58 (2): 14–18.

Horsey, Richard. 2009. "Strategy and Priorities in Addressing the Humanitarian Situation in Burma." Paper presented at the Burma/Myanmar: Views from the Ground and the International Community, Senate Office Building, Washington, DC, May 8. nbr.org.

———. 2011. "Myanmar's Political Landscape Following the Elections: Glass Nine-Tenths Empty?" Paper presented at the 2011 Myanmar/Burma Update Conference, Australian National University, May 16–17. asiapacific.anu.edu.au.

Hoselitz, Bert F. 1952. "Non-economic Barriers to Economic Development." *Economic Development and Cultural Change* 1 (1): 8–21.

Hossain, Naomi, and Mick Moore. 2002. *Arguing for the Poor: Elites and Poverty in Developing Countries*. IDS Working Paper 148. Brighton, UK: Institute of Development Studies, University of Sussex. ids.ac.uk.

Houtman, Gustaaf. 1999. *Mental Culture in Burmese Crisis Politics: Aung San Suu Kyi and the National League for Democracy*. Tokyo: ILCAA Study of Languages and Cultures of Asia and Africa, Tokyo University of Foreign Studies. tesco.net.

Howse, Robert L., and Jared M. Genser. 2008. "Are EU Trade Sanctions on Burma Compatible with WTO Law?" *Michigan Journal of International Law* 29:165–96.

Hseng, Sai Zom. 2011. "Suu Kyi Welcomes Suspension of Myitsone Dam." *The Irrawaddy*, September 30. irrawaddy.org.

ICG. 2001. *Myanmar: The Role of Civil Society.* Asia Report No. 27. Bangkok/Brussels: International Crisis Group. crisisgroup.org.

———. 2002. *Myanmar: The Politics of Humanitarian Aid.* Asia Report No. 32. Bangkok/Brussels: International Crisis Group. crisisgroup.org.

———. 2003. *Myanmar Backgrounder: Ethnic Minority Politics.* Asia Report No. 52. Yangon/Brussels: International Crisis Group. crisisgroup.org.

———. 2004. *Myanmar: Sanctions, Engagement or Another Way.* Asia Report No. 78. Yangon/Brussels: International Crisis Group. crisisgroup.org.

———. 2006. *Myanmar: New Threats to Humanitarian Aid.* Asia Update Briefing No. 58. Yangon/Brussels: International Crisis Group. crisisgroup.org.

———. 2008. *Burma/Myanmar after Nargis: Time to Normalise Aid Relations.* Asia Report No. 161. Yangon/Brussels: International Crisis Group. crisisgroup.org.

———. 2009. *Myanmar: Towards the Elections.* Asia Report No. 174. Yangon/Brussels: International Crisis Group. crisisgroup.org.

———. 2010a. *China's Myanmar Strategy: Elections, Ethnic Politics and Economics.* Asia Briefing No. 112. Jakarta/Brussels: International Crisis Group. crisisgroup.org.

———. 2010b. *The Myanmar Elections.* Asia Briefing No. 105. Jakarta/Brussels: International Crisis Group. crisisgroup.org.

———. 2011a. *Myanmar: Major Reform Underway.* Asia Briefing No. 127. Jakarta/Brussels: International Crisis Group. crisisgroup.org.

———. 2011b. *Myanmar's Post-Election Landscape.* Asia Briefing No. 118. Jakarta/Brussels: International Crisis Group. crisisgroup.org.

———. 2011c. *Myanmar: A New Peace Initiative.* Asia Report No. 214. Yangon/Brussels: International Crisis Group. crisisgroup.org.

———. 2012. *Reform in Myanmar: One Year On.* Asia Briefing No. 136. Jakarta/Brussels: International Crisis Group. crisisgroup.org.

Ife, Jim. 2010. "Reconceptualising Development: Modernity and Democracy." Paper presented at the Reconceptualising Development Workshop, Centre for Citizenship, Development and Human Rights, Deakin University, Melbourne, October 29.

Igboemeka, Adaeze. 2005. *Aid Effectiveness in Burma/Myanmar: Study on Development Agency Perceptions.* UK Department for International Development, South East Asia.

IHLCA. 2007. *Integrated Household Living Conditions Survey in Myanmar (2003–2005) Poverty Profile.* Yangon: Integrated Household Living Conditions Assessment Project Technical Unit. With support of Ministry of National Planning and Economic Development and the United Nations Development Programme.

———. 2011. *Integrated Household Living Conditions Survey in Myanmar (2009–2010) Poverty Profile.* Yangon: Integrated Household Living Conditions Assessment Project Technical Unit. Joint Project of Myanmar Ministry of National Planning and Economic Development, United Nations Development Programme, United Nations Children's Fund, and Swedish International Development Agency.

ILO. 1998. *Forced Labour in Myanmar (Burma) Report of the Commission of Inquiry Appointed under Article 26 of the Constitution of the International Labour Organization to Examine the Observance by Myanmar of the Forced Labour Convention, 1930 (No. 29).* Geneva: International Labour Organisation, International Labour Office.

———. 2002. *Understanding between the Government of the Union of Myanmar and the International Labour Office Concerning the Appointment of an ILO Liaison Officer in Myanmar.* Geneva: International Labour Organisation. ilo.org.

———. 2007. *Supplementary Understanding between the Government of the Union of Myanmar and the International Labour Office.* Geneva: International Labour Organisation. ilo.org.

———. 2008. *Supplementary Understanding between the Government of the Union of Myanmar and the International Labour Office.* Geneva: International Labour Organisation. ilo.org.

———. 2009. *Supplementary Understanding between the Government of the Union of Myanmar and the International Labour Office.* Geneva: International Labour Organisation. ilo.org.

———. 2010. *Supplementary Understanding between the Government of the Union of Myanmar and the International Labour Office.* Geneva: International Labour Organisation. ilo.org.

———. 2011. *Supplementary Understanding between the Government of the Union of Myanmar and the International Labour Office.* Geneva: International Labour Organisation. ilo.org.

IMF. 2009. *World Economic and Financial Surveys: World Economic Outlook Database.* International Monetary Fund. imf.org.

IMGHD. 2003. *Principles and Good Practice of Humanitarian Donorship.* Paper presented at the International Meeting on Good Humanitarian Donorship, Stockholm, June 16–17. reliefweb.int.

International Alert, Saferworld, and IDRC. 2000. *Peace and Conflict-Sensitive Approaches to Development.* A briefing for the OECD Task Force on Conflict, Peace and Development Cooperation and the Conflict Prevention and Reconstruction Network. London: International Alert, Saferworld, and the International Development Research Centre. international-alert.org.

Inwood, Paul Douglas. 2008. "International Humanitarian Assistance to Myanmar." MPh diss., Massey University, New Zealand.

Irrawaddy. 2011. " 'An Opportunity for Change': Suu Kyi." *The Irrawaddy,* September 15. irrawaddy.org.

Ishizawa, Jorge. 2004. "On Local Communities and Megaprojects: The Cultural Challenge." *Development* 47 (1): 58–63.

Jackson, Terrence. 2003. *Cross-Cultural Management and NGO Capacity Building: Why Is a Cross-Cultural Approach Necessary?* PraxisNote No. 1. Oxford: INTRAC. intrac.org.

Jagan, Larry. 2010. "Burma: China's Most Important Strategic Ally in Southeast Asia." In *Myanmar: Prospect for Change,* edited by Li Chenyang and Wilhelm Hofmeister. Singapore: Select Publishing.

James, Helen. 2004. "King Solomon's Judgment." In *Reconciling Burma/Myanmar: Essays on U.S. Relations with Burma,* edited by John H. Badgley, vol. 15, no. 1, 55–66. Seattle, WA: NBR Analysis, The National Bureau of Asian Research.

Jordt, Ingrid. 2001. "Mass Lay Meditation and State-Society Relations in Post-Independence Burma." PhD diss., Harvard University.

———. 2003. "From Relations of Power to Relations of Authority: Epistemic Claims, Practices, and Ideology in the Production of Burma's Political Order." *Social Analysis* 47 (1): 65–76.

Kaldor, Mary. 1999. *New and Old Wars: Organised Violence in a Global Era.* Cambridge: Polity Press.

Kanwal, Gurmeet. 2010. "A Strategic Perspective on India Myanmar Relations." In *Myanmar/ Burma: Inside Challenges, Outside Interests*, edited by Lex Rieffel, 134–49. Washington, DC: Konrad Adenauer Foundation/Brookings Institution.

Kasongo, Emmanuel. 1998. "From Development by Effects to Development by Contexts via Communication." *Development in Practice* 8 (1): 30–39.

Keesing, R. M., and Andrew J. Strathern. 1998. *Cultural Anthropology: A Contemporary Perspective*. 3rd ed. Fort Worth, TX: Harcourt Brace College Publishers.

Khin Maung Nyo. 2011. "Taking Stock of the Myanmar Economy in 2011." Chief Editor *World Economic Journal* (Yangon), paper presented at the 2011 Myanmar/Burma Update Conference, Australian National University, May 16–17. asiapacific.anu.edu.au.

Kilby, Patrick. 2010. "Development Studies, Development and Aid Effectiveness: Advice to Donors." Paper presented at the conference Development and Aid Effectiveness: Interrogating Pedagogies in International Development Studies, University of Canberra, November 18–19.

Kingsbury, Damien. 2008a. "Community Development." In *International Development: Issues and Challenges*, edited by Damien Kingsbury et al. New York: Palgrave Macmillan.

———. 2008b. "Introduction." In *International Development: Issues and Challenges*, edited by Damien Kingsbury et al. New York: Palgrave Macmillan.

Kipling, Rudyard. 1889. *Letters from the East*. Pioneer of India.

Klasen, Stephan. 2006. "What Is Equity." In *Equity and Development: Berlin Workshop Series 2006*, edited by Gudrun Kochendörfer-Lucius and Boris Pleskovic, 69–78. Washington, DC: World Bank.

Klotz, Audie. 1996. "Norms and Sanctions: Lessons from the Socialization of South Africa." *Review of International Studies* 22 (2): 173–90.

Koenig, William J. 1990. *The Burmese Polity, 1752–1819: Politics, Administration, and Social Organization in the Early Kon-Baung Period*. Michigan Papers on South and Southeast Asia No. 34. Ann Arbor: University of Michigan.

Korten, David C. 1990. *Getting to the 21st Century: Voluntary Action and the Global Agenda*. West Hartford, CT: Kumarian Press.

Kraft, Charles. 1979. *Christianity in Culture: A Study in Dynamic Biblical Theologizing in Cross-Cultural Perspective*. Maryknoll, NY: Orbis Books.

———. 1996. *Anthropology for Christian Witness*. Maryknoll, NY: Orbis Books.

———. 2005. "Meaning Equivalence Contextualisation." In *Appropriate Christianity*, edited by Charles Kraft, 155–68. Pasadena, CA: William Carey Library.

Kramer, Tom. 2009. *Neither War nor Peace: The Future of the Cease-Fire Agreements in Burma*. Amsterdam: Transnational Institute.

Kreimer, A., J. Eriksson, R. Muskat, M. Arnold, and C. Scott. 1998. *The World Bank's Experience with Conflict Reconstruction*. Washington, DC: World Bank.

Kroeber, A. L., and C. Kluckhohn. 1952. *Culture: A Critical Review of Concepts and Definitions*. Papers of the Peabody Museum of American Archaeology and Ethnology, Vol. XLVII. Cambridge, MA: Harvard University Press.

Kudo, Toshihiro. 2007. "Myanmar's Economic Relations with China: Who Benefits and Who Pays?" In *Myanmar: The State, the Community, the Environment*, edited by Monique Skidmore and Trevor Wilson, 87–109. Canberra: ANU E Press and Asia Pacific Press.

Labonne, Julien, and Robert S. Chase. 2009. "Who Is at the Wheel When Communities Drive Development? Evidence from the Philippines." *World Development* 37 (1): 219–31.

Latour, Bruno. 2005. *Reassembling the Social: An Introduction to Actor-Network-Theory*. Oxford: Oxford University Press.

Leider, Jacques P. 2009. *King Alaungmintaya's Golden Letter to King George II (7 May 1756): The Story of an Exceptional Manuscript and the Failure of a Diplomatic Overture*. Hannover: Gottfried Wilhelm Leibniz Bibliothek. gwlb.de.

Lerner, Daniel. 1958. *The Passing of Traditional Society: Modernizing the Middle East*. Glencoe, IL: Free Press.

Lewis, W. Arthur. 1955. *Theory of Economic Growth*. London: Allen and Unwin.

Li, Chenyang, and Lye Liang Fook. 2010. "China's Policies towards Myanmar: A Successful Model for Dealing with the Myanmar Issue?" In *Myanmar: Prospect for Change*, edited by Li Chenyang and Wilhelm Hofmeister. Singapore: Select Publishing.

Liddell, Zunetta. 1997. "No Room to Move: Legal Constraints on Civil Society in Burma." In *Strengthening Civil Society in Burma: Possibilities and Dilemmas for International NGOs*. Amsterdam: Transnational Institute and the Burma Centrum Nederland.

Lieberman, Victor. 1980. "The Political Significance of Religious Wealth in Burmese History: Some Further Thoughts." *Journal of Asian Studies* 39 (4): 753–69.

Lintner, Bertil. 1991. *Aung San Suu Kyi and Burma's Unfinished Renaissance*. Bangkok: White Lotus.

Linton, Ralph. 1936. *The Study of Man*. New York: D. Appleton-Century.

Löfving, Annami. 2011. *The Force for Change: Achievements of the Fellowship Programme in Myanmar*. Yangon: ActionAid Myanmar.

Lorch, Jasmin. 2007. "The (Re)-Emergence of Civil Society in Areas of State Weakness: The Case of Education in Burma/Myanmar." In *Dictatorship, Disorder and Decline in Myanmar*, edited by Monique Skidmore and Trevor Wilson, 151–86. Canberra: ANU E Press.

LRC and Oxfam. 2010. *Progressing through Partnerships: How National and International Organizations Work Together in Myanmar*. Yangon: Local Resource Centre and Oxfam.

Luzbetak, Louis J. 1963. *The Church and Cultures: An Applied Anthropology for the Religious Worker*. Techny, IL: Divine Word.

Lynch, Colum. 2010. "An End to Engagement? U.S. to Push for Burma Inquiry." *Foreign Policy*, August 17.

Malik, Nadeem. 2011. "Development Studies: Discipline or Interdisciplinary Field." In *International Development: Linking Academia with Development Aid and Effectiveness*, edited by Tahmina Rashid and Jason Flanagan. Saarbrucken: LAP Lambert Academic.

Malinowski, Bronislaw. 1929. "Practical Anthropology." *Africa* 2 (1): 22–38.

Marris, Peter. 1970. "Social Perspectives." In *Development in a Divided World*, edited by Dudley Seers and Leonard Joy. Middlesex: Penguin Books.

Marshall, Katherine. 2001. "Religion and Development: A Different Lens on Development Debates." *Peabody Journal of Education* 76 (3–4): 339–75.

Mathie, Alison, and Gord Cunningham. 2003. "From Clients to Citizens: Asset-Based Community Development as a Strategy for Community-Driven Development." *Development in Practice* 13 (5): 474–86.

Matthews, Bruce. 1998. "The Present Fortune of Tradition-Bound Authoritarianism in Myanmar." *Pacific Affairs* 71 (1): 7–23.

Maung Aung Myoe. 2006. *The Road to Naypyidaw: Making Sense of the Myanmar Government's Decision to Move Its Capital*. Working Paper Series No. 79. Singapore: Asia Research Institute.

Maung Htin Aung. 1967. *A History of Burma.* New York: Columbia University Press.

Maung Htin Aung, and Michael A. Aung-Thwin. 2008. *Myanmar.* Chicago: Encyclopædia Britannica.

Maung Maung Gyi. 1983. *Burmese Political Values: The Socio-political Roots of Authoritarianism.* New York: Praeger.

Maykut, Pamela, and Richard Morehouse. 1994. *Beginning Qualitative Research: A Philosophic and Practical Guide.* London; Washington, DC: Falmer Press.

McCarthy, Stephen. 2008. "Overturning the Alms Bowl: The Price of Survival and the Consequences for Political Legitimacy in Burma." *Australian Journal of International Affairs* 62 (3): 298–314.

McDermid, Charles. 2009. "Missing the Point on Myanmar: Interview with Thant Myint-U." *Asia Times Online,* July 2.

McGillivray, Mark. 2008. "What Is Development." In *International Development: Issues and Challenges,* edited by Damien Kingsbury et al. New York: Palgrave Macmillan.

McGillivray, Mark, and Simon Feeny. 2008. *Aid and Growth in Fragile States.* Research Paper No. 2008/03. Helsinki, Finland: United Nations University World Institute for Development Economics Research.

McKenzie, Stephen. 2004. *Social Sustainability: Towards Some Definitions.* Working Paper Series No. 27. Magill: University of South Australia, Hawke Research Institute. unisa.edu.au.

McLeish, John. 1969. *The Theory of Social Change: Four Views Considered.* London: Routledge and Kegan Paul.

Miller, S. M. 2002. "Best Practices: Scepticism and Hope." In *Best Practices in Poverty Reduction: An Analytical Framework,* edited by Else Øyen, 51–67. London and New York: CROP International Studies in Poverty Research, ZED Books.

Miller, Terry, and Kim R. Holmes. 2011. *Index of Economic Freedom.* Washington, DC; New York: Heritage Foundation and Dow Jones and Company. heritage.org.

Min Zin. 2010. "Opposition Movements in Burma: The Question of Relevancy." In *Finding Dollars, Sense and Legitimacy in Burma,* edited by Susan L. Levenstein, 77–94. Washington, DC: Woodrow Wilson International Center for Scholars.

Minear, Larry, and Thomas G. Weiss. 1993. *Humanitarian Action in Times of War: A Handbook for Practitioners.* Boulder, CO: Lynne Rienner.

Minye Kaungbon. 1994. *Our Three Main National Causes.* Rangoon: News and Periodicals Enterprise.

Mitchell, Derek. 2011. "Press Conference in Rangoon." Special Representative and Policy Coordinator for Burma, US State Department, September 14. state.gov.

Mizzima. 2011. "Sanctions on Burma: A Review." February 8. mizzima.com.

MoH. 2008. *Health in Myanmar 2008.* Naypyidaw: Ministry of Health, Union of Myanmar.

Mohan, Giles. 2007. "Participatory Development: From Epistemological Reversals to Active Citizenship." *Geography Compass* 1 (4): 779–96.

Moore, Richard. 2009. "Discussant to Keynote Speech by Dr. William Sabandar." Deputy Director General (Asia) for AusAID in response to paper presented at the 2009 Myanmar/Burma Update Conference, Australian National University, August 17–18.

———. 2011. "Discussant Comments: The Continued Importance of International Assistance." First Deputy Director for AusAID in response to paper presented at the 2011 Myanmar/Burma Update Conference, Australian National University, May 16–17. asiapacific.anu.edu.au.

Mosse, David. 2001. " 'People's Knowledge,' Participation and Patronage: Orientations and Representations in Rural Development." In *Participation: The New Tyranny?*, edited by Bill Cooke and Uma Kothari, 16–35. London and New York: ZED Books.

Murphy, Brian K. 2000. "International NGOs and the Challenge of Modernity." *Development in Practice* 10 (3–4): 330–47.

Murray, Suellen, and Matthew Clarke. 2008. "Improving the Capacity to Respond: Examining the Experiences of Tsunami Relief Workers." *Journal of International Development* 20 (4): 466–80.

Mya Maung. 1991. *The Burma Road to Poverty*. New York: Praeger.

———. 1999. "The Burma Road to the Past." *Asian Survey* 39 (2): 265–86.

Mya Than, and Myat Thein. 2007. "Transitional Economy of Myanmar: Present Status, Developmental Divide, and Future Prospects." *ASEAN Economic Bulletin, Singapore* 24 (1): 98–119.

Naw, Angelene. 2001. *Aung San and the Struggle for Burmese Independence*. Chiang Mai, Thailand: Silkworm Books.

Naylor, Larry L. 1996. *Culture and Change: An Introduction*. Westport, CA; London: Bergin and Garvey.

Nelson, Paul J. 2007. "Human Rights, the Millennium Development Goals, and the Future of Development Cooperation." *World Development* 35 (12): 2041–55.

Newell, P. 2002. "Taking Accountability into Account: The Debates So Far." In *Rights, Resources and the Politics of Accountability*, edited by P. Newell and J. Wheeler. London: ZED Books.

NGOs in the Golden Land. 2010. *NGOs in the Golden Land*. ngoinmyanmar.org.

Nida, Eugene. 1954. *Customs and Cultures*. New York: Harper and Bros.

———. 1960. *Message and Mission*. New York: Harper and Row.

Nisbet, Robert A. 1969. *Social Change and History: Aspects of the Western Theory of Development*. Oxford: Oxford University Press.

NLM. 2003. "Prime Minister General Khin Nyunt Clarifies Future Policies and Programmes of State." *New Light of Myanmar*, August 31.

———. 2009. "Habits of Exploitation of Human Rights by Certain Powerful Countries as a Pretext for Meddling in Internal Affairs of Member States Still Linger On." *New Light of Myanmar*, July 20, p. 16.

———. 2011a. "Cancellation for Validity of Registered Vehicles and Substitution." *New Light of Myanmar*, September 11, p. 9.

———. 2011b. "President U Thein Sein Delivers Inaugural Address to Pyidaungsu Hluttaw." *New Light of Myanmar*, March 31.

———. 2011c. "Press Conference on Overage Vehicles to Be Written Off, New Cars to Be Imported." *New Light of Myanmar*, September 11. Online edition.

———. 2011d. "Workshop Successfully Concludes with Package of Pragmatic Ideas." *New Light of Myanmar*, August 22, p. 1.

Nussbaum, Martha Craven. 2000. *Women and Human Development: The Capabilities Approach*. Cambridge: Cambridge University Press.

Nyamu-Musembi, Celestine, and Andrea Cornwall. 2004. *What Is the "Rights-Based Approach" All About? Perspectives from International Development Agencies*. IDS Working Paper 234. Brighton, UK: Institute of Development Studies, University of Sussex. ids.ac.uk.

Oakley, Peter. 1991. *Projects with People: The Practice of Participation in Rural Development*. Geneva: ILO.

Odendahl, Teresa, and Aileen M. Shaw. 2001. "Interviewing Elites." In *Handbook of Interview Research: Context and Method*, edited by Jaber F. Gubrium and James A. Holstein, 299–316. Thousand Oaks, CA: Sage.

OECD. 1997. *DAC Guidelines on Conflict, Peace and Development Cooperation*. Paris: Organisation for Economic Co-operation and Development.

———. 2007a. *Concepts and Dilemmas of State Building in Fragile Situations: From Fragility to Eesilience*. OECD/DAC Discussion Paper. Paris: Organisation for Economic Co-operation and Development. oecd.org.

———. 2007b. *Principles for Good International Engagement in Fragile States*. Paris: Organisation for Economic Co-operation and Development, Development Co-operation Directorate. oecd.org.

Oehlers, Alfred. 2004. "Sanctions and Burma: Revisiting the Case Against." *Burma Economic Watch* 1 (2): 36–46.

OHCHR. 2006. *Frequently Asked Questions on a Human Rights-Based Approach to Development Cooperation*. New York and Geneva: Office of the United Nations High Commissioner for Human Rights.

O'Leary, Moira, and Meas Nee. 2001. *Learning for Transformation: A Study of the Relationship between Culture, Values, Experience and Development Practice in Cambodia*. Phnom Penh: Krom Akphiwat Phum (funded by Oxfam GB, Dan Church Aid, ICCO, and VBNK).

Orwell, George. 1934. *Burmese Days*. New York: Harper.

Ossewaarde, Ringo, Andre Nijhof, and Liesbet Heyse. 2008. "Dynamics of NGO Legitimacy: How Organising Betrays Core Missions of INGOs." *Public Administration and Development* 28 (1): 42–53.

Øyen, Else. 2002. "A Methodological Approach to Best Practices." In *Best Practices in Poverty Reduction: An Analytical Framework*, edited by Else Øyen, 1–28. London; New York: CROP International Studies in Poverty Research, ZED Books.

Paldron, Mario. 1987. "Non-government Development Organisations: From Development Aid to Development Cooperation." Supplement. *World Development* 15:69–71.

Patterson, Thomas C. 1998. *Change and Development in the Twentieth Century*. Oxford: Berg.

Patton, Michael. 1990. *Qualitative Evaluation and Research Methods*. London: Sage.

Pe Maung Tin, and Gordon H. Luce. 1923. *The Glass Palace Chronicle of the Kings of Burma*. London: Oxford University Press.

Pedersen, Morten B. 2008. *Promoting Human Rights in Burma: A Critique of Western Sanctions Policy*. Lanham ML; Plymouth UK: Rowman and Littlefield.

———. 2009. "Setting the Scene: Lessons from Twenty Years of Foreign Aid." Paper presented at the conference Burma/Myanmar: Views from the Ground and the International Community, Senate Office Building, Washington, DC, May 8. nbr.org.

———. 2010. "Burma, the International Community, and Human Rights (with Particular Attention to the Role of Foreign Aid)." In *Finding Dollars, Sense and Legitimacy in Burma*, edited by Susan L. Levenstein, 114–28. Washington, DC: Woodrow Wilson International Center for Scholars.

Perry, Peter John. 2007. *Myanmar (Burma) since 1962: The Failure of Development*. Aldershot, UK: Ashgate.

Pettit, Jethro. 2000. "Strengthening Local Organisation: Where the Rubber Hits the Road." *IDS Bulletin* 31 (3): 57–67.

Philp, Janette. 2004. "Cultural Politics and the Appropriation of Theravada Buddhism in Contemporary Burma (Myanmar)." PhD diss., Melbourne, Deakin University.

Pinheiro. 2006. "Report of the Special Rapporteur on the Situation of Human Rights in Myanmar, Paulo Sérgio Pinheiro: Situation of Human Rights in Myanmar." A/61/369, United Nations General Assembly.

Platteau, Jean-Philippe, and Frédéric Gaspart. 2003. "The Risk of Resource Misappropriation in Community-Driven Development." *World Development* 33 (10): 1687–703.

Pomfret, John. 2010. "U.S. Supports Creation of U.N. Commission of Inquiry into War Crimes in Burma." *Washington Post*, August 17.

Purcell, Marc. 1997. "Axe-Handles or Willing Minions? International NGOs in Burma." Paper presented at the conference Strengthening Civil Society in Burma: Possibilities and Dilemmas for International NGOs, Royal Tropical Institute, Transnational Institute and the Burma Centrum Nederland, Amsterdam, December 4–5.

Pye, Lucian W. 1962. *Politics, Personality, and Nation Building: Burma's Search for Identity*. New Haven, CT: Yale University Press.

Quintana, Tomas Ojea. 2011. "Press Conference by Special Rapporteur on Human Rights in Myanmar." Released by UN Department of Public Information, October 20.

Radcliffe, Sarah A. 2006a. *Culture and Development in a Globalizing World: Geographies, Actors and Paradigms*. London; New York: Routledge.

———. 2006b. "Culture in Development Thinking: Geographies, Actors and Paradigms." In *Culture and Development in a Globalizing World: Geographies, Actors and Paradigms*, edited by Sarah A. Radcliffe, 1–29. London; New York: Routledge.

Redfield, Robert, Ralph Linton, and Melville J. Herskovits. 1936. "Memorandum for the Study of Acculturation." *American Anthropologist* 38 (1): 149–52.

Rice, Susan E., and Stewart Patrick. 2008. *Index of State Weakness in the Developing World*. Washington, DC: Brookings Institution.

Risse, Thomas, and Kathryn Sikkink. 1999. "The Socialization of International Human Rights Norms into Domestic Politics." In *The Power of Human Rights: International Norms and Domestic Change*, edited by Thomas Risse et al., 1–38. Cambridge: Cambridge University Press.

Rist, Gilbert. 2002. *The History of Development: From Western Origins to Global Faith*. 2nd ed. London: ZED Books.

Rogers, Everett M. 2003. *Diffusion of Innovations*. 5th ed. New York: Free Press.

Rostow, Walt W. 1960. *The Stages of Economic Growth: A Non-communist Manifesto*. Cambridge, MA: Cambridge University Press.

Rotberg, Robert I. 1998. *Burma: Prospects for a Democratic Future*. Washington, DC: Brookings Institution.

Rozenberg, Guillaume. 2009. "How 'the Generals' Think: Gustaaf Houtman and the Enigma of the Burmese Military Regime." *Ase'anie* 24 (December): 11–31.

Rüland, Jürgen. 2001. "Burma Ten Years after the Uprising: The Regional Dimension." In *Burma: Political Economy under Military Rule*, edited by Robert H. Taylor, 119–36. New York: Palgrave.

Sadandar, William. 2010. "Cyclone Nargis and ASEAN: A Window for More Meaningful Development Cooperation in Myanmar." In *Ruling Myanmar: From Cyclone Nargis to National Elections*, edited by Nick Cheesman et al. Singapore: Institute of Southeast Asian Studies.

Santiso, Carlos. 2001. "Good Governance and Aid Effectiveness: The World Bank and Conditionality." *The Georgetown Public Policy Review* 7 (1): 1–22.

Save [the Children] in Myanmar & Matt Desmond. 2009. "Data Salad: Headlining the Development Economy." A discussion paper for the INGO Forum, October 2009.

Schech, Susanne, and Jane Haggis. 2000. *Culture and Development.* Malden, MA: Blackwell.

Schineller, Peter. 1990. *A Handbook on Inculturation.* New York: Paulist Press.

Schober, Juliane. 2011. *Modern Buddhist Conjunctures in Myanmar: Colonial Narratives, Colonial Legacies and Civil Society.* Honolulu: University of Hawai'i Press.

Schumpeter, Joseph. (1911) 1962. *The Theory of Economic Development: An Inquiry into Profits, Capital, Credit, Interest, and the Business Cycle.* Translated by Redvers Opie. Cambridge, MA: Harvard University Press.

Seekins, Donald M. 2005. "Burma and US Sanctions: Punishing an Authoritarian Regime." *Asian Survey* 45 (3): 437–52.

———. 2009. " 'Runaway Chickens' and Myanmar Identity: Relocating Burma's Capital." *City* 13 (1): 63–70.

Seers, Dudley. 1969. "The Meaning of Development." *International Development Review* 11 (4): 2–6.

———. 1977. "The New Meaning of Development." *International Development Review* 19 (3): 2–7.

Seers, Dudley, and Leonard Joy, eds. 1970. *Development in a Divided World.* Middlesex: Penguin Books.

Sein Htay. 2006. *Burma Economic Review 2005–2006.* Rockville, MD: The Burma Fund, National Coalition Government of the Union of Burma.

Selinger, Leah. 2004. "The Forgotten Factor: The Uneasy Relationship between Religion and Development." *Social Compass* 51 (4): 523–43.

Selth, Andrew. 2002. *Burma's Armed Forces: Power without Glory.* Norwalk, CT: EastBridge.

———. 2007a. *Burma and Nuclear Proliferation: Policies and Perceptions.* Regional Outlook Paper No. 12. Brisbane: Griffith Asia Institute, Griffith University.

———. 2007b. *Chinese Military Bases in Burma: The Explosion of a Myth.* Regional Outlook Paper No. 10. Brisbane: Griffith Asia Institute, Griffith University.

———. 2008a. *Burma and the Threat of Invasion: Regime Fantasy or Strategic Reality?* Regional Outlook Paper No. 17. Brisbane: Griffith Asia Institute, Griffith University.

———. 2008b. "Even Paranoids Have Enemies: Cyclone Nargis and Myanmar's Fears of Invasion." *Contemporary Southeast Asia* 30 (3): 379–402.

———. 2009. *Burma's Armed Forces: Looking down the Barrel.* Regional Outlook Paper No. 21. Brisbane: Griffith Asia Institute, Griffith University.

———. 2010a. *From Coup d'état to "Disciplined Democracy": The Burmese Regime's Claims to Legitimacy.* Regional Outlook Paper No. 23. Brisbane: Griffith Asia Institute, Griffith University.

———. 2010b. "Modern Burma Studies: A Survey of the Field." *Modern Asian Studies* 44 (2): 401–40.

Sen, Amartya Kumar. 1993. "Capability and Well-being." In *The Quality of Life*, edited by Martha Craven Nussbaum and Amartya Kumar Sen, 30–53. Helsinki, Finland: World Institute for Development Economics Research.

———. 1999a. *Development as Freedom.* Oxford: Oxford University Press.

———. 1999b. "The Value of Democracy." *Development Outreach* (Summer). devoutreach.com.

————. 2004. "How Does Culture Matter?" In *Culture and Public Action*, edited by Vijayendra Rao and Michael Walton. Palo Alto, CA: Stanford University Press.

Shihong, Bi. 2010. "Chance of Challenge: Japan's Policies towards Myanmar in the Post-Cold War Era." In *Myanmar: Prospects for Change*, edited by Li Chenyang and Wilhelm Hofmeister. Singapore: Select Publishing.

Shutt, Cathy. 2009. *Changing the World by Changing Ourselves: Reflections from a Bunch of BINGOs*. Brighton, UK: Institute of Development Studies, University of Sussex.

Shwe Rooms. 2011. "Shwe Rooms." shwerooms.com.

Silverstein, Josef. 1977. *Burma: Military Rule and the Politics of Stagnation*. Ithaca, NY: Cornell University Press.

————. 1996. "The Idea of Freedom in Burma and the Political Thought of Daw Aung San Suu Kyi." *Pacific Affairs* 69 (2): 211–28.

Skidmore, Monique. 2003. "Darker Than Midnight: Fear, Vulnerability, and Terror Making in Urban Burma (Myanmar)." *American Ethnologist* 30 (1): 5–40.

————. 2004. *Karaoke Fascism: Burma and the Politics of Fear*. Philadelphia: University of Pennsylvania Press.

————, ed. 2005. *Burma at the Turn of the Twenty-First Century*. Honolulu: University of Hawai'i Press.

SLORC. 1990. *Declaration No. 1/90 of July 27, 1990*. Issued by the State Law and Order Restoration Council, Yangon. In the *Working People's Daily*, July 29, 1990. burmalibrary.org.

Smith, Martin J. 1994. *Ethnic Groups in Burma: Development, Democracy and Human Rights*. London: Anti-Slavery International.

————. 1997. "Ethnic Conflict and the Challenge of Civil Society in Burma." In *Strengthening Civil Society in Burma: Possibilities and Dilemmas for International NGOs*. 2nd ed. Royal Tropical Institute, Amsterdam: Transnational Institute and the Burma Centrum Nederland.

————. 1999. *Burma: Insurgency and the Politics of Ethnicity*. London: ZED Books.

Smith, Stephen. 2010. "Ministerial Statement on Burma." Speech delivered by Stephen Smith MP Australian Minister for Foreign Affairs, Australian Parliament, February 8.

South, Ashley. 2004. "Political Transition in Myanmar: A New Model for Democratization." *Contemporary Southeast Asia* 26 (2): 233–55.

————. 2008a. *Civil Society in Burma: The Development of Democracy amidst Conflict*. Policy Studies 51 (Southeast Asia). Washington: East-West Centre.

————. 2008b. *Ethnic Politics in Burma: States of Conflict*. London: Routledge.

Spiro, Melford E. 1982. *Buddhism and Society: A Great Tradition and Its Burmese Vicissitudes*. 2nd ed. Berkeley: University of California Press.

State Dept. 2011. "Daily Press Briefing." Victoria Nuland, Spokesperson, US State Department, October 6.

Steinberg, David I. 1982. *Burma: A Socialist Nation of Southeast Asia*. Boulder, CO: Westview.

————. 1997. "A Void in Myanmar: Civil Society in Burma." In *Strengthening Civil Society in Burma: Possibilities and Dilemmas for International NGOs*. Amsterdam: Transnational Institute and the Burma Centrum Nederland.

————. 2001. "The Burmese Conundrum: Approaching Reformation of the Political Economy." In *Burma: Political Economy under Military Rule*, edited by Robert H. Taylor, 41–69. New York: Palgrave.

————. 2006. *Turmoil in Burma: Contested Legitimacies in Myanmar*. Norwalk, CT: Eastbridge.

———. 2007. "The United States and Its Allies: The Problem of Burma/Myanmar Policy." *Contemporary Southeast Asia* 29 (2): 219–32.

———. 2009. *Testimony to the U.S. Senate Subcommittee on Asia and Pacific Affairs.* Hearings on Burma, Washington, DC, September 30. foreign.senate.gov.

———. 2010a. "Anticipations and Anticipated Responses: The United States and the 2010 Burmese Elections." In *Finding Dollars, Sense and Legitimacy in Burma*, edited by Susan L. Levenstein, 129–48. Washington, DC: Woodrow Wilson International Center for Scholars.

———. 2010b. *Burma/Myanmar: What Everyone Needs to Know.* Oxford; New York: Oxford University Press.

Steward, Julian H. 1955. *The Theory of Culture Change.* Urbana: University of Illinois Press.

Stiglitz, Joseph E. 1999. "The Role of Participation in Development." *Development Outreach* (Summer). devoutreach.com.

Stokes, Deborah. 2010. "Keynote Address." Paper presented at the conference Development and Aid Effectiveness: Interrogating Pedagogies in International Development Studies, by First Assistant Secretary, Australian Department of Foreign Affairs and Trade, University of Canberra, November 18–19.

Streeten, Paul. 1970. "More on Development in an International Setting." In *Development in a Divided World*, edited by Dudley Seers and Leonard Joy. Middlesex: Penguin Books.

Sumner, Andy, and Michael Tribe. 2008. *International Development Studies: Theories and Methods in Research and Practice.* Los Angeles: Sage.

Suu Kyi, Aung San. 1991. *Aung San of Burma: A Biographical Portrait by His Daughter.* 2nd ed. Edinburgh: Kiscadale.

———. 1995a. "Freedom, Development, and Human Worth." *Journal of Democracy* 6 (2): 11–19.

———. 1995b. *Freedom from Fear and Other Writings.* London: Penguin Books.

———. 1996. *Letters from Burma.* London: Penguin Books.

———. 2010. "At the Crossroads: A Dialogue with Aung San Suu Kyi." A conversation with academics from the London School of Economics: Al Jazeera–English, December 22, 2010.

Suzuki, Naoke. 1998. *Inside NGOs: Learning to Manage Conflicts between Headquarters and Field Offices.* London: Intermediate Technology.

Tadros, Mariz. 2009. *Advocacy in the Age of Authoritarianism: Adjustments of All Sorts in Egypt.* Working Paper 337. Brighton, UK: Institute of Development Studies, University of Sussex. ids.ac.uk.

Tambiah, Stanley J. 1976. *World Conqueror and World Renouncer: A Study of Buddhism and Polity in Thailand against a Historical Background.* Cambridge: Cambridge University Press.

Taylor, Peter, Andrew Deak, Jethro Pettit, and Isobel Vogel. 2006. *Learning for Social Change: Exploring Concepts, Methods and Practice.* Brighton, UK: Institute of Development Studies, University of Sussex. ids.ac.uk.

Taylor, Robert H. 1987. *The State in Burma.* London: C. Hurst.

———. 1995. "Disaster or Release? J. S. Furnivall and the Bankruptcy of Burma." *Modern Asian Studies* 29 (1): 45–63.

———. 2001a. *Burma: Political Economy under Military Rule.* New York: Palgrave.

———. 2001b. "Stifling Change: The Army Remains in Command." In *Burma: Political Economy under Military Rule*, edited by Robert H. Taylor, 5–14. New York: Palgrave.

———. 2004. "Myanmar's Political Future: Is Waiting for the Perfect the Enemy of Doing the Possible?" In *Reconciling Burma/Myanmar: Essays on U.S. Relations with Burma*, edited by John H. Badgley, vol. 15, no. 1, 29–40. Seattle, WA. NBR Analysis, The National Bureau of Asian Research.

———. 2005. "Pathways to the Present." In *Myanmar: Beyond Politics to Societal Imperatives*, edited by Kyaw Yin Hlaing et al., 1–29. Singapore: Institute of Southeast Asian Studies.

———. 2008. "Finding the Political in Myanmar, a.k.a. Burma." *Journal of Southeast Asian Studies* 39 (2): 219–37.

———. 2009. *The State in Myanmar*. London: Hurst.

TCG. 2008. *Post-Nargis Recovery and Preparedness Plan*. Myanmar: Tripartite Core Group: Government of the Union of Myanmar, the United Nations, and ASEAN.

Tegenfeldt, David. 2001. "International Non-government Organizations in Burma." In *Burma: Political Economy under Military Rule*, edited by Robert H. Taylor, 109–18. New York: Palgrave.

Than Tun. 1983. "Social Life in Burma in the 16th Century." *Southeast Asian Studies* 21 (3): 267–74.

Thant Myint-U. 2001. *The Making of Modern Burma*. Cambridge: Cambridge University Press.

———. 2009a. "Missing the Point on Myanmar." Interview with Thant Myint-U by Charles McDermid, *Asia Times Online*, July 7.

———. 2009b. "Prepared Testimony by Dr. Thant Myint-U before the East Asia Sub-committee of the Senate Foreign Relations Committee." Speech delivered at Hearings on Burma, Washington, DC, September 30. foreign.senate.gov.

———. 2011. "White Elephants and Black Swans: Thoughts on Burma/Myanmar's Recent History and Its Possible Futures." Paper presented at the 2011 Myanmar/Burma Update Conference, Australian National University, May 16–17. asiapacific.anu.edu.au.

TI. 2011. *Corruption Perceptions Index 2011*. Berlin, Germany: Transparency International. transparency.org.

Titchen, Angie, and Dawn Hobson. 2005. "Phenomenology." In *Research Methods in the Social Sciences*, edited by Bridget Somekh and Cathy Lewin, 121–30. London: Sage.

TNI. 2010. *Burma's 2010 Elections: Challenges and Opportunities*. Amsterdam: Transnational Institute and Burma Centrum Netherlands.

Treasury, HM. 2011. "Burma/Myanmar." March 8. treasury.gov.uk.

Turnell, Sean. 2007a. "Assessing the Economic Situation after the 2001–2 Banking Crisis: Myanmar's Economy in 2006." In *Myanmar: The State, the Community, the Environment*, edited by Monique Skidmore and Trevor Wilson, 108–34. Canberra: ANU E Press and Asia Pacific Press.

———. 2007b. "Natural Gas Exports and the Missing Billion." *Burma Economic Watch* 4 (1): 1–3.

———. 2008. "Burma's Economy 2008: Current Situation and Prospects for Reform." *Burma Economic Watch*, Macquarie University.

———. 2010a. "Burma's Poverty of Riches: Natural Gas and the Voracious State." In *Burma or Myanmar: The Struggle for National Identity*, edited by Lowell Dittmer, 207–30. Singapore: World Scientific.

———. 2010b. "Finding Dollars and Sense: Burma's Economy in 2010." In *Finding Dollars, Sense and Legitimacy in Burma*, edited by Susan L. Levenstein, 20–39. Washington, DC: Woodrow Wilson International Center for Scholars.

———. 2011. "Known Knowns, New Knowns and Known Unknowns: Capital Formation and Burma's Economy in 2011." Paper presented at the 2011 Myanmar/Burma Update Conference, Australian National University, May 16–17. asiapacific.anu.edu.au.

Turnell, Sean, Wylie Bradford, and Alison Vicary. 2009. "Burma's Economy 2009: Disaster, Recovery . . . and Reform?" *Asian Politics and Policy* 4 (1): 631–59.

Turnell, Sean, Alison Vicary, and Wylie Bradford. 2007. "Migrant-Worker Remittances and Burma: An Economic Analysis of Survey Results." In *Dictatorship, Disorder and Decline in Myanmar*, edited by Monique Skidmore and Trevor Wilson, 63–86. Canberra: ANU E Press.

Tylor, Edward. 1958. *Primitive Culture: The Development of Mythology, Philosophy, Religion, Art and Customs*. New York: Harper and Row. First published 1871.

Tyndale, Wendy. 1998. *Key Issues for Development: A Discussion Paper for the Contribution by the World Faiths Development Dialogue (WFDD) to the World Bank's "World Development Report 2001."* Occasional Paper No. 1. Oxford, UK: World Faiths Development Dialogue. developmentandfaith.org.

———. 2000. "Faith and Economics in 'Development': A Bridge across the Chasm?" *Development in Practice* 10 (1): 9–18.

U Myint. 2007. "Myanmar's GDP Growth and Investment: Lessons from a Historical Perspective." In *Dictatorship, Disorder and Decline in Myanmar*, edited by Monique Skidmore and Trevor Wilson, 51–62. Canberra: ANU E Press.

———. 2010. *Myanmar Economy: A Comparative View*. Stockholm-Nacka: Institute for Security and Development Policy. isdp.eu.

———. 2011. "Reducing Poverty in Myanmar: The Way Forward." Chief Economic Advisor to the President. Paper presented at the Workshop on Rural Development and Poverty Alleviation in Myanmar, Myanmar International Convention Center, Naypyitaw, May 20–21.

U Soe Tha. 2006. "Press Conference on Economic Growth of Myanmar, Implementation of Millennium Goals and Cooperation with UN Agencies and Internal and International NGOs: Implementation of MDGs and Cooperation with UN Agencies and INGOs." Nay Pyi Taw, Press Briefing. Minister for National Planning and Economic Development, Government of Myanmar, December 17.

UN. 1951. *Measures for the Economic Development of Under-developed Countries*. New York: United Nations.

———. 1986. Declaration on the Right to Development. Resolution A/RES/41/128, of the United Nations General Assembly.

———. 1991. *The Realization of the Right to Development: Global Consultation on the Right to Development as a Human Right*. HR/PUB/91/2. New York: Centre for Human Rights (Geneva), United Nations.

———. 1993. *Vienna Declaration and Programme of Action*. UN Document A/Conf.157/23 of the United Nations General Assembly, World Conference on Human Rights.

UNDP. 1990. *Human Development Report: Concept and Measurement of Human Development*. New York: United Nations Development Programme.

———. 1994. *Human Development Report: New Dimensions of Human Security*. New York: United Nations Development Programme.

———. 1996. *Human Development Report: Economic Growth and Human Development*. New York: United Nations Development Programme and Oxford University Press.

————. 1997. *Governance for Sustainable Human Development.* UNDP Policy Papers Series. New York: United Nations Development Programme.

————. 2003a. *Human Development Report 2003. Millennium Development Goals: A Compact among Nations to End Human Poverty.* New York: United Nations Development Programme.

————. 2003b. *Poverty Reduction and Human Rights: A Practice Note.* New York: United Nations Development Programme.

————. 2004. *Human Development Report 2004: Cultural Liberty in Today's Diverse World.* New York: United Nations Development Programme.

————. 2007. *Human Development Report 2007/2008: Fighting Climate Change.* New York: United Nations Development Programme.

————. 2009. *Human Development Report 2009: Overcoming Barriers—Human Mobility and Development.* New York: United Nations Development Programme.

————. 2010. *Human Development Report 2010: The Real Wealth of Nations—Pathways to Development.* New York: United Nations Development Programme.

————. 2011. *Human Development Report 2011—Sustainability and Equity: A Better Future for All.* New York: United Nations Development Programme.

UNESCO. 1995. *Our Creative Diversity.* Report of the World Commission on Culture and Development, July 1996. Paris: UNESCO Culture and Development Co-ordination Office.

————. 2001. *Universal Declaration on Cultural Diversity.* Paris: UNESCO Culture and Development Co-ordination Office.

————. 2010. *Culture and Development: A Response to the Challenges of the Future?* Paris: UNESCO Culture and Development Co-ordination Office.

UNFPA. 2010. "Partnering with Faith-Based Organizations: Using Culturally Sensitive Approaches." unfpa.org.

UNICEF. 2003. "Child-Friendly Schools in Area-Focused Townships in Myanmar." UNICEF.

UNU. 2008. *Failed States.* Research Brief No. 3. Helsinki, Finland: United Nations University World Institute for Development Economics Research.

Uphoff, Norman, Milton Esman, and Anirudh Krishna. 1998. *Reasons for Success: Learning from Instructive Experiences in Rural Development.* West Hartford, CT: Kumarian Press.

USAID. 2011. *FY 2011 Foreign Operations Budget Request: Congressional Budget Justification for Foreign Operations.* Washington, DC: US Department of State. usaid.gov.

Ver Beek, K. A. 2002. "Spirituality: A Development Taboo." *Development in Practice* 10 (1): 31–43.

Vicary, Alison. 2007. "Revisiting the Financing of Health in Burma: A Comparison with the Other ASEAN Countries." *Burma Economic Watch* 4 (1): 4–10.

————. 2010. "The Relief and Reconstruction Programme Following Cyclone Nargis: A Review of SPDC Policy." In *Ruling Myanmar: From Cyclone Nargis to National Elections,* edited by Nick Cheesman et al., 208–35. Singapore: Institute of Southeast Asian Studies.

Wallace, Tina, Lisa Bornstein, and Jennifer Chapman. 2006. *The Aid Chain: Coercion and Commitment in Development NGOs.* London: Intermediate Technology/Practical Action.

Ward, Victoria. 2011. "Burmese Letter to King George II Deciphered after More Than 250 Years." *Daily Telegraph,* January 14.

Ware, Anthony. 2010. "Human Rights and the Right to Development: Insights into the Myanmar Government's Response to Rights Allegations." In *Crises and Opportunities: Proceedings of the 18th Biennial Conference of the ASAA 2010*, edited by Elizabeth Morrell and Michael D. Barr. Canberra: Asian Studies Association of Australia, University of Adelaide. adelaide.edu.au.

———. 2011. "The MDGs in Myanmar: Relevant or Redundant?" *Journal of the Asia Pacific Economy* 16 (4): 580–97.

Watson, Elizabeth E. 2006. "Culture and Conservation in Post-Conflict Africa: Changing Attitudes and Approaches." In *Culture and Development in a Globalizing World: Geographies, Actors and Paradigms*, edited by Sarah A. Radcliffe, 58–82. London; New York: Routledge.

WCED. 1987. "Our Common Future." Report of the World Commission on Environment and Development, annex to UN General Assembly document A/42/427, Development and International Co-operation: Environment, August 2.

Webster, Anthony. 2000. "Business and Empire: A Reassessment of the British Conquest of Burma in 1885." *The Historical Journal* 43 (4): 1003–25.

Weitz, R. 1986. *New Roads to Development*. New York: Greenwood Press.

Wells, Tamas. 2009. *Doing Harm to Civil Society: Cautionary Tales from Paung Ku*. Yangon: Paung Ku.

Wesley, Michael. 2008. "State of the Art on the Art of State Building." *Global Governance* 14:135–56.

WFDD. 2001. *Cultures, Spirituality and Development*. Oxford, UK: World Faiths Development Dialogue.

WHO. 2008. *Health Action in Crises: Myanmar, August 2009*. Geneva: World Health Organization. who.int.

———. 2009. *WHO Statistical Information System (WHOSIS) Core Health Indicators*. Geneva: World Health Organization. who.int.

Wilde, Oscar. 1922. *For Love of the King: A Burmese Masque*. London: Methuen.

Williams, Lewis. 2004. "Culture and Community Development: Towards New Conceptualizations and Practice." *Community Development Journal* 39 (4): 345–59.

Williams, Raymond. 1993. *Keywords*. New York: Oxford University Press. pubpages.unh.edu.

Wilson, Trevor. 2012. *Australian Aid Can Make a Difference in Burma*. Development Policy Blog, Crawford School of Economics and Government, Australian National University, March 12. devpolicy.org.

Wintle, Justin. 2007. *Perfect Hostage: Aung San Suu Kyi, Burma and the Generals*. London: Arrow Books.

———. 2010. "Aung San Suu Kyi Freed: What Happens Now?" *The Daily Telegraph*, November 13. telegraph.co.uk.

Wolfensohn, James. 1998. "Culture and Sustainable Development: Investing in the Promise of Societies." In *Culture in Sustainable Development: Investing in Cultural and Natural Endowments*, edited by Ismail Serageldin and Joan Martin-Brown, 5–7. Proceedings of the conference hosted by World Bank and UNESCO, September 28–29. Washington, DC: World Bank.

———. 2000. "Opening Keynote Address." In *Culture Counts: Financing, Resources, and the Economics of Culture in Sustainable Development*. Proceedings of the conference held in Florence, Italy, October 4–7,1999. Washington, DC: World Bank.

World Bank. 1989. "Involving Nongovernmental Organizations in World Bank–Supported Activities." Operational Directive 14.70, of the World Bank. *World Bank Operational Manual*. gdrc.org.

———. 2005. *World Development Report 2006: Equity and Development*. Washington, DC: World Bank and Oxford University Press.

———. 2006. *Community-Driven Development in the Context of Conflict-Affected Countries: Challenges and Opportunities*. Report No. 36425 GLB. Washington, DC: World Bank, Social Development Department.

———. 2009. *Statistical Capacity Indicator*. Washington, DC: World Bank. worldbank.org.

Yasuaki, Onuma. 1999. "Toward an Intercivilizational Approach to Human Rights." In *East Asian Challenge for Human Rights*, edited by Joanne R. Bauer and Daniel A. Bell, 103–23. Cambridge: Cambridge University Press.

Yohome, K. 2010. "The Changing Discourse on China–Myanmar Bilateral Relations." In *Myanmar: Prospect for Change*, edited by Li Chenyang and Wilhelm Hofmeister. Singapore: Select Publishing.

Yonekura, Yukiko. 2000. "Partnership for Whom? Cambodian NGOs' Supporting Schemes." *IDS Bulletin: Questioning Partnership: The Reality of Aid and NGO Relationships* 31 (3): 35–47.

Zarni, Maung. 2007. "Confronting Burma/Myanmar's Security Dilemma: An Integrated Approach to National and Human Security Issues." In *Civil Society, Religion and Global Governance: Paradigms of Power and Persuasion*, edited by Helen James, 202–12. New York: Routledge.

———. 2011. "Outrageously Optimistic." *Himāl Magazine*, April 8.

Index